SLAVES OF THE STATE

Slaves of the State

. . . .

Black Incarceration from the Chain Gang to the Penitentiary

Dennis Childs

University of Minnesota Press
Minneapolis
London

Chapter 1 was previously published as "'You Ain't Seen Nothin' Yet': *Beloved*, the American Chain Gang, and the Middle Passage Remix," *American Quarterly* 61, no. 2 (June 2009): 271–97; reprinted with permission of *American Quarterly*.

Portions of chapter 3 were previously published as "Angola, Convict Leasing, and the Annulment of Freedom," in *Violence and the Body: Race, Gender, and the State*, ed. Arturo Aldama (Bloomington: Indiana University Press, 2003); reprinted by permission of Indiana University Press.

Published by the University of Minnesota Press
111 Third Avenue South, Suite 290
Minneapolis, MN 55401-2520
http://www.upress.umn.edu

Library of Congress Cataloging-in-Publication Data
Childs, Dennis.
Slaves of the state : black incarceration from the chain gang to the penitentiary /
Dennis Childs.
Includes bibliographical references and index.
ISBN 978-0-8166-9240-8 (hc : alk. paper) — ISBN 978-0-8166-9241-5 (pb : alk. paper)
1. African American prisoners—History. 2. Slavery—United States—History.
3. Discrimination in criminal justice administration—United States.
4. United States—Race relations. I. Title.
HV9471.C473 2015
365′.608996073—dc23
2014019929

Printed in the United States of America on acid- free paper

The University of Minnesota is an equal-opportunity educator and employer.

For Saranella and Kahlil,
and all prison slaves past and present

Contents

"Inhuman Punishment"

The *(Un)dead Book* of Chattel Carcerality

Slavery and freedom
They is mostly the same
No difference hardly
Except in the name.

—Georgia chain-gang song (c. early 1900s)

The administrators have stripped us of all but the bare necessities
and are now taking those also. The beating and rapes don't help mat-
ters either. The male guards treat us as if we were chattel.

—Elizabeth B., *Revolutionary Prisoners Speak* (1999)

THIS BOOK REPRESENTS MY ATTEMPT at answering a call I first
heard many years ago as a graduate student living in Oakland,
California—one emitting from an article by Angela Davis entitled "Racialized Punishment and Prison Abolition." The radical, counter-historical
directive I received from this piece is crystallized most succinctly at a
moment in which Davis distinguishes her neo-abolitionist encounter with
the U.S. carceral state from that of Michel Foucault on the basis of the culturally and legally crafted "soulless" character of the captive "Negro":

> If, as Foucault suggests, the locus of the new European mode of
> punishment shifted from the body to the soul, black slaves in the
> US were largely perceived as lacking a soul that might be shaped
> and transformed by punishment. *Within the institution of slavery,*
> *itself a form of incarceration,* racialized forms of punishment devel-
> oped alongside the emergence of the prison system within and as a
> negative affirmation of the "free world." . . . As white men acquired
> the privilege to be punished in ways that acknowledged their

equality and the racialized universality of liberty, the punishment of black slaves was corporeal, concrete and particular.[1]

Within the institution of slavery, itself a form of incarceration. I had read my Foucault before encountering this hugely significant yet largely unengaged black radical epistemic phrase; before reading *Soledad Brother*; before reading Assata Shakur's autobiography; before I finally recognized that Toni Morrison's *Beloved* is *not* solely concerned with pre-1865 formations of chattel slavery; before my initial conversation with Robert Hillary King of the "Angola 3" following his hard-won release from nearly thirty years of solitary confinement; before hearing the spectral neoslave soundings of Odea Mathews and Robert Pete Williams; before being summoned to a national white supremacist tourist site situated at the threshold of a fully operational eighteen-thousand-acre slave plantation by one of its historically anonymous and unceremoniously buried black captives. While Foucault barely makes mention of slavery in his compelling history of the modern prison, the writings, soundings, and survival practices of Davis and countless other black prisoners and former prisoners define chattel slavery as a primordial and tenaciously undead carceral regime of Euro-American modernity—as the legal, political, architectural, and cultural linchpin of racial capitalist misogynist imprisonment in the United States as it has morphed from the slave-ship holds and barracoons of the Middle Passage, to the portable boxcar cages of early Jim Crow apartheid, to the coffin-simulating boxcar cells of today's prison–industrial complex (PIC).[2] Indeed, when read as one overarching, cross-fertilizing, and temporally unfixed network of racial and spatial terror, the U.S. system of mass imprisonment represents a centuries-old regime of chattelized prison–industrial genocide that began well before the term PIC was ever uttered—a liberal white supremacist misogynist "shit-stem," as Peter Tosh might have dubbed it, that has submitted an as yet uncalculated (nor completed) number of black people and other racially and criminally stigmatized groups to collectivized natal alienation, excremental internment, (un)productive forced labor, serialized corporeal rupture, legally unredressable sexual violence, coerced performance, and manifold forms of death, ranging from the social, to the civil, to the biological.[3]

Notwithstanding the tendency within U.S. juridical, legislative, and penal law to disavow the chattel origins of modern incarceration, there have been key moments in which postbellum liberal legal discourse has offered boldface articulation of the state's enslaving and murderous bearing toward criminally and racially stigmatized bodies. In *Ruffin v. Commonwealth* (1871), Justice J. Christian supplies just this sort of open declaration of the law's re-chattelizing functionality vis-à-vis former slaves in his ostensibly color-blind construction of the civilly dead nonposition of the criminally branded felon: "He has, as a consequence of his crime, not only forfeited his liberty, but all his personal rights except those which the law in its humanity accords to him. He is for the time being the *slave of the State*. He is *civiliter mortuus* [civilly dead]; and his estate, if he has any, is administered like that of a dead man."[4] What would the law's incantatory proclamation of penal enslavement in respect to all criminally branded subjects mean for those beings who had been defined as metaphysically incorrigible, legally fungible, and socially disposable for generations before 1871? As suggested in Davis's discussion of the racialized dimensions of chattel imprisonment, the abject status of civil death would be taken to its zero degree as postbellum white supremacist law set its sights on those putatively soulless subjects whose slavery and social death rested at the very foundation of free/white social, civil, and cultural life in the United States since its inception as a genocidal colony of the British Empire. Far from representing a juridical anomaly or an anachronistic throwback to the feudal origins of Euro-American common law, *Ruffin* constituted an all-too-accurate racial gothic omen of the terroristic trajectories of modern imprisonment as it has been waged against former slaves and putatively "free" black people—from convict leasing, to chain gangs, to peonage camps, to the prison plantation, to the penitentiary. In attempting to offer an aperture of necromantic address for the (living) dead of U.S. neoslavery, however, this book considers what amounts to a collectively issued refutation of the organizing fascist logic within J. Christian's matter-of-fact pronouncement of the civilly dead status of the prison slave; that is, what the spectral voices, testimonies, and survival practices of black prisoners make clear is that racialized prison slavery has had little to do with the alleged criminal acts of individual black people and everything to do with the socially constructed crime of being born black (or Indigenous or brown or poor) in apartheid "America."[5]

The *Temporal Boxes* of Neoslavery

If, as Saidiya Hartman suggests, "the grand narrative of Emancipation continues to hold sway over our imagination," notwithstanding the forms of chattelized legal and extralegal terror that proliferated in freedom's wake, then the writings, testimonies, soundings, and lifeways of black neoslaves from 1865 to the present offer a nearly inexhaustible, if largely unheeded, set of ghostly demystifications of that time-honored master narrative.[6] I want to be clear here that when I use the term *ghostly* I am not speaking metaphorically. My use of the term is in keeping with Avery Gordon's pivotally important assertion that, in the name of social and historical justice for the perilously alive and the desecrated dead, we must attempt to offer *gracious, hospitable, and attentive listening* to the countless material revenants that have accumulated under the long-standing criminal reign of racial capitalist misogyny.[7] This book calls our attention to how the law's gothic transmutation of living, nominally rights-bearing, human beings into "slaves of the state" has produced an unaccounted-for excess in the form of a subterranean poetics, politics, and epistemics of the living dead—an unquietly buried assemblage of black neoslave sound and theory (and legally disappeared bodies) that constitutes a haunting *unhistorical* counter to the well-entrenched U.S. national fable of slavery's nineteenth-century demise.[8]

In a piece entitled "Teetering on the Brink: Between Death and Life," the black radical political prisoner Mumia Abu-Jamal offers just this sort of spectral disenchantment of the fictive slavery/freedom borderline. He does so by outlining the degree to which collectivized natal alienation—one of the foundational elements of world-historical slavery and social death that is performed through the slave's systematic severance from loved ones—insinuated itself into the late twentieth century for himself and others whom he describes as being *"entombed in a juridical, psychic, and temporal box."* He expresses how this chattelizing technique resurfaced through the state's proscription of familial touch for those it has branded as condemned felons:

> The ultimate effect of noncontact visits is to weaken, and finally to sever, family ties. Through this policy and practice the state skillfully and intentionally denies those it condemns a fundamental element and expression of humanity—that of touch and physical contact—and slowly erodes family ties already made tenuous by the distance between home and the prison. Thus prisoners are as isolated psychologically as they are temporally and spatially. By state action, *they become "dead" to those who know and love them, and therefore dead to themselves.*[9]

From the abject legal position of being cargoed within a *juridical, psychic, and temporal box* situated inside Pennsylvania's death row, the imprisoned black radical intellectual theorizes neoslavery as a ritualized predicament of living death wrought through the mutually constitutive state-terror modalities of temporal dislocation, structural dehumanization, and collectivized natal alienation. In this sense, the cellular zone of living burial, state-murder preparation, and familial rupture that Abu-Jamal describes as the "temporal box" enacts both a time/body freeze—with the death-simulating routine of imprisonment initiating a virtual stoppage of time—and a time/body warp, wherein the civil death of penal entombment performs horrifying repetition of the social death of chattel enslavement.[10] Here we see how Abu-Jamal's theoretical voice, like those of other incarcerated black radicals such as Angela Davis, Assata Shakur, Sundiata Acoli, George Jackson, and Herman Wallace, calls upon us to recognize the fact that the birthplace of epistemic articulations of and against neoslavery has not been the liberal bourgeois academy (an institution centrally implicated in the cross-generational mass production and consumption of criminally racialized human beings), but the space of neoslavery itself. As Joy James asserts in her groundbreaking work on (anti)prison radicalism, the neoslave narrative, and the theoretical component of what she describes as "captive insurgent abolitionism," the term "'public intellectual' encompasses the oft-forgotten 'prison intellectual'. Like his or her visible counterparts, the imprisoned intellectual reflects upon social meaning, ethics and justice; only s/he does so in detention centres and prisons which function as intellectual and political sites unauthorised by the state."[11]

However, if incarcerated and formerly imprisoned black radicals such as Abu-Jamal, Shakur, Acoli, Davis, Jackson, and Wallace represent relatively submerged voices of black intellectualism and neo-abolitionism, then what terms do we have at our disposal to describe the sonic, written, performative, and resistive practices of the countless historically anonymous black neoslaves who were subjected to chattelism's post-1865 return for generations before the advent of the 1960s and 1970s Movement era; who have un-Google-able names such as Harriet Purdy, Gassaway Price, John McElroy, James Bruce, and Aubert LaCarlton Collins; whose stories cannot be traced by way of book barcodes or ISBN numbers; and whose terrorized lives and unceremonious deaths have rarely been categorized as "political," "radical," or "intellectual"? Was something like a theory of "neoslavery" produced long before George Jackson coined and theorized the term while being held deep within the bowels of what he described as one of California's land-based slave ships? In what ways was the neo-abolitionist impulse that we rightly associate with black, Indigenous, Latina/o, and other allied radical formations of the Movement era prefigured in the cultures and politics of those subjected to the original systems of U.S. neoslavery such as the chain gang, the convict lease camp, the prison plantation, and the publically cultivated brands of privatized neochattelism known as peonage and criminal surety? What do the unrequited dead of prison slavery's past have to tell us about our current moment of prison–industrial genocide, namely, since every one of the more than 2.3 million human beings currently entombed under today's PIC (both domestically and globally) represents nothing if not a renewed desecration of the unnamable, unheralded, and unromanticizable casualties of earlier formations of neoslavery? Here I am suggesting the possibility that if indeed the dead have yet to be saved from the defiling repetition of the ravages of the past within our current moment, then the perilous present is also unclear of the re-membering and wailing, and presence(s) of those whose remains lie buried within the unmarked graves of a prison plantation sugarcane field and the sepulcher-like temporal boxes of the master archive.[12]

One such incompletely interred voice of early neoslavery still calls out from among a mountain-sized pile of boxes collected and filed away by the U.S. Department of Justice in respect to its investigation of peonage cases from 1901 to 1945—black apparitional testimony from Laronia, Georgia, in the form of a letter addressed to President Theodore Roosevelt, in October 1903:

Mr. President,
Dear Sir:
   I write you this letter to inform you that my husband (Jackson Morrison, col'd) is being made to serve an unlawful term at Col. James M. Smith's camp at Smithonia, Ga., in Oglethorpe county,
   Events of the case:
   (1) He was sentenced at Carnsville, Ga. to the [chain] Gang for 12 months from Sept. 27th, 1901, or pay a fine of $100.00.
   (2) He was bought out by a Mr. Mose Jordan of Corner, Ga. to whom he gave 8 months which made 20 months.
   (3) Mr. Jordan, after working Morrison only two months sold him to Col. James M. Smith, on Nov. 30th, 1901.

(4) Col. Smith agreed to liberate Morrison on the 30th day of May 1903.

(5) Col. Smith also induced me to work by saying that if I labored on his farm he would pay me for my work, or else he would allow it to be credited to my husband sents. in order to shorten his term, but he did not do either. I worked for 18 months hard labor and he (Col. Smith) did not pay me anything neither did credit any of my time to . . . that of my husband.

(6) I went to Col. Cmith's Camp on Nov. 30th, 1901, and stayed there till July 7th 1903, and worked all the time and when I left he took all of my household possessions.

(7) My husband, Jackson Morrison's time expired on May 30th 1903, but Smith would not turn him free. He, (Morrison) worked on till July 7th on which day he left the camp.

(8) On Sept. 11, 1903 he, Morrison, was captured by Smith's sheriff and carried back to the camp and then lodged in the Lexington jail in Oglethorpe county.

(9) Col. Smith inflicts inhuman punishment on the person of his convicts, and whips them unmercifully.

(10) Mr. President, I appeal to you, as the Executive Head of our Nation to please do something for my husband. Will you please cause an investigation of that Camp to be made in the future, and while doing so it will be found that there are numbers of persons (both men and women) serving as slaves there for many months and days after their terms have expired. I have one child 3 years old and am in great need of my husband's assistance.

> I have the honor to be, Sir,
> Your obedient Servant,
> Mentha Morrison, Col'd[13]

We will never know whether Mentha Morrison and her three-year-old child ever saw Jackson Morrison again. We will also never know the full breadth of unspeakable terror that is made to fall under the sign of "inhuman punishment" in section 9 of Mentha's ten-point appeal to the president of the United States to "do something" about her husband's (and her own) enslavement. What we do know is that besides what she describes as the modern reintroduction of the antebellum punitive measure of the plantation whip, neoslaves were routinely subjected to rape; "long-chaining," boxcar and stockade "tight-packing;" "can't to can't see" labor and terror in the house, field, or mine; coffling over great distances; bloodhound maulings; outright murder; and coerced musical and theatrical performance. What we also know is that—similar to the overwhelming majority of cases in which black subjects attempted to make substantive use of late nineteenth- and early twentieth-century legal proscriptions of (fictive) debt peonage—executive, legislative, and juridical arenas of U.S. liberal white supremacist law ultimately did absolutely nothing to redress the grievances of Mentha Morrison, her husband, and their newly fatherless child. In fact, as noted above in reference to *Ruffin,* these branches of U.S. national law and governance are centrally implicated in each of the horrifying regimes of public and private neoslavery that occurred at places such as James Smith's twenty-thousand-acre industrialized neoslave plantation (otherwise known as "Smithonia"), the "Gang" that Jackson Morrison was able to avoid only by being converted into fungible courthouse chattel, and the jail in which he was held after attempting to escape from the neoplantation. Indeed, as I discuss in chapter 2, the very document that signaled the de jure liberation of African slaves some thirty-six years before Jackson Morrison's arrest and courtroom "sale" in 1901—the Thirteenth Amendment to the U.S. Constitution—actually served as the sine qua non of his penal enslavement and that of untold numbers of other putatively "free" black people. As Mentha Morrison's gripping entreaty makes clear, the *slavery or involuntary servitude as punishment for a crime* exception within the "Emancipation Amendment" allowed courthouses of Jim Crow apartheid to function as virtual auction blocks in which criminally branded black people were either disappeared to the public profiteering venues of the chain gang, the levee camp, and the state prison plantation, or in which, like Jackson Morrison, they were submitted to the designs of enterprising white planters and industrialists who could literally purchase, lease, or sublease the bodies of black men, women, and children through the publically brokered "private" machinations of convict leasing, peonage, the "fine/fee system," and criminal surety.

The postbellum experience of racialized criminal sanction that the Morrisons endured, as well as an untabulatable number of other black people, speaks to the routinized manner by which white supremacist juridical, statutory, and penal law conjured the nominally free black civil subject into a criminalized, natally alienated, and fungible commodity.[14] Indeed, notwithstanding the other horrifying aspects of Mentha Morrison's testimony, one is struck by the utterly banal nature of her gestures toward the arrest, conviction, courthouse sale, and private subleasing of her husband's "col'd" body/flesh as would-be chain-gang prisoner and fictively indebted peon. How does the rather matter-of-fact nature of her "rememory" of her husband being arrested, sentenced to the chain gang, only to be "bought" and "sold" to a prison plantation as a piece of criminally branded merchandise alter our understanding of the living history of southern neoslavery?[15] If the Thirteenth Amendment was the primary legal weapon of black neoslavery, then what were the ideologically determining factors that allowed for the profits and pleasures associated with the auctioning, leasing, and subleasing of black bodies in the courthouse, the plantation field, and the coal mine in the age of emancipation?

Studies of the southern postbellum turn to "convict labor" have often explained the unprecedented demographic shift in the South's official spaces of incarceration that occurred after the Civil War—with the number of officially imprisoned black people increasing from less than one percent before 1861 to as much as 90 percent in certain counties and states after 1865—in terms of political economy. According to this line of analysis, the move to prison slavery fulfilled the need for the recuperation of a formerly enslaved labor force and the restoration and modernization of a war-torn and "backward" southern economy.[16] The ultimate message of this interpretive framework has been: if racism was an important immediate/local factor in the new southern prison system, then the national and global macroeconomic factors of capitalist profit and industrial modernization were its determinant historical forces. However, Morrison's unhistorical account of the courthouse auctioning of her husband calls upon us to recognize that the corporeal economies of white supremacy and black fungibility represented fundamental conditions of possibility for the formations of terror, subjection, and genocidal domination that black people have endured under convict leasing, the chain gang, the prison plantation, fictive-debt peonage, and the penitentiary. To invoke Sylvia Wynter, the liberal white supremacist cultural manufacture of blackness as *metaphysical affliction* was the social and philosophical edifice upon which southern capitalist neoslavery was built and the ideological driving force behind the routinized disappearance and reenslavement of nominally "free" black civil subjects.[17] Mentha Morrison's testimony illustrates how the inhuman quality of postbellum punishment was a product of the nationally projected ontological mythos of the "Negro" or "Nigger" as *incorrigible and inhuman being*—a fatal, material, and socially determining fable that had been forged at law and custom for hundreds of years before her husband's courthouse auctioning.[18] Finally, the fact that Jackson Morrison's criminally branded and sold body ended up being coffled to a geography of racial internment that had been in operation since well before the Civil War underlines how the supposed historical shift in penal demography that occurred after 1865 was not really so much of a shift at all—that Africans had faced mass inhuman punishment and industrialized plantation imprisonment on grounds such as Smithonia, Parchman (Mississippi), and "Angola" (Louisiana) for generations before the openly declared turn to "Negro convict labor."

Given her all-too-acute lived understanding of the ways in which the U.S. system of inhuman punishment did indeed amount to a predicament of de jure reenslavement for her own family and others within her circle, we can imagine that Mentha Morrison knew full well that there was little chance that a single "Col'd" woman's missive to one of the most powerful white men on the planet would yield anything more than it did. However, it is our recognition of her likely understanding of the very impossibility of her task of calling on national white supremacist law to free her husband from local white supremacist law that underlines the haunting future-orientation of the neo-abolitionist appeal that can still be heard emitting from her letter well over a century after its composition. A strident black apparitional demand on the neoslavery present from deep within the neoslavery past can be heard most clearly in section 10— *Will you please cause an investigation of that Camp to be made in the future, and while doing so it will be found that there are numbers of persons (both men and women) serving as slaves there.* If Morrison's appeal can be taken as less of a dead letter than an undead indictment of a past that has never perished, of a living History that continues to see massive *numbers of persons (both men and women* [and gender-nonconforming people]) *serving as slaves* in modern living death camps such as those that currently entomb one out of every nine black men in the United States between the ages of twenty and thirty-four[19]—or the scores of immigrant detention camps that now line "America's" hypermilitarized and imperially erected border with Mexico—then it forces us to understand that formations of chattelized imprisonment such as Smithonia (Georgia), Cummins (Arkansas), Banner Mine (Alabama), Parchman (Mississippi), and Angola (Louisiana) are not anachronistic figments of southern white supremacist exceptionalism or premodern anachronism, but legal, methodological, and cultural foundations of the current U.S. mass production, consumption, and inhuman punishment of incarcerated black, Indigenous, brown, poor, and Muslim bodies.

Here I want to clarify that my engagement with the neo-abolitionist demand of those such as Morrison, Abu-Jamal, and Davis for us to recognize the vicious continuities of racialized incarceration as it has reached across the well-entrenched boundaries of liberal bourgeois historical periodization is not an argument for a flattening or eliding of political, experiential, or social difference between the past and present of U.S. racial genocide. Rather, the apparitional voices of slaves of the state demand that we pay serious attention to the ways in which the chattel principle has infused the sociality of black freedom from the moment of its de jure birth.[20] Again, in the spirit of purposeful repetition, the inseparability of freedom and reenslavement is analogized most audaciously within the Janus-headed language of the very legal document that is advertised as the genesis of black civil personhood and the extinguishment of "Negro" chattelhood. My reading of liberal legality and modern racialized carcerality through the theoretical, epistemological, and pedagogical guidance of neoslaves past and present presupposes a concentric/accumulative view of history rather than a linear/sequential one—an experientially informed conception of the dynamic interfacing of penal time, racialized carceral space, and terrorized black unfree experience that discerns grim congruence in the very places that the liberal white supremacist state implants the socially seductive illusion of progress and the repressive ideological machinery of "postracial" amnesia.[21] The adamant refusal of the liberal white nationalist narrative of progress that unfolds within this book does not treat the past and present as homological (or exactly the same); rather, it represents a politically interested unveiling of the gothic presence of chattel slavery at the material substratum of U.S. modernity—a presence that embodies not a "premodern" or "precapitalist" mode of production, but an undead source of modern social reproduction and the genealogical matrix of our current catastrophe of mass inhuman entombment. When encountered in this light, the voices heard throughout this book ultimately signal how the racial capitalist misogynist state has subjected millions of black people and other racially and criminally stigmatized peoples to conditions that render the differences between past and present modes of domination virtually indecipherable, if not completely nonexistent.

Robert Pete Williams beckons us further into necessary reckoning with the vertiginous continuities of the *then* of "southern" prison slavery and Black Atlantic chattel slavery, and the *now* of U.S. (inter)national prison–industrial genocide, in "Prisoner's Talking Blues," a song he performed on a day in the late 1950s while held captive at the last of the prison plantations mentioned above—Louisiana's "Angola"—an eighteen-thousand-acre plot of fertile Mississippi river-bottom land that has operated as a slave plantation since the early nineteenth century and now serves as the largest maximum-security prison in the country:

> Lord, I feel so bad sometime,
> Seems like that I'm weakenin' every day.
> You know I've begin to grey since I got here
> Well a whole lot of worryin' causin' that
> But I can feel myself weakenin'
> I don't keep well no more . . . I keeps sickly.
> I takes a lot of medicine but it don't look like it do no good.
> All I have to do is pray, that's the only thing that'll help me
>   here.

> One foot in the grave it look like
> And the other one out.
> Sometime it look like my best days, gotta be my last days.
> Sometimes I feel like I'ma never see, my little ol' kids anymore.
> But if I don't ever see 'em no more, leave 'em in the hands of
>   God. . . .

> In a way, I was glad my poor mother had 'ceased'
> because she suffered with heart trouble, and trouble behind me
> sure would have went hard with her.
> But if she were livin', I could call on her sometime.
> But my ol' father dead too.
> That make me, be motherless and fatherless. . . .

> Lord my worry, sure carryin' me down
> Lord my worry, sure is carryin' me down
> Sometime I feel like, baby, committin' suicide
> Yah, sometime I feel, feel like committin' suicide

I got the nerve, if I just had somethin' to do it with.
I'm goin' down slow, somethin' wrong with me.
Yes, I'm goin' down slow, somethin' wrong with me.[22]

As with Mentha Morrison and Mumia Abu-Jamal, the black apparitional words of Williams illuminate the degree to which the experience of neo-slavery shuttles the living, breathing, loving subject to an insufferable life/death borderland—a zone of civil murder erected through the legal interfacing of natal alienation and racialized criminal sanction. Except in Williams's case, the intensity of the neoslave's written articulation of the experiences of familial rupture and plantation terror is heightened by the added aesthetic dimensions of Delta-inflected "worried notes" and the haunting chorus-like tones of a twelve-string guitar. In listening to the recording, one is immediately struck by the ways in which the semantic depth, epistemic force, and spectral urgency of Williams's self-addressed dirge are felt as much, if not more, in the wheezes of his throat and the reverberating tones of his guitar (melancholic sounds that hover at the margins of nearly every lyrical line) than in the words themselves. In fact, these elements of nonverbal prison slave communication work to pro-duce a cloaked expansion of meaning rather than a transparent exposure of meaning.[23] Here, as in my later discussions of black incarcerated perfor-mance, I am suggesting how our attentive listening to the aesthetic and political remains of the dead and living dead must take into account the fact that the full range of unhistorical meaning, pedagogical purpose, and terrorized experience held within their soundings, testimonies, and sur-vival practices is necessarily unavailable to us, even as we accept the urgent responsibility of hearing and acting upon what these specters of neoslav-ery still need to say.

In this respect, the words of Saidiya Hartman, following Edouard Glis-sant, regarding the opacity, or resistive nontransparency, of the songs that issued from the "orchestrated amusements" of the chattel slave are vitally instructive for our engagement with the punitive performances of the prison slave:

[T]he significance of opacity [is] precisely that which enables something in excess of the orchestrated amusements of the enslaved and which similarly troubles the distinctions between joy and sorrow and toil and leisure. For this opacity, the subterranean

and veiled character of slave song must be considered in relation
to the dominative imposition of transparency and the degrading
hyper-visibility of the enslaved, and, by the same token, such
concealment should be considered a form of resistance.[24]

The direct relationship between the hypervisibility of the enslaved and
the recessed semantic aspects of chattelized performance is fundamentally
germane to our understanding of the circumscribed, fraught, and pained
characteristics of postbellum black prisoner performance in spaces such
as the Angola prison plantation, or "The Farm," as it is euphemistically and
pastorally designated by the state. Indeed this dynamic is redolent in the
very moment of neoslave abolitionist sound that Williams produced in
"Prisoner's Talking Blues." That is, as much as we are able to glean a redressive or resistive quality in Williams's sonic renaming, redefining, and
reclamation of his experience of imprisonment—with his voice and guitar
performing a counter-conjuration of the legal narrative of "Negro" criminality and inhuman incorrigibility into a black apparitional story of kidnapping, neoslavery, living death, and state criminality[25]—the conditions
in which the field recording was made limn the long-standing imbrications
of (neo)slave performance and punishment, leisure and terror, and imprisoned privilege and punitive sufferance that Hartman charts so masterfully
in *Scenes of Subjection.* Here what I am gesturing toward are the ways in
which the melancholic strains heard on the Williams recording were as
attributable to the vexed conditions under which they were produced as
to the other horrifying regiments of black neoslave labor that the singer
endured on "The Farm." Specifically, on the day that "Prisoner's Talking
Blues" was recorded, and Williams was ordered out of the cane fields,
to leave his domestic duties in the house of an Angola prison plantation
guard, or to temporarily suspend some other quotidian neoplantation
task, and told to grab hold of his twelve-string guitar and sing for a white
folkloric prison plantation tourist, the blues maestro was functioning in a
role that had been established on the plantation since the nineteenth
century—that of "musical slave." Indeed, on that day in the late 1950s, Robert Pete Williams was the latest in a long line of black subjects who had
been allotted the perverse privilege of entertaining white folkloric and
nonacademic tourists, politicians, local townspeople, fellow prisoners, and
prison-guard families and their guests at the plantation—the most famous
of whom were Williams and Huddie Ledbetter (aka Lead Belly), who were

"discovered" at the prison plantation as a folk and blues prodigy by John and Alan Lomax in the early 1930s.[26]

While the incarcerated performances of Williams and Lead Belly have attained something of a legendary status within histories of blues and folk music, the relationship between such moments of white academic prison plantation enjoyment and "discovery" to spectacles of coerced performance during chattel slavery has gone completely unmentioned. By outlining the ways in which performative "privilege" and punitive recreation have been deployed as central mechanisms of prison management, perverse pleasure, and free white civil subject formation, I consider the paradoxical fact that the neoslave's very attempt at fashioning something of a "selfhood" through sonic, theatrical, or testimonial redress is also what qualifies the postbellum experience of imprisonment as so dubiously reminiscent of chattel enslavement. Similar to the ritualized punitive theatrics of the antebellum period, when slaves were forced to sing and dance on the decks of slave ships, auction blocks, and during plantation holiday celebrations in order to simulate the African's "contentedness" with bondage, black postbellum prisoners have been regularly used as theatrical, musical, athletic, and filmic showpieces at Angola and other zones of neoslavery. Along with being forced to work in the plantation homes of Angola guards and local townspeople as field laborers and domestic servants, those late nineteenth- to mid-twentieth-century neoslaves who were considered artistically talented were used by Angola guard and warden families—or rented out to whites in the "free world"—as private musical slaves. While relatively well-known imprisoned folk and blues artists such as Williams and Lead Belly were recognized as prodigies by white folklorists—a label that in Williams's case led directly to his release on "servitude parole" to a local white landowner—most of the musical, theatrical, and athletic prisoners at Angola and other sites of neoslavery have never succeeded in singing, dancing, acting, or rodeo-ing their way to freedom or historical recognition. Indeed, rather than being a modality of public acclaim, early prison release, or recreational levity, incarcerated performance and other forms of punitive privilege at chain gangs, prison plantations, levee camps, and penitentiaries have actually been part and parcel of prison slave management, terror, and racialized public and private dishonor. I ultimately consider how this largely overlooked history of black incarcerated performance demonstrates the degree to which the (un)productive travails of slaves of the state on plantation house porches, in guard family kitchens, and other less visible venues, such as the prison master's bedroom, have been as fundamental to the liberal white supremacist penal and social order as their "productive" labors in railroad camps, levee camps, iron-ore mines, cotton rows, and penitentiary sweatshops.[27]

Again, this is not to underestimate the inarguably central role that profit-making and productive labor have played under U.S. carceral modernity, but to register the degree to which chattelized incarceration has always been catalyzed in a poly-determinant fashion involving dialectics of unfree labor expropriation and bodily subjection, economic dispossession and legalized domination, and rationalized profit and sadistic private and public enjoyment. Here the words of William Goodell in respect to the *res*, or object, status of the chattel slave are disturbingly prescient to our encounter with the seemingly infinite social, political, psychological, and visceral utility of the black neoslave in the United States since 1865: "Slaves, as Property, may be *used,* absolutely by their owners at will, *for their own profit or pleasure.*"[28] Indeed, even when the monetary profits of prison plantations such as Angola began to wane in the early twentieth century, and it became clear that southern states would be unable to match the huge profits that convict-leasing companies cleared in the late nineteenth-to early twentieth-century, the free/white civil subject continued to gain innumerable forms of bodily enjoyment, psychic pleasure, and identificatory self-augmentation through the hypervisibility, disposability, and fungibility of (in)human state property.

While looking through another of the infinite temporal boxes that offer historically muted exposure of the mythological divide of slavery and freedom, I encountered a photograph (Figure 1) that speaks volumes vis-à-vis the perverse private and public pleasures associated with black neo-enslavement. The image features a hunted black man, in prison stripes, attempting to climb a tree in the middle of a slave plantation field, while a white Angola guard captain sicks a pack of penitentiary bloodhounds on his body. In looking at the photograph, the viewer is immediately confronted with what I referred to above as the time-bending power of the racialized carceral. That is, aside from the time-locating effect of the prison stripes, which were surely sown by black women who were imprisoned at the neoplantation until 1966, the moment could have been snatched from any day in the more than two-hundred-year history of Angola or any other slave plantation, chain gang, convict lease camp, or prison plantation. Indeed, as Sara Johnson reveals in her superb treatment of the use of dogs as weapons of racial warfare from the fifteenth century through the current U.S. invasion/occupation of Afghanistan and Iraq (and elsewhere), such scenes of inhuman punishment have occurred throughout the Western Hemisphere from the very outset of chattel slavery and U.S. colonial genocide.[29]

However, a closer look at the photograph allows the viewer to engage with the long-standing tradition of private and public enjoyment that has accrued to the spectacular performance of race terror and the degree to which such rituals of racial domination have never been restricted to the "private" domains of extralegal lynching. Along these lines, I want to consider the overtly staged quality of an image that casts itself as an action shot of a prison plantation official fulfilling the heroic duty of apprehending a black fugitive neoslave. This is rendered most clearly in the guard's visible smirk—a look suggestive of how this moment was as much about the racial self-realization and self-aggrandizement of the free white lawman as an official documentation of an escaped black prisoner's apprehension. Along these lines, we can be sure that this photo, like the incalculable

Figure 1. Hellhound of Neoslavery: A fugitive neoslave "treeing," Louisiana State Prison Plantation, c. 1930s. Henry L. Fuqua, Jr., Lytle Photograph Collection and Papers, Louisiana and Lower Mississippi Valley Collections, LSU Libraries, Baton Rouge.

number of other horrific images just like it, was placed in a family photo album, scrapbook, or on a plantation house wall as an item of familial and social enjoyment long before it ever became a part of the historical archive. Another clear indication of the dramatized aspect of the photo is the way in which the guard's horse is shown in the background calmly grazing on plantation grass at a moment of supposed frenetic pursuit. These elements of punitive staging are joined by something, or rather someone, positioned at the margins of the photograph—the penitentiary's *Negro dog-sergeant*— an absent presence whose task as inmate guard (or "Trusty plantation Negro") would have involved guiding the four bloodhounds in pursuit of his fellow black prisoner ahead of the heroic white man on horseback.

The visible and invisible theatrics of the photo leave us to wonder just how long the white guard, the prisoner, the dog-sergeant, and the photographer would have been positioned near this tree in order to achieve this scene. Just who is the person behind the camera and how long did it take for him to set up this dramatic shot? Is the prisoner who is about to be mauled an actual would-be fugitive or one of the many black men on the neoplantation who avoided cane and cotton field labor by assuming the role of dog-sergeant's assistant, or "dog-boy"—captive men who bore the violative and coercive privilege of simulating neoslave hunts by allowing themselves to being chased, bitten, and "treed" by plantation bloodhounds in training? Did the "Negro" prisoner have to climb the tree multiple times in order to capture just the right look of unassailable power on his captor's face? Was the guard captain joined on this particular neoslave hunt by friends, family, and tourists enjoying a prison plantation holiday? And just how many such treeings of fugitive neoslaves culminated in all-out legal lynchings? At issue here is the virtual indistinguishability of neoslave punishment, incarcerated performance, and white supremacist pleasure. The elements of punitive contrivance and perverse amusement registered within this moment of neoplantation portraiture suggest how the legal atrocity of prison slavery has been evacuated through the pastoralizing, criminalizing, and dehumanizing lens of white supremacist mnemonic reproduction. Stated differently, the imaging of racial dominance presented here was both an ideological weapon—whereby black reenslavement and neoslave rebellion were conjured into the liberal white nationalist legends of "Negro" incorrigibility, un-dishonorability, and servile tractability— and an ontological tool, involving the visual projection of the dominative social position of the white prison master and other free white subjects who reaped psychological satisfaction and racist enjoyment from the open display of such photographs in prison plantation homes and local newspapers. As such, the visual mementos of racial state terror serve a similar purpose to the more often discussed pictorial and corporeal relics of extralegal lynchings that were exchanged between white subjects throughout the country until the mid-twentieth century—that is, they performed the racialized ontological function of solidifying the dominative and free status of whiteness through the visual reproduction of black enslavement, corporeal rupture, and dehumanization.[30] In fact, such images of southern neoslavery and the circumstances of punitive abjection that informed them actually point to the ways in which structural white supremacy stripped the word "dehumanization" of any social value in respect to the prison slave through the ideological reproduction of black subhumanity.

But, as stated above, the spectral voices of American neoslavery will not allow us the liberal nationalist comfort of receiving this image as an embalmed social artifact or a relic of a prehistoric racial past. Rather, they demand that we view this socially haunting object and the system of inhuman punishment that it symbolizes as an emblem of the experiential communion between yesterday's neoslaves and those who continue to face such rituals of legal violence in our current moment. Lest we unhear this element of the neo-abolitionist theoretical challenge posed by the words, sounds, and resistive cultural practices of prisoners such as Mumia Abu-Jamal, Mentha Morrison, and Robert Pete Williams, I want to draw attention to a news item that appeared in the *Savannah News-Press* (Georgia), from November 18, 1990:

A Prison Nightmare: Inmate Used as Bloodhound Bait
Austin, Texas. Richard Kaelin was *a prison 'dog boy'* in Texas and he has the scars to prove it.

All across his hands. And his arms.

Even on the back of his legs where snapping hounds drew blood as he served as human "bait"—a controversial practice he said he participated in about two dozen times during a 10-month stint in [Eastham] prison.

"It was a nightmare," said Kaelin, a 32-year-old father of three who was paroled five months ago.

"I've had to fight off 10 or 12 attacking dogs with no protective clothing whatsoever. Seen dogs rip chunks out of another convict's

leg. Seen them pull a man to the ground, tear open the padded
clothing.

"I've got bit every time I went out". . . .

He said he initially asked for the assignment, because he had
trained Dobermans for years—and because he knew it carried with
it a highly prized trusty status within the prison system. . . .

Kaelin said he asked for a transfer, but prison officials made it
clear that his next job would be undesirable work—like cleaning
out hog pens or cattle barns. And he could lose his trusy status,
which gives inmates increased responsibilities in return for more
good-time credits to be applied toward parole.[31]

Here the experiences of a Bush 41–era "dog-boy" in Lovelady, Texas, present horrifying evidence of the future-haunting power of the managerial and
punitive methodologies depicted in a long-buried photograph from Angola,
Louisiana. More specifically, this publically disseminated and socially disqualified dispatch from a late twentieth-century prison plantation expresses
the absolute inapplicability of notions of hegemonic consent in respect to
the predicament of modern chattel imprisonment. Like their antebellum
predecessors, spaces of U.S. neoslavery have functioned as *pseudohegemonic* arenas of domination wherein carceral privilege, volition, and "good-
time(s)" have amounted to coerced self-immolation, punitive abjection,
and living death.

However, along with issuing a temporal theory that allows us to view
the neoslave-treeing photograph as a marker of abject experiential communion between yesterday's neoslaves and those who face such rituals
of legal terror as I write these words, the historically muted voices of U.S.
neoslavery also offer an essential lesson in political geography—one that
calls for us to receive such images not as peculiarly "southern" horrors but
as unhistorical freeze-frames of a national process of ritualized state terror that has extended from Angola, to Attica, to Abu Ghraib (and back
again). Furthermore, anyone who has seen one of the countless cable television documentaries advertised as exposés of the "realities" of life inside
U.S. jails and prisons—or who has watched one of the seemingly infinite
stand-up routines, television shows, and Hollywood films that deploy the
"don't drop the soap" ritual of transposing prison rape and sex trafficking
into sources of comedic pleasure—understands that the spectaculariza-
tion and banal public enjoyment of racial state terror, natal alienation, and

inhuman punishment are far from distinctly southern phenomena.[32] Indeed, the constant bombardment of the U.S. social field with such criminalizing and dehumanizing imagery has a great deal to do with the fact that modern mass entombment remains both socially acceptable and socially pleasurable. As stated above, the images, sounds, and testimonies of neoslavery within this book are not to be received as relics of a dead "southern" history, but as ghostly reminders of the ways in which the violence of the past continues to be visited upon the lives of millions of black, brown, and poor people every day—whether performed by a modern K-9 unit on a ghetto or barrio street corner, or by a prison riot-squad in a SHU "exercise" yard that is hidden in plain sight.[33]

This book's engagement with the material ghosts of U.S. chattel imprisonment and racial capitalist misogynist terror as unleashed on both sides of the Mason-Dixon line and the fictive historical border of 1865 has been greatly influenced by the aesthetic *and* epistemic interventions of Toni Morrison—particularly as expressed in her most acclaimed novel, *Beloved*. In chapter 1, "'You Ain't Seen Nothin' Yet': *Beloved* and the Middle Passage Carceral Model," I offer a reassessment of this often-revisited text, one that examines the ways in which it represents a critically important epistemic and unhistorical guide into the workings of chattelized incarceration on both sides of the fictive 1865 border. Many critics have described the text as a "neoslave narrative," a generic tag that denotes a set of modern novels that offers retrospective accounts of chattel slavery from a postslavery context. I challenge this reading by describing *Beloved* as a *narrative of neoslavery,* a term I use—in a manner similar to the leading critical prison studies scholar Joy James—to describe prison and chain-gang-centered soundings, writings, testimonies, and social practices in which the unsettling continuities of slavery and freedom are brought into overt relief.[34] When read in relation to Morrison's portrayal of the Middle Passage, the novel's chain-gang scene focalizes the interconnections of ante- and postbellum formations of incarceration—namely, insofar as it illustrates the uncanny similarity between chattelized penal architectures such as the barracoon, the slave-ship hold, the slave pen, the chain-gang cage, and the solitary-confinement cell. This discussion of the tandem operation of racial and spatial terror across supposedly static historical borders lends itself to a theoretical discussion of the ways in which racialized architectures subject neoslaves to states of legalized exception that are grounded in the cultural branding of blackness as a biometaphysical exception to white, normative humanity. Along with suggesting the "for-ward haunting" propensities of chattel carcerality, Paul D's chain-gang experience unveils the paradoxical fact that sites of neoslavery have often doubled as spaces of black vernacular cultural production. As such, his performance of chain-gang songs throughout the text qualifies him as a narrative analogue of scores of black blues and folk artists who were "dis-covered" while being held as public slaves at chain gangs and prison plantations—and who used music as a means of retrieving something of a life out of conditions bordering on death. In laying out the theoreti-cal and counter-historical terrain of the entire book, my discussion of *Beloved* allows for a new understanding of Morrison's novel as a critically important epistemological, theoretical, and counter-historical document expressive of the long-standing centrality of racialized incarceration within Euro-American modernity.

Chapter 2, "'Except as Punishment for a Crime': The Thirteenth Amendment and the Rebirth of Chattel Imprisonment," focuses on the legislative and juridical history of the emancipation amendment and how this moment of putative black liberation actually signaled the condition of possibility for public reenslavement and the legal rebirth of the Middle Passage carceral model. The amendment's punitive exception allowing for "slavery and involuntary servitude" upon one's "due conviction" of a crime has represented one of the most devastating moments of liberal legal dis-course in U.S. history. The exception clause was the primary mechanism whereby an untold number of black subjects were legally disappeared into convict lease camps, chain gangs, prison plantations, and peonage camps. By tracing the origins of the Thirteenth Amendment's punitive excep-tion to the statutory and legislative handling of precariously "free" black bodies during the antebellum period, and to the congressional debates that attended the legislation's passing, the chapter allows for new understand-ing of a document of progressive dehumanization that, in spite of its dev-astating impact, has received only episodic treatment by prisoners, prison activists, and a small number of legal historians and prison studies schol-ars. The chapter concludes by considering the shrouded presence of the punitive exception within moments of apparent liberal legalism, such as *US v. Reynolds* (1914), a largely ignored Supreme Court case that dealt with the socialized form of neoslavery known as "peonage." By discussing the Supreme Court's problematic contention that a version of peonage called "criminal-surety" was strictly a "private" or contractual domain, I uncover how the state reasserted its divine right to transmute the free civil subject into a civilly dead object even within those moments when it seemed to offer a modicum of legal protection to a collectively terrorized and dispossessed black population.

The devastating real-life outcomes of the law's transmutation of chattel slavery into penal neoslavery are also the subject of chapter 3, "Angola Penitentiary: The Once and Future Slave Plantation." Here I focus specifically on the historical and present-day manifestations of neoslavery at "Angola" prison plantation—the *still-operational* eighteen-thousand-acre slave plantation that was converted into Louisiana's state penitentiary following the Civil War. The chapter centers on the neoplantation's blackface minstrel troupe and my ghostly encounter with its leader during a research trip to the prison's on-site museum. I discuss how the practice of forcing prisoners to act as musical and theatrical slaves led to an unaccounted-for excess in the form of a spectral poetics of living death and a subterranean politics of resistance. This section of the chapter is also where I begin to incorporate queer-of-color critique in order to register the hypercriminalization and differential terror faced by bodies branded as both racially and sexually aberrant. I also show how modern-day Angola continues to combine punitive leisure and terror through public spectacles such as the prison rodeo and invisible modalities of violence such as indefinite solitary confinement. I conclude that such practices mark Angola as a geographic analogue of the impossible severance of *southern* and *northern*— and *premodern* and *modern*—modalities of chattelized incarceration.

The fourth and final chapter, "The Warfare of Northern Neoslavery in Chester Himes's *Yesterday Will Make You Cry*," offers a reading of Himes's most critically ignored novel, a fictional autobiography of the writer's seven-year imprisonment in the Ohio State Penitentiary. I argue that Himes's fictionalized treatment of his actual experience as a survivor of the Easter Monday penitentiary fire of 1930 suggests that the Depression-era northern prison represented a repressive analogue of rather than a disciplinary exception to the chain gangs and prison plantations of the South. Himes exposes the degree to which the northern prison, like its more notorious southern counterpart, amounted to a regime of domestic warfare against those branded as contaminating elements within the social body. The spectacular sacrifice of prisoners' bodies in the fire scene represents a dramatic instantiation of the banal practice or premature, living, and civil death in zones of neoslavery, a quotidian operation that is represented most clearly in the novel by the state's hypercriminalization of racialized and nonheteronormative bodies. As in chapter 3, I deploy the theoretical rubric of queer-of-color critique as a means of uncovering the sexualized and gendered dimensions of racialized incarceration—particularly as they are expressed in the state's punitive response to the main character's romantic bond with a black migrant chain-gang survivor named "Prince Rico." By exposing the dynamic interplay between white supremacist, capitalist, and homo/transphobic state terror in the Depression-era penitentiary, the chapter sheds light on a totally ignored element of gender and sexual complexity within the oeuvre of a "hard-boiled" black writer most commonly portrayed as simplistically heteronormative and hypermasculinist. The chapter concludes by discussing the degree to which Prince Rico's presence in the text as both imprisoned writer and singer of chain-gang work songs gestures toward the haunting presence of the black migratory subject in the novel, and the insidiously successful migration of putatively southern models of racial capitalist misogynist homo/transphobic imprisonment into northern topographies of neoslavery. I hope that in offering a small opening of unhistorical reentry for neoslaves ranging back to 1865, this book will serve as a black apparitional genealogy of our current moment of prison–industrial genocide—one that represents an opportunity for us to be pushed further toward accepting the melancholic cue offered by Mentha Morrison and countless other historically anonymous neoslaves for all of us to *do something* in the name of prison slavery abolition and collective social liberation even as the racial capitalist misogynist state *has not* (yet) *ceased to be victorious.*[35]

"You Ain't Seen Nothin' Yet"

Beloved and the Middle Passage Carceral Model

There is a law of progressive dehumanization *in accordance with which henceforth on the agenda of the bourgeoisie there is—there can be—nothing but violence, corruption, and barbarism.*

—Aimé Césaire, *Discourse on Colonialism*

Worse than the taunts and the threats of the jailers, worse than the tortures they inflicted upon me, worse than the horrible conditions under which I lived, was the way time dragged and dragged for me. Every minute became an eternity of suffering.

—Angelo Herndon, *Let Me Live*

IN NOVEMBER 1994, as the number of prisoners in the United States was about to reach 1.6 million,[1] the North Carolina Department of Correction (DOC) issued a press release announcing that it had unearthed a relic of America's carceral past at one of its facilities. The release read in part: "[The] Community Resource Council for the Alexander Correctional Center arranged for the National Guard to forklift the cage out of the mud and vines. The original three-inch concrete floor, a small toilet and braided metal bars are all that remain of the prison cage where 12 convicts slept."[2] The news item goes on to point out that "the cage" is one of the two remaining examples in the state of the portable prisons within which, until the 1930s, chain-gang captives were hauled from place to place as they were working to build the North Carolina highway system (Figure 2). It then relates how such cages were purchased for $500 apiece from a Georgia company called "Manly Jail Works," which in its advertisement for the "moving prisons" boasted that a "bucket of disinfectant once or twice a month and a bucket of paint once a year will keep this cage clean, sanitary and vermin proof," and that the cage was "officially endorsed by state and county prison boards all over the South."

Early twentieth-century North Carolina chain-gang and prison officials more than corroborated the company's claims, stating that the cage allowed for fewer guards at the chain-gang camps and that it actually became a source of captive comfort and good cheer: "As soon as we began to use cages our men at once improved in health and spirits. They have proved themselves to be cool in summer, warm and well ventilated in the winter, and the men are much more comfortable than when housed in tents or the stockade."[3] After alluding to the horrifying statistic that the average life expectancy of those working on the state's chain gang was no more than five years, the DOC press release concludes by relating how the state planned to enshrine one of the two uncovered chain-gang cages in a transportation museum: "At least one of these cages should be restored as a stark reminder of how far we have come in penology in this century." This chapter considers how the unburial of the chain-gang iron cage in 1994 was actually anticipated seven years earlier by its literary resurrection in *Beloved,* Toni Morrison's most acclaimed novel. As the largely ignored experience of Paul D and his forty-four fellow chain-gang captives in the novel reveals, nothing about the chain-gang experience was "clean," "sanitary," or "vermin proof."

Even though the gangs came about as a "Progressive Era" reform of convict leasing, the transfer of southern states' mostly black prison and jail populations from private to state control represented a continuance rather than an abatement of racial capitalist terror and abjection. As Alex Lichtenstein points out in *Twice the Work of Free Labor,* his pathbreaking book on Jim Crow apartheid convict labor, the history of the American chain gang illuminates the degree to which northern liberalism and southern chauvinism, liberal bourgeois modernity and "backward" southern barbarity, have been mutually constitutive under U.S. empire. In so doing, Lichtenstein points to the central role of the federal government in supporting what was to have been a modernizing reform of the convict lease system: "With the help and encouragement of federal intervention [in the form of funding and logistical support], the progress embodied in a modern transportation network and the tradition of unfree black labor proved symbiotic."[4] He goes on to relate how, through the propagation of a mythos of black indolence—that is, the idea that freed blacks were only suited for "nigger work" and would only work by coercive means such as flogging, "stretching," and a modern version of the feudal stocks—the South was

Figure 2. The Land-Based Slave Ship. Outside view of a chain-gang cage in Georgia, early 1930s. Photograph by John Spivak. The original caption read: "The Cage: where convicts are herded like beasts in the jungle. The pan under it is the toilet receptacle. The stench of it hangs like a pall over the whole area" (*John Spivak,* Georgia Nigger *[Montclair, N.J.: Patterson Smith, 1969]*). *Photography Collection, Harry Ransom Center, University of Texas at Austin.*

able to progress toward economic modernization through prison slavery with county chain gangs playing a central role in projects such as railroad and highway construction, coal and iron-ore mining, and forest industries. As one former prisoner of a Florida chain gang recounts, captives experienced a banality of terror that blurred the line between life and death and offered a dubious replay of coerced performance spectacles that took place on the slave ship, the coffle, and the plantation: "We were sent to the swamps to do logging and lay rails. After 24 hours there *we prayed for death*. . . . If we did not work fast enough we were whipped cruelly. [And] after beating us all week [the guard captain] and *his guards would come and make us sing and dance for them*."[5]

In *Beloved*, Morrison's depiction of the slave ship, the plantation, and the chain gang disallows a reading of formations of racial terror and genocide as aberrant or premodern exceptions to the rule of U.S. capitalism, Western penology, and modernity. The resurfacing of the chain-gang cage in her novel, along with its resurrection of a ghostly survivor of the Middle Passage, exemplifies the centrality of architectures such as the slave-ship hold, the antebellum slave plantation, and chain-gang cage with respect to U.S. empire. Her work expresses what I describe as the "Middle Passage carceral model"—a paradigm of racial capitalist internment and violence that necessitates a shifting of white-subject–centered penal historiography. This remapping of the carceral through the lens of epochal race terror reads the barracoons, maroon Depósitos, coffles, slave holds, and plantations of the Middle Passage and plantation slavery as central to the Euro-American imperialist project—as spatial, ideological, ontological, and economic analogues of modern punishment that haunted their way into the present by way of formations of spatial violence such as the chain-gang cage.[6] Along these lines, I want to consider the degree to which *Beloved* represents as much of an epistemic intervention as a narrative one—how it can be conceived as offering a kind of black diasporic counter-penology that not only disinters largely unheard aspects of the unhistorical predicament of early black neoslavery, but that also offers a fundamental reassessment of the present moment of mass (in)human entombment through its centering of chattel slavery and the chain gang as primary sources of modern racial capitalist misogynist imprisonment.[7]

What I describe as the "forward-haunting" aspects of Morrison's ostensibly past-obsessed text also suggest that gothic penal architectures such as the chain-gang cage are not ready to be memorialized in museums as emblems of a bygone era of white supremacy and nascent southern capitalism—that is, if such memorialization within the context of white supremacist culture can amount to anything more than a disqualification of the survivals of unfreedom. *Beloved* underscores that the terror modalities of chattel slavery have not only survived the putatively static borderline of 1865, but have in fact reached their apogee with the "Security Housing Units" and "Supermax" prisons of today's prison–industrial complex.[8] Through this new approach to Morrison's most critically scrutinized text, I argue that formations of chattel slavery have resurfaced in updated forms in the context of a system of mass living death and human *incapacitation* (to use Ruth Wilson Gilmore's term)—which, as of this writing, entombs more than 2.3 million human beings—and, more specifically, a modern penitentiary system that now encages one out of every nine black men in the United States between the ages of twenty and thirty-four.[9]

The Narrative of *Neoslavery*

Literary critical discussions of Toni Morrison's *Beloved* often describe the text as a "neoslave narrative." This designation signifies an African American narrative mode of retrospection, whereby modern black writers such as Margaret Walker, David Bradley, Gayl Jones, Octavia Butler, and Ishmael Reed have offered re-visions of the violence and subjection of the transatlantic slave trade through the lens of the "post" slavery moment.[10] In what follows, I problematize this prevailing conception of temporality and historicity with respect to Morrison's most acclaimed novel and to U.S. history in general. I do so by reading the text not as a neoslave narrative but rather as a "narrative of neoslavery," a term that signifies narrative, sonic, testimonial, and performative expressions of postbellum racialized incarceration that unveil the horrifying methodological intimacies of chattel and penal enslavement.[11] The internment experiences of those such as Beloved, Sethe, Paul D (and Sethe's mother, who is lynched aboard a slave ship) underscore how for the African and those of African descent, the modern prison did not begin with Jeremy Bentham's Panopticon, the Walnut Street Jail, or the Auburn System, but with the coffles, barracoons, slave ships, and slave "pens" of the Middle Passage. As Dylan Rodríguez argues in this regard:

> A genealogy of the contemporary prison regime awakens both
> the historical memory and the sociopolitical logic of the Middle

Passage. The prison has come to form a hauntingly similar spatial and temporal continuum between social and biological notions of life and death, banal liberal civic freedom and totalizing unfreedom, community and alienation, agency and liquidation, the "human" and the subhuman/nonhuman. In a reconstruction of the Middle Passage's constitutive logic, the reinvented prison regime is articulating and self-valorizing a commitment to efficient and effective bodily immobilization within the mass-based ontological subjection of human beings.[12]

In *Beloved*, the transactional relationship between carceral spaces situated on opposing sides of the 1865 border underlines a mode of radical counterhistorical theorization within Morrison's text. That is, the central role of prison architectures vis-à-vis the novel's overall severing of linear temporality underlines its role as narrative reorientation of occidental penology by way of a nondiachronic, black diasporic timeline—or, more properly speaking, a temporal circularity, about which ostensibly obsolete or premodern terror modalities resurface right along with the text's putatively dead ghost-child.

As Robert Broad has pointed out, Beloved represents the return not only of Sethe's "crawling already" baby, but also of all those who were murdered as a direct result of their entombment in the holds, half-, and quarterdecks of slave ships during the Middle Passage—the "60 million and more" referred to in the novel's epigraph.[13] Beloved makes reference to her horrifying transatlantic experience in a stream-of-consciousness interlude that occurs well into the text:

> All of it is now it is always now there will never be a time when I am not
> crouching and watching others who are crouching too I am always
> crouching the man on my face is dead his face is not mine . . . some
> who eat nasty themselves . . . at night I cannot see the dead man
> on my face . . . small rats do not wait for us to sleep someone is
> thrashing but there is no room to do it in if we had more to drink
> we could make tears . . . we are all trying to leave our bodies
> behind . . . in the beginning we could vomit now we do not now we
> cannot . . . someone is trembling . . . he is fighting hard to leave his body
> which is a small bird trembling there is no room to tremble so he is not
> able to die . . . those able to die are in a pile.[14]

Compare Beloved's testimony to that given in 1788 by the Reverend John Newton after he had witnessed conditions aboard European slave vessels. He describes the spaces in which the captives were packed,

> sometimes more than five feet high and sometimes less; and this height is divided toward the middle for the slaves lie in two rows [on platforms] one above the other, on each side of the ship, close to each other like books on a shelf. I have known them so close that the shelf would not easily contain one more.
>
> The poor creatures, thus cramped, are likewise in irons for the most part which makes it difficult for them to turn or move or attempt to rise or to lie down without hurting themselves or each other. Every morning . . . *more instances than one are found of the living and the dead fastened together.*[15]

Both testimonies describe a Western philosophy of imprisonment that was used from the early modern period through the nineteenth century aboard slave vessels, a system known as "tight-packing." The teleology of this mass-internment system had to do with maximizing the profitability of the trade in human commodities by requiring that slaves be crammed into every inch of available space. The bodies of slave-ship prisoners were horizontally pressed together and vertically stacked upon each other in a manner that immobilized captive men, women, and children to such an extent that shifting one's position or sitting up straight was often impossible. Those entombed in the slave hold were often forced to lie in their own excrement for the entire transatlantic journey. Such methods of sadistic racial capitalist misogynist architectural calculation are evidenced in the now-infamous sketch of the Liverpool slaver *Brookes*. The diagram pictures 451 cartoon-like black figures placed "spoon" style into the holds and tiered platforms of the ship, a number that was three short of what in 1788 was deemed legal for a ship of its size. This sardine-like tiering of human cargo theoretically allotted a space of six feet long by sixteen inches wide (and approximately two feet high) for every man; five feet, ten inches long by sixteen inches wide for every woman; five feet by fourteen inches for every boy; and four feet by six inches for every girl. That the *Brookes* carried as many as 609 prisoners (155 more than its capacity) across the Atlantic before the 1788 law was passed exemplifies the dehumanizing spatial techniques by which early modernity's first racialized prisons produced mass biological death of genocidal proportions.[16] Between 15 percent and 20 percent of those who began the "passage" in the coffles and barracoons of Africa perished before reaching the Americas—a figure that amounted to at least 12 million premature deaths.[17]

For my purposes, however, it is important to recognize how the incidence of biological death that occurred in the coffles, barracoons, "factories," ships, and "pens" of the Middle Passage does not offer a complete measure of the genocidal nature of modern white supremacist carcerality.[18] That both Beloved and Dr. Newton speak of the living and the dead being piled on top of one another and fastened together by chains in the holds of slave ships graphically testifies to how the killing of the African slave involved more than the taking of her biological life. Stated simply, Black Atlantic and "New World" mass internment, enslavement, and genocide were and *are* produced as much through the mass reproduction of *living death* as through the production of biologically expired bodies. Here we might think of the radical import of Sethe's only monologue, in which she explains the untold reason behind her ostensibly insane act of infanticide: "*If I hadn't killed her she would have died* and that is something I could not bear."[19] If we take into account living death as a fundamental aspect of Middle Passage and plantation imprisonment, then the number of those killed in the trade does indeed approach the seemingly miscalculated death count of "60 million and more" that appears in Beloved's epigraph. And, as we shall see below, 60 million and more becomes an even more accurate count if we consider how slavery's death toll reaches across the border of Emancipation. The inclusion of the category of living death within the techniques of state and corporate killing also allows us to attend to the ways in which today's modern version of mass human warehousing— the white supremacist capitalist misogynist penitentiary—represents an extension of rather than an antithesis to Middle Passage genocide. As Colin Dayan states with respect to the connected positionalities of slave and criminal: "Death takes many forms, including loss of status beyond which life ceases to be politically relevant."[20]

The status loss that accompanied the mass entombment and natal alienation of transatlantic imprisonment was enacted on the ideological and ontological level through the questioning of the slave's membership in the community of humans.[21] In other words, if the captive could be projected as inhuman or subhuman, then *dehumanization* could be emptied of any semantic value, thereby disqualifying black injury.[22] Sylvia Wynter uses the term *biological idealism* to describe the ideological system that transmuted African humanity into quasi-bestiality and black personhood into objecthood. For her, the "nigger" was made to represent "the ultimate zero degree category of an ostensibly *'primal'* human nature whose differentiation from a lurking bestiality was dangerously imprecise and uncertain, so uncertain as to call for a question mark to be placed with respect to the humanity of this zero-degree category."[23] The repeated references to the dispossession of manhood and womanhood on the part of Sethe, Paul D, and the rest of the "Sweet Home men"—*you got two legs not four; I had a bit in my mouth*"—represent the reintroduction within the "post" slavery moment of the ideological construct of black subhumanity, discursive branding processes that began with chattel slavery and that were specifically inaugurated with the mass physical branding, rape, and cargoing of human beings aboard the slave ship. Consequently, the realm of ideology—the casting of blackness as an anthropology of metaphysical deficit[24]—was as much a devastating weapon in the production of mass social and living death as whips, chains, and pistols.[25]

In one installment of a series of epistolary narratives from 1795 to 1796, George Pinkard, a British medical doctor, attests to the warfare functionality of racist ideology through his very attempt at eliding the terror of the Middle Passage. After insinuating that a group of African women aboard a slave ship flirted with him and other white male ship tourists by giving them "an expressive look . . . or significant gesture," Pinkard attempts a rationalization of slave ship terror that prefigures the plantation romances of late nineteenth- and twentieth-century American literary and popular culture:

> Their sleeping berths were the naked boards. Divided into two crowded parties they reposed, during the night, upon the bare planks below—the males on the main deck—the females upon the deck of the aft cabin. In the day time they . . . were kept mostly upon the open deck, where they were made to exercise, and encouraged by the music of their beloved banjor [sic], to *dancing and cheerfulness*. We saw them dance and heard them sing. In dancing they scarcely moved their feet, but threw about their arms and twisted and writhed their bodies into a multitude of disgusting and indecent attitudes. Their song was a wild and savage yell, devoid of all softness and harmony, and loudly chanted in monotony.

Their food is chiefly rice which they prepare by plain and simple boiling. At the time of messing they squat around the bowl in large bodies, upon their heels and haunches, *like monkies* [*sic*], each putting his paw into the platter to claw out with his fingers. We saw several of them employed in beating the red husks off the rice, which was done by pounding the grain in wooden mortars. . . . This appeared to be a labor of cheerfulness. *They beat the pestle in time to the song and seemed happy; yet nothing of industry marked their toil;* for the pounding was performed by indolently raising the pestle and then leaving it fall by its own weight.[26]

Here the physical branding that slaves received upon their kidnapping onto the coffle and slave ship is coupled with their epistemic branding as animalistic, infantile, and lazy; as such, the forebears of the plantation "darky" are incapable of feeling the pain of internment, of recognizing the enormity of their dispossession, or of performing industrious labor without the spur of punishment. For those humans branded as savage "monkeys," terror and collective disappearance are an occasion for joviality, merriment, and song. As in the testimony above of a twentieth-century chaingang captive, what is absent from this account is that such "happiness" on the part of the slave-ship prisoner was only made possible through the enactment or threat of physical terror. In contrast, as Saidiya Hartman suggests, what was at issue for the slavery apologist (and often the self-avowed liberal abolitionist) when acting as spectator of black suffering was not veracity with respect to the experience of the enslaved but the transmutation of black sufferance into a stage of enjoyment: "The terms of this disavowal are something like: No the slave is not in pain. Pain isn't really pain for the enslaved, because of their limited sentience, tendency to forget, and easily consolable grief. Lastly the slave is happy and . . . his happiness exceeds our own . . . the initial revulsion and horror induced by the sight of shackled and manacled bodies gives way to reassurances about black pleasure."[27]

Whether through its stagings of black inurnment to pain or through the direct enactment of collective terror, the slave ship symbolized the manner in which natal alienation, the slave's total banishment from lines of kinship and modes of sociocultural life, catalyzed mass living death, the zero degree of enslavement's serialized social death. In so doing, it functioned as an unprecedented penological configuration of early modernity, one that turned the Atlantic into a *necropolitical* geography (to use Achille Mbembe's term), an oceanic death-scape, wherein the border separating life and death became virtually indecipherable.[28]

Beloved's presence in Morrison's novel takes on a new meaning if we attend to how her undead or dead-living state represents the obverse of the living death condition of Middle Passage prisoners. Her lived remembrance of transatlantic imprisonment gives us a prime example of how inanimate spaces can acquire devastating agency through radical asymmetries of power. In the case of the slave ship, a transfer of subjectivity took place wherein an inanimate architecture acquired "a life of its own" by siphoning the life of the captive. In Beloved's monologue, we see how the cramped conditions of the slave ship played a determining role in social relations even as they were a product of those relations. In terms of its violent and dehumanizing effects on the captive body, the slave/prison ship carried what Louis Althusser would describe as a "relative autonomy" vis-à-vis the reproduction of relations of dominance.[29] This powerful agency of place is represented elsewhere in *Beloved* by Denver's reaction whenever she approached 124, a house that she regarded "as a person rather than a structure. A person that wept, sighed, trembled and fell into fits."[30] In her narrative re-creation of the slave-ship hold, Morrison exposes a space whose subjectivity and purpose were defined by the power to immobilize, torture, and kill.

Literary critiques of the relationship between personal memory and collective history in *Beloved* have often described characters' reliving of the experience of slavery in strictly symbolic terms. According to this approach, the presence of the Middle Passage in the text represents the need of those such as Sethe and Paul D to revisit repressed horrors of the past in order to begin the process of self-possession and to initiate the healing process. In Sethe's case, Beloved's presence initiates her recollection of a conversation she had with Nan regarding the repeated rape of Sethe's mother aboard a slave ship. Thus, in such a psychoanalytical approach, the first line of Beloved's monologue—*"All of it is now . . . it is always now . . . there will never be a time when . . . I am not crouching and watching others who are crouching too"*—would represent how the memory of the atrocities of the Middle Passage and, by extension, of "Sweet Home" plantation is still alive within the psyche of the newly freed black subject. Although the validity of this argument is in large measure valid, I want to suggest how it might also be incomplete. A closer look at the relationship between

Beloved's monologue and the novel's chain-gang scene requires us to re-examine Morrison's rendering of the slave ship and plantation as sites of African diasporic living memory, or what Sethe describes as her "remem-ory." The transactional relationship of Black Atlantic, plantation, and Jim Crow prison architectures across boundaries of space and time registers the salience of Stephanie Smallwood's theoretical assertion of the tempo-ral boundlessness of the Middle Passage—that, while trapped within the prison-ship hold, it was "enormously difficult for Africans to clearly dis-tinguish the phases of their journey, or to anticipate the end of one phase and the beginning of another." The experience of Paul D and forty-five other black men in a chain-gang camp in Alfred, Georgia, registers the possibility that what Smallwood describes as the "temporal and spatial entrapment" of the Middle Passage never ended—that indeed, *it is always now*—even, or especially, after the Civil War.[31]

In a section of the novel that has received little critical attention (and that is also conspicuously absent from Jonathan Demme's cinematic adap-tation of the text), Paul D recounts his experience of being sold by School-teacher—a punishment that resulted from his attempted escape from Sweet Home. While being led in a coffle across the state border from Kentucky to Virginia with ten other slaves, Paul D attempts to kill Brandywine, his new owner. His efforts fail; and, as a result of the "crime" of attempting to attain freedom, he is sent to a pre–Civil War chain-gang camp in Georgia. Morrison opens the chain-gang chapter with a description of the method that was used to warehouse Paul D and his forty-five fellow prison slaves:

> The ditches, the one thousand feet of earth—five feet deep, five
> feet wide, into which wooden boxes had been fitted. A door of
> bars that you could fit on hinges like a cage opened into three walls
> and a roof of scrap lumber and red dirt. Two feet of it over his
> head; three feet of open trench in front of him with anything
> that crawled or scurried welcome to share *that grave calling itself
> quarters.*[32]

For Paul D, the trauma of living burial within the prison camp "box" man-ifests itself physically in the form of uncontrollable body movements. The narrator describes the point at which "they shoved [D] into the box and dropped the cage door down, his hands quit taking instruction. On their own they traveled. Nothing could stop them or get their attention. They would not hold his penis to urinate or a spoon to scoop lima beans. . . . The miracle of their obedience came with the hammer at dawn."[33] Tellingly, the word Morrison uses in this chapter and other sections of the text to describe the uncontrollable physical signs of Paul D's trauma-inducing experience of underground living burial is *trembling*, the very same word that Beloved uses repeatedly to describe the condition of a fellow captive in the underwater tomb of the slave-ship hold—*someone is trembling . . . he is fighting hard to leave his body which is a small bird trembling . . . there is no room to tremble so he is not able to die . . . those able to die are in a pile.* That Paul D, the chain-gang prisoner, and the anonymous slave-ship prisoner are described as having an identical somatic response to captivity suggests how spaces of racist terror have as much spectral force in the novel as Sethe's ghost-child—that what Morrison describes as Beloved's "miraculous resurrection" is coincident with and contingent upon the revival of the Middle Passage carceral model within the experiential present of characters in the text.[34]

This new understanding of the relationship between epochal racial and spatial violence and the ineluctable resurfacing of the dead in the novel offers an alternative point of entry into the meaning of Beloved and Paul D's sexual engagements. Most critical inquiries into this sexual bond have treated it solely from the perspective of Paul D. His physical encounters with the ghost-child-woman in the very shed where she was killed represent the beginning of his confrontation with the emotional contents of an injured selfhood that he has kept hidden, or repressed, within what Morrison describes as his "tobacco tin"—his sealed-off heart.[35] An element of this bond that critics have largely ignored until now, however, is its meaning from the point of view of Beloved. What little has been written on the subject has focused on its obvious meaning: her instigation of the union simply reflects her jealousy with respect to D's intimacy with Sethe. This would suggest that Beloved uses sex with Paul D as a pragmatic tactic, one that she knows will lead to D's self-imposed banishment from 124, a place that, from her perspective, has no room for the presence of a man— namely, one whose initial entrance into the dwelling led to her own temporary banishment, and, more important, one who represents a competing force for the attention of Sethe.

However, if we keep in mind Beloved's stream-of-consciousness rememory of her slave-ship experience, we realize that sex with Paul D represents much more than a mere fit of jealousy over Sethe's love. Along with the man who is described as "trembling," and who dies while pressed against Beloved's body on the slave ship, Beloved also remembers another slave-hold prisoner who was an object of her affection, a sentiment that results from this particular unnamed man's gift of song: "Storms rock us and mix the men into the women and the women into the men that is when I begin to be on the back of the man. . . . I love him because he has a song when he turned to die I see the teeth he sang through . . . his singing was soft . . . his song is gone now I love his pretty teeth instead."[36] This description reminds us that one of Paul D's defining characteristics is his tendency to break out into the songs he learned while slaving on the chain gang at any given moment, his uncanny ability to tap into Sethe's own repressed memories and feelings: "Emotions sped to the surface in his company. Things became what they were: drabness looked drab; heat was hot. Windows suddenly had view. *And wouldn't you know he'd be a singing man.*"[37] From Beloved's perspective, Paul D's singing voice represents the possibility that the singing man she had lost to death in the slave-ship hold has been reincarnated—that she is not the only embodied ghostly passenger of the Middle Passage who has materialized in the space of 124. Beloved and Paul D's lovemaking thereby signifies an attempt on Beloved's part at re-creating the *mixing of man and woman* that occurred aboard the slave vessel on something close to her own terms rather than those imposed by the slave trader. She desires a consummation of two "living" bodies rather than the commingling of the dead and living dead that occurred in the hold. In this sense, Beloved's spectral role is one not just of indiscriminate rage, jealousy, and "break-neck possessiveness": her yearning for (re)union with Paul D is an expression of how slaves attempted to fashion sexual agency, intimacy, and love out of conditions bordering on death. For my purposes, the question of whether Paul D is actually the singing man whom Beloved desired (or the trembling man who did not have enough room to achieve biological death) during the Atlantic crossing is immaterial. What I am concerned with is the ways in which the experience of terror that D faced as a chain-gang prisoner elicited the sort of somatic signs, emotional responses, and musical soundings that could easily be (mis)recognized as emanations of the slave-ship experience.[38]

In discussing the recurrence of something perilously akin to the slave ship within the experiential present of characters in the text, several questions arise. Why does Morrison choose to focus on the chain-gang camp as the primary connecting link to the "past" horrors of the slave ship?

What is the function of the southern prison camp in a novel fixated on the haunting power of "Sweet Home" slave plantation? What does the law's conjuring of Paul D and Sethe's attempts at escaping bondage into criminal offense say about the nature of black freedom after formal emancipation? And, finally, how do the expressions of a politics of wounded radicality on the part of those such as Sethe, Paul D, and his fellow chain-gang captives represent the vexing contours of agency within zones of collective unfreedom? Again, I am interested in how the experience of Paul D and his forty-five fellow chain-gang captives in particular, along with the dynamics of racialized imprisonment in the text in general, reveals how Morrison's characters and action are haunted as much by the future as they are by the past.[39] Put another way, I am interested in how Morrison's characters experience a cyclical or back-and-forth temporality and historicity wherein the past, present, and future exist in constant interface. From the perspective of the novel's late antebellum plot, the labeling of the runaway slave as a transgressing *criminal* represents an ominous prefiguration of the postbellum branding of the black "criminal" as *slave of the state*.[40] Moreover, *Beloved* registers how acts of collective racial capitalist misogynist terror and enslavement have not been (and will not be) received without radical, if injurious, responses on the part of the unfree.

The Racial Exception as Rule of American Law: The Radical Resurrection of the "Alfred 46"

In one of *Beloved*'s numerous flashbacks, Paul D recalls how, after the collective escape attempt of himself, Sethe, Halle, Sixo, Paul A, and Paul F had been foiled, Schoolteacher placed a bit in his mouth. He was subsequently dragged away from Sweet Home by a rope, one end of which was lassoed around his neck, with the other attached to the back of his new owner's carriage. It was at this moment that he caught a glimpse of "Mister," the plantation rooster—a bird who in the estimation of Paul D had been free to express more "manhood" than he had at Sweet Home. D remembers the look on Mister's face as the former was being hauled away from the plantation: "Then he saw . . . the rooster, smiling as if to say, *You ain't seen nothing yet.* How could a rooster know about Alfred, Georgia?" Mister's foreboding expression is corroborated by the treatment Paul D receives immediately upon his arrival at the prison camp, a point symbolized by the fact that it was the experience of living burial at Alfred, Georgia—not his enslavement at Sweet Home—that led to D's trembling fits. Indeed, the narrator alludes to the peculiar effects of the camp early in the text, the day after D arrives at 124, well before the chain-gang scene actually unfolds: "The box had done to him what Sweet Home had not; Drove him crazy so he wouldn't lose his mind."[41]

I want to pursue the possibility that the dubious look of knowing in the rooster's eyes as Paul D is being hauled away from the slave plantation refers to much more than D's imminent experience of terror and dehumanization in Georgia—that the "you" of the *you ain't seen nothin' yet* has a collective resonance that reaches forward into the actual lived reality of black people after Emancipation. When viewed from the experiential present of the novel's main characters—and from the present context of the prison–industrial complex—Mister's glance not only portends Paul D's personal encounter with the chain gang but also heralds the collective ordeal of many freed men, women, and children who have been subjected to prison slavery and to an overall state of siege and domestic warfare after the attainment of de jure freedom. Read in this light, the omen Paul D garners from Mister's stare registers the unsettling reality that the transition from slavery to freedom would lead to an amplification rather than abatement of injury, living death, and murder for many former slaves. This is symbolized by the clear correlation between Morrison's antebellum chain-gang camp and the county chain-gang camps of the postbellum era.

To fully understand what I mean by the "future orientation" of *Beloved* and the role of imprisonment in producing the forward-haunting aspects of the novel, we must first identify what can be thought of as Morrison's use of *strategic anachronism* in the chain-gang scene. With this term, I am referring to her intentional placement of a punitive regime normally associated with the late nineteenth to mid-twentieth century into the context of the late antebellum period. The mechanism that the Alfred, Georgia, prison-camp authorities use to entomb Paul D and his fellow captive fugitives, the "box" that "resembles a cage," has a real postbellum historical referent: the portable chain-gang "cage," or "moving prison," many of which were built in Georgia and distributed throughout the southern states. Both radical scholarship and muckraking accounts of early Jim Crow apartheid belie the earlier referenced claims on the part of chain-gang administrators to the "comfort" and "sanitary" nature of the moving prison. In a *Harper's Monthly Magazine* article from 1933, Walter Wilson offers a more accurate picture:

The steel cage . . . wagon is ordinarily about 18 feet long, 8 feet high, and 8 feet wide with two or three tiers of bunks in each cage. This is the sleeping and living room for about 20 men. Because it can easily be moved with the progress of the job, the cage is especially suited for road work, if one doesn't consider the welfare of the prisoners. It is a sight not soon forgotten to see the cages, which look all the world *like animal cages in a circus* . . . as they move to another job. Country people flock to the front gates to watch and listen as the procession of cages, loaded with vermin infested men, creaks and rasps along the hot, sandy, dusty road. In rainy weather a tarpaulin flap is dropped over the walls of the cage to shut out the water; it also shuts off ventilation and light. A tub underneath a hole in the floor is the toilet. A horrible stench arises from it. . . . On Sundays, nights, and holidays the men are locked in the cages. *A long chain is passed through the leg chains of each prisoner*—these latter are permanently riveted on by the blacksmith. In this way all the prisoners are fastened to a single chain and can be released only by a guard unlocking them. Obviously such an arrangement has its good points, for fewer guards are necessary to watch fettered prisoners in a steel cage, and money is saved.[42]

The portable aboveground version of Morrison's box was designed to hold from twelve to twenty-four men or boys. To fit so many prisoners into such a small space, the "cage" consisted of two parallel sections of three-tiered bunks with an access path running down the center and a hole cut in the middle of the walkway, through which prisoners were forced to urinate and defecate into a bucket placed on the ground below. The outer shell of these structures was either a lattice of wooden or metal bars that left the chain-gang captive open to surveillance by camp guards and the public or four windowless wooden walls (Figure 3).[43] This latter version of the rolling cage left prisoners with no view of the outside world and allowed them only a minuscule supply of breathable air—through a narrow slit running along the top of the structure.[44] As in the case of the slave ship, the moving cage immobilized its chained prisoners to such an extent that sitting up straight was impossible.

The dehumanizing and suffocating aspects of these spaces of racial capitalist terror register the affiliations of the prison architectures of slavery and freedom. More specifically, in terms of its properties of defilement

Figure 3. Two prison slaves chained inside a Georgia chain-gang "box," early 1930s. Photograph by John Spivak. Photography Collection, Harry Ransom Center, University of Texas at Austin.

and tier-style human cargoing, the land-based moving prison of Jim Crow apartheid revived, on a smaller scale, the horror endured by those entombed within the water-based moving prisons of the Atlantic. That Morrison situates her version of the chain-gang cage within the late antebellum period rather than its "proper" place in postslavery history analogizes the porous and vertiginous nature of the 1865 border from the standpoint of black captives. The doubling of racialized prison architectures across ostensibly separate historical junctures highlights the temporal and spatial dislocation that the enslaved prisoner experienced, whereby any attempt at distinguishing past and present modalities of entombment is rendered nearly impossible.

Like Paul D and his forty-five fellow prisoners in the late antebellum chain gang, those free black people who were rounded up and detained at chain-gang camps for misdemeanor "crimes" such as vagrancy, breach of contract, petty larceny, loitering, public nuisance, drinking, and gambling faced circumstances bordering on, and crossing the border into, what Giorgio Agamben describes as "conditio inhumana."[45] For Agamben, the horrifying conditions of the Nazi concentration camp resulted from a "state of exception"—an extreme political situation wherein the sovereign or state executive suspends constitutional rights and the rule of law in order to "protect" the state against a reputed enemy. The declaration of the exception in relation to Jews, Gypsies, queer subjects, communists, and others labeled as "internal and external enemies of the state" resulted in the Nazi concentration camp, a space wherein human "life" was turned into an approximation of death. As Agamben explains, "Because [camp prisoners] were lacking almost all the rights and expectations that we customarily attribute to human existence, and yet were still biologically alive, they came to be situated at a limit zone between life and death."[46] He adds that these conditions of living death, along with the serialized murder that took place at the camp, represented the deployment by the Nazi state of what he calls "thanatopolitics," a more openly coercive and sanguinary form of Foucault's "biopolitics," where modern state power has more to do with the power to kill than it does with the micromanagement and disciplining of the living. Along these lines, a main function of state sovereignty in the modern era has to do with crafting an enemy so defamed that they come to represent a "life that may be killed without the commission of homicide."[47] For Agamben, the concentration camp is the ultimate symbol of the zone of exception, whose place outside law clearly distinguishes it from what Foucault describes as "the modern prison." Agamben insists that the exception is exemplified in the "camp—and *not the prison,*" that "*prison law constitutes a particular sphere of penal law and is not outside the normal order,* the juridical constellation that guides the camp . . . is martial law and the state of siege. This is why it is not possible to inscribe the analysis of the camp in the trail opened by the works of Foucault."[48]

In *Beloved,* Morrison's portrayal of the carceral according to a black diasporic historical and temporal axis blurs any such clear distinction between the exceptional conditions of the concentration camp and the various formations of imprisonment to which black captives and other Third World peoples have been subjected from the colonial period in the Americas through the present.[49] A major problem with Agamben's comparison of "the camp" to "the prison" has to do more with historiography than methodology. He relies upon Michel Foucault's prison history, one that somehow manages to offer a detailed account of Western carceral regimes from feudalism to modernity without giving as much as a passing reference to how slavery or colonialism fit into the picture: prison spaces such as the barracoon, the slave ship, slave pen, plantation, and chain-gang camp are not counted as nodes on what he describes as the Western "carceral archipelago." These glaring omissions disclose how the feudal-modern polarity outlined in *Discipline and Punish* depends on a complete disregard for the centrality of slavery and colonialism in the production of Western carceral formations and in the unfolding of occidental modernity as a whole. Morrison's centering of the Middle Passage and the plantation as primal sites of racialized punishment forces us to reevaluate what we are referring to when we speak of the "modern prison." She reveals how the slave ship and the plantation operated as spatial, racial, and economic templates for subsequent models of coerced labor and human warehousing— as America's original prison–industrial complex. Her characters' experiences symbolize the degree to which, from slavery to neoslavery, surveillance, incarceration, and collective punishment have made *normal life* tantamount to a state of siege, if not all-out war, for those branded as internal aliens or natural-born enemies of the state on the basis of the social construct of race.[50]

As Joy James has pointed out in respect to the dominative nature of legal and extralegal terror against black people, analysis of the integral functionality of white supremacy in relation to U.S. carceral modes in particular, and to Western imperialist mass violence in general, short-circuits the major historical claim of Foucault's project—that with the transition from feudalism to modernity, punishment became less public and physically repressive, and more psychologically coercive, refined, and "administratively decent."[51] This historical and theoretical blind spot explains Foucault's mistaken claim that the chain gang was discontinued as a punitive institution in the early nineteenth century, when it ended in France, an ironic historiographic oversight considering that America's more repressive brand of the chain-gang system would operate well into the twentieth century: that is, until some two decades before the publication of *Discipline and Punish*.[52] Although the theoretical import of Foucault's analysis of modern disciplinary regimes cannot be denied, the experience of Africans, indigenous peoples, and other colonized and enslaved collectives within locales of Western imperialism belie any categorical separation of premodern and modern methods of violence and social domination. Here we are reminded of Cedric Robinson's assertion in *Black Marxism* of the ever-encroaching and decidedly undead presence of slavery within Euro-American modernity: "The expansion of slavery into the nineteenth century was not an anachronism but a forewarning."[53] Again, the measure of necropolitics and the state of legalized exception in spaces such as the slave-ship hold, the chattel-slave plantation, the postbellum prison plantation, and the portable chain-gang camp cannot be reduced to biological death rates—though, as David Oshinsky has pointed out, such rates in the case of postbellum prison camps ranged from 10 percent to 40 percent.[54] For those such as Paul D and the real-life referents for his experience of neoslavery, conditions of terror and abjection made biological life tantamount to living death. To limit our conception of thanato- or necropolitics to biological death counts is to negate the genocidal reach of imperialist sovereignty in its protean methodologies of killing.

If the radical temporality of Morrison's narrative of neoslavery is registered largely by its exposition of the time-bending capacities of racialized imprisonment, then its full measure cannot be understood without attending to the modes of resistance within the text that function as replays of transatlantic and plantation rebellion. In a moment that recalls the perilous and tenuous nature of collective rebellion during chattel slavery, the "Alfred 46" are delivered from their underground living burial. As the waters of a torrential rainstorm fill the muddy trench in which they are buried, the forty-six chain-gang captives act in unison to release themselves by yanking the "long-chain" that held them in the underground cage: "They talked through the chain like Sam Morse and . . . they all came up. Like *the unshriven dead,* zombies on the loose, *holding the chains in their hands,* they trusted the rain and the dark, yes, but mostly . . . each other."[55]

Morrison's description of the newly freed men as "zombies" registers both the paradoxical capacities of attempted agency and collective action on the part of those facing the most abject forms of dominance and how, within the context of continued collective subjection, the "success" of such acts of rebellion cannot most often be measured by a "clean break" from unfreedom. Indeed, as the *arwhoolie,* or work song, that the forty-six men perform before their prison break makes clear,[56] the history of black diasporic resistance to formations of prison terror has as much to do with the reclamation of the story of one's servitude as it does with a miraculous inversion of power dynamics. During the song, they imagine beating their chain-gang boss to a pulp, even as they sound their collective state of living death: "More than the rest, they killed the flirt whom folks called Life for leading them on. Making them think the next sunrise would be worth it; that another stroke of time would do it at last."[57] Paul D's rearrest and enslavement in Delaware by a company tellingly called "*Northpoint* Bank and Railway" soon after his escape from the chain gang brings into stark relief the tenaciousness of formations of slavery, even for those who reach points north of the Mason-Dixon line. Moreover, Paul D's tendency to re-sound the songs he learned in Alfred, Georgia, throughout the novel expresses how Morrison conceived of D and her other chain-gang characters as fictive emblems of the countless (and mostly nameless) black men who have attempted to steal moments of expressive refuge in the face of unendurable horror in chain gangs, levee camps, prison plantations, and solitary-confinement cells from 1865 to the present.

Again, notwithstanding the emotive power of black (anti)prison songs as they have extended from the spirituals and field hollers of antebellum slaves, to the chain-gang and prison plantation songs of incarcerated blues maestros, to the prison-centered verses of modern hip-hop artists—the historical enormity of Middle Passage imprisonment in the United States and its continued accretion into our current moment both domestically and globally disallows any model of tidy or triumphalist resistance. In her literary exhumation of the American chain-gang box from the Georgia mud (and from the dustbin of racist liberal historiography), Morrison resounds Amílcar Cabral's warning to global freedom fighters to "claim no easy victories."[58] Cabral's reminder is especially relevant in respect to the realities that real-world black prisoners have faced in the wake of the Thirteenth Amendment, bodies whose transmutation into state-crafted slaves have rarely led to anything close to the miraculous escape of the "Alfred 46," and whose most viable forms of resistance have tended to render the word "victory" virtually meaningless.

For those who, up to the point of this writing, continue to contend with modern reconfigurations of the slave ship and the chain-gang box, what Saidiya Hartman defines as "redressive action," can often be indexed only at the level of the captive's ability to render an alternative truth to that which led to her captivity—a de-marginalization of disqualified stories.[59] Morrison's narrative unburial of the chain-gang box shows how the act of subverting master narratives of black criminality and notions of liberal progress is a main mechanism by which redress can be enacted even as state biological and living death counts continue to mount and collective substantive freedom seems all but impossible. It involves asserting the right to testify to one's own situation of abjection rather than allowing it be transmuted into the well-worn national fable of natural-born black criminality. In this light, the ownership of one's own story of terror—a testifying to one's own pain—signals a branch of black and subaltern agency that reaches as far back as the slave ship. This element of circular temporality represents the incomplete nature of domination and the degree to which the Middle Passage carceral model produces its own excesses, "zombies" whose resurfacing challenges white supremacist plotlines of history.[60] In his reunion with Sethe at the close of Beloved, Paul D recognizes his own hard-won power of narrating, of saying the unsayable that he has repressed for so long: "Only this woman Sethe could have left him his manhood. . . . He wants to put his story next to hers."[61] Read in this light, Morrison's narrative of neoslavery—the placement of the stories of the Middle Passage, the plantation, and the chain gang at the center of U.S. nation building—represents a radical reclamation of stolen histories and bodies. Indeed, her counter-historical reclamation project held vital (if largely ignored) political urgency given the fact that black bodies were being legally kidnapped into U.S. penitentiaries en masse at the very moment of Beloved's publication in 1987.

As Joy James reminds us, modes of radical theorization are not the sole property of academics—radical epistemologies (or what the late VèVè Clark often described as "epistemic breaks")—often emerge from spaces of death and abjection rather than from those of liberal bourgeois privilege.[62] No work written from the position of entombment better captures the explosion of facile models of diachronic history by the neoslavery narrative than George Jackson's *Soledad Brother* (1970), an epistolary manifesto composed while he was a political prisoner in California penitentiaries for ten years, seven of which were spent in solitary confinement. From this perspective, Jackson's letters represent what can be thought of as moments in which a real-world Paul D was able to tell his own stolen story and theory of racial capitalist incarceration. In fact, Jackson's subjection to protracted isolation operated as the condition of possibility for what, to my knowledge, constitutes the first full theorization of what he defines as *neoslavery*. However, whereas much of the black radical socialist's discussion of the term reflects a Marxist interpretation of class relations in the United States, whereby working-class black people such as his father were turned into "wage slaves," Jackson's experience of indefinite isolation produces a poetic theory of neoslavery that exceeds the explanatory capacities of his socialist training insofar as it underlines how white supremacist incarceration submits the racially/criminally stigmatized subject to a predicament akin to the supposedly premodern experience of chattel slaves.[63]

In a letter dated April 1970, composed after he had already endured seven years of solitary confinement for his interracial organizing and radical writings from behind prison walls, Jackson registers in poetic form the continuities of his experience and that of slave-ship prisoners:

> *My recall is nearly perfect, time has faded nothing.* I recall the very first kidnap. *I've lived through the passage, died on the passage,* lain in the unmarked, shallow graves of the millions who have fertilized the Amerikan soil with their corpses; cotton and corn growing out of my chest, "unto the third and fourth generation," the tenth, the hundredth. My mind ranges back and forth through the uncounted generations, and *I feel all that they have felt, but double.* I can't help it; there are too many things to remind me of the 23½ hours [a day] that I'm in this cell. Not ten minutes pass without a reminder. In between, I'm left to speculate on what form the reminder will take.[64]

Jackson's corporealized total recall of chattel slavery is catalyzed by the material and experiential imbrications of the slave *hold* and prison *hole*— with the process of carceral dehumanization forcing a definition of neoslavery that derives less from an intellectual engagement with the black subject's place in proletarian labor history than Jackson's embodied feeling of being shuttled to a supposedly dead place in chattelized carceral history. The solitary prisoner is not only removed from lines of biological kinship but from social contact altogether, a fact that explains his testimony of feeling everything that chattel slaves felt "but double." Like the chain-gang cage, Middle Passage imprisonment expressed as indefinite solitary involves a radical disorientation of temporal experience; in other words, the articulation of racial and spatial terror in the context of the modern prison warps time insofar as the experiential present is haunted in a material fashion by *past*, or *southern*, modes of racial capitalist domination.[65] As Colin Dayan suggests, although "the resurrection of slavery is often discussed in the turn to convict labor and the criminalization of blacks in the postbellum South . . . the penitentiary . . . especially 'solitary,' also known as 'the discipline' or 'the separate system'—offered an unsettling counter to servitude, an invention of criminality and prescriptions for treatment that turned humans into the living dead."[66] The unsettling continuities between Jackson's experience and that of chattel slaves past is registered in his poetic remapping of the "passage" as more than simply a southern or water-based phenomenon. For him, "the millions who have fertilized the Amerikan soil" cannot be separated from the countless bones lining the Atlantic. Through his experientially based poetics of living death, Jackson insists that the process of mass murder that began on the Atlantic continued right through his own entombment in a "land-based slave ship" on the liberal West Coast, a space of white supremacist terror that he also repeatedly described as a "concentration camp."

Again, the purpose of reading the Middle Passage as foundational to Western carceral formations is not to treat of spaces such as the slave ship, the plantation, the U.S prison camp, and the German concentration camp as homological, as exactly the same, but to recall Césaire's critically important assertion that the systematic reproduction of banishable, enslavable, and murderable masses by way of racist ideological warfare is a process that did not begin with or end with the defeat of the Third Reich.[67] Along with the colonized peoples of the Global South, the "free" black subject of the Jim Crow apartheid era represented life that had been devalued to the extent that it could be reenslaved, killed, dispossessed, or subjected to living death with impunity. The existence of the moving prison—and its direct relation to the dehumanizing carceral space of the slave ship— reveals how, in the United States, what Agamben describes as *conditio inhumana* has often been a function of rather than an exception to the "normal" processes of law and order. In the words of Walter Benjamin, the experiences of those entombed within such racial capitalist misogynist architectures signify how the "tradition of the oppressed teaches us that the 'state of emergency' in which we live is not the exception but the rule."[68] Indeed, such conditions for blacks under both the law of slavery and the law of neoslavery have had to do not with the state's creation of an exception to the law, but with the fact that the "Negro" subject has historically been viewed as a *biological and metaphysical exception to the rule of (white) humanity*—as the antithesis of order, rationality, morality, and productivity—and as a natural-born enemy or "Problem" of the state.[69]

In terms of the chain gang and early postbellum prison slavery in general, the ideological construction of blacks as quasi-human was not simply an example of southern anachronism, a fact indexed by the direct funding of the chain gang by federal public-roads monies. One particular engineer representing the federal Office of Public Roads registered northern culpability with respect to southern neoslavery in a way that rivaled the worst paternalism of plantation slavery. He argued that the "*human material dealt with* [on the chain gang] *is . . . so radically different* from other sections" that it demanded techniques that would be considered inhumane if deployed against whites.[70] Only in this case, as Lichtenstein points out, chain-gang neoslavery differed uniquely from its agrarian forerunner in that the enslaved would be exploited in the service of revamping the southern economy in the image of northern modernity and industrialization.

The direct correlation between Morrison's "box" and the postbellum "cage" suggests that, in creating the chain-gang scene, Morrison was acutely aware of how the dehumanizing methods found on the slave ship not only reemerged in antebellum spaces of horror such as Sweet Home plantation, but that the slave ship also haunted the experience of black people after emancipation. Along these lines, Stephanie Smallwood's theorization of the insufficiency of linear models of space-time in reference to the slave's experience of transatlantic imprisonment applies directly to the black experience of collective entombment after Emancipation. As Smallwood points out, "The slave ship chartered no course of narrative continuity between the African past and the American present, but rather memorialized an *indeterminate passage* marked by *the impossibility of full narrative closure.*"[71]

That the chattelized carceral practices depicted in *Beloved* continued to defy narrative and material closure in the United States by haunting their way forward into the lives of black people after the advent of de jure free-dom is represented in chilling fashion in *Westbrook v. The State* (1909), a relatively obscure legal case from the early twentieth century that in many respects represents a spectral materialization of Morrison's chain-gang scene.[72] At the same time, the long-forgotten events that led to this case also signal how no fictionalized portrait of neoslavery can begin to approach the horrors of the real as experienced in places like an American chain-gang camp in the early 1900s. The case involved the conviction of a black man named Cleveland Westbrook for the murder of a fellow prisoner, another black man named James Davis, at an actual Georgia chain gang in the southern region of the state. After the Tift County superior court issued a guilty verdict, Westbrook challenged his conviction on the homi-cide charge in the state supreme court based on his contention that his killing of the man coffled next to him on the long-chain actually amounted to self-defense—that he had stabbed Davis in a last-ditch desperate re-sponse to being whipped by the camp's warden and having the camp's long-chain tightened around his legs and ankles by his fellow prisoners.

Westbrook's version of the events leading to his murder conviction is ultimately corroborated by the chain-gang warden, J. M. Davis, who upon cross-examination by the prisoner's attorney, revealed that he had whipped Westbrook repeatedly across his face while ordering members of the chain-gang coffle to lay hold of their chains and squeeze Westbrook into compli-ance with his orders for the latter to drop a knife he had been using to carve a piece of wood. After relating how he always allowed his prisoners to sing and play games around a campfire before riveting them inside their "car"—the Tift County version of the chain-gang rolling cage—the camp's war-den offered this account of what occurred after he had overheard an appar-ent altercation between some of his "boys on the chain":

> When I went out there I had my strap in my hand. When I told him to get ready for the whipping he had the knife in his hand. He stepped out and pulled off his coat and laid it on the bench, and stepped back a step or two and looked at the chain and looked at me and said "I don't think you ought to whip me." I said to him "Throw the knife out here and get down across the bench." He dropped his head and thought a minute and said, "No, sir, you or no other man don't whip me.' *The boys began tightening the chain* . . . . I called on Mr. Davis, the trusty, and the boys on the

chain, to assist in getting the knife away from him. He just made a spring at that boy, the first one on the chain next to him; after he had cut at him he rushed over at me; when he stabbed to hit the boy I struck him in the face with my strap, and he made at me. He hadn't attempted to strike me before that. He told them to stand back or he would kill the first one that came at him. Then I struck him in the face, and he turned on me. I hit him some eight or ten times; then he turned and stabbed the boy, and then turned back on me. I hit him over the head; *they kept tightening the chain.* Then he turned and stabbed the boy again.[73]

Here the sense of communal recognition and collective resistance expressed in the liberation of the "Alfred 46" is contorted through the unspeakable lens of the real. Rather than communicating with one another in unified resistance to premature death, the chain-linked Morse code enacted by the "ten or twelve" black men riveted to one another at the Tift County camp represents the degree to which neoslaves—like their pre-1865 counterparts— have often been coerced into acting as terroristic proxies of the master in securing one another's experience of ritualized rupture. In this sense, Westbrook's status as an individually recalcitrant neoslave—one whose "resistance" amounted simply to an adamant refusal to bend over a bench for a hiding by the warden or a "negro trusty"—offers a terribly instructive documentary refraction of Paul D's internal monologue at the moment of his liberation: *Somebody yanked the chain . . . hard enough to cross his legs and throw him in the mud. He never figured out how he knew—how anybody did—and he took both his hands and yanked the length of chain at his left, so the next man would know.* Fully receptive of the knowledge that he received from every yank of the chain that his own fellow slaves of the state were acting as a collectivized extension of the prison master, Westbrook chose the only available avenue of self-defense in the moment by stabbing the sole body that the tightening coffle would allow his arms to reach.

In reversing the lower court's decision, the state supreme court ulti-mately found that the judge in the earlier case had erred in neglecting to offer the jury instructions as to statutory provisions that would have allowed for the charge of homicide to be reduced to voluntary manslaughter. In his opinion for the case, J. Atkinson cited penal code 1147 (1895), which repre-sented the state's de jure regulation of the practice of whipping in its chain-gang and convict lease camps: "No whipping shall be administered to a convict by a whipping-boss or other officer or person, except in cases where it is reasonably necessary to enforce discipline or compel work or labor by the convict."[74] For the court, Westbrook's violent response to being whipped and squeezed by the long-chain represented an understandable "passionate" reaction to the warden's assault on his person—a claim that could be made at law because of the fact that the "convict" was a "human" and not a slave:

> The convict occupies a different attitude from the slave toward society. He is not mere property without any civil rights, but has all the rights of an ordinary citizen that are not expressly or by necessary implication taken from him by law. While the law does take his liberty, and imposes a duty of servitude and observance of discipline for the regulation of convicts, it does not deny his right to personal security against unlawful invasion. The convict is human, and his passions are subject to influence and as liable to become uncontrollable as if he were not a convict. The law which provides for reducing a homicide from murder to voluntary manslaughter makes no exception of a convict, but contemplates that no homicide by any person shall be classed as murder where there is an absence of malice. . . . While it is the duty of a convict to faithfully execute his sentence and observe the rules of discipline lawfully fixed for his government, he is not bound to submit to unauthorized acts of violence perpetrated or attempted against his person.[75]

Although cited in contemporaneous legal texts as a refutation of the pronouncement in *Ruffin v. Commonwealth* (1871) that the convict is a "slave of the state," the *Westbrook* decision unveils the degree to which the law's very disavowal of neoslavery is as potent an exemplar of its necropolitical power to re-chattelize the "free" black civil subject as Justice Christian's open expression of this commonly practiced divine right in *Ruffin*. In an astounding example of what Dayan refers to as the occult rhetorical practice of the law, the court's deployment of the discourses of regulatory efficiency and liberal legal humanism shroud the substantive realities that overdetermined the death of James Davis, the torture of Cleveland Westbrook, and the neo-enslavement of an untold number of black people in the state of Georgia and throughout the United States after 1865.

That is, in proffering an ostensible juridical check on an isolated instance of what it deemed to be an irregular and "unreasonable" application of the whip, the court reinscribes the penal sovereign's power to submit the black subject to every form of chattelized entombment that took place at spaces such as the Tift County chain gang. This is represented clearly in the exception clause of the very statutory measure upon which the court bases its decision—that which allowed for the whipping of chain-gang captives in "reasonably necessary" cases wherein such terror was found to have been deployed in the service of labor compulsion or normal penal discipline. According to this standard of reasonable necessity, Westbrook's appeal would have never been heard were it only to have occurred as a result of his refusal to go to work, which represents the single most common reason that penal administrators have used to rationalize their deployment of the whip and other forms of corporeal rupture on chain gangs, convict lease camps, prison plantations, and modern penitentiaries from their inception. The liberal legal proscription of a single instance of "irregular" whipping and "unlawful invasion" thereby offers a backdoor normalization of the very condition of possibility for Westbrook's torture and James Davis's biological death—that is, the chain-gang system itself.

When read along with the portrayal of the chain gang in *Beloved*—and against the backdrop of the actual experiences of Georgia's black prisoners who faced the quotidian *lawful invasions* of whipping, scatological cargoing in rolling cages, natal alienation, serialized sexual violence, and perpetual coffling during both productive and "unproductive" moments of chattelized imprisonment—the court's positing of a definitive line between the social death of slavery and the civil death of imprisonment rings cynical at best. One wonders how liberal legal assurances that the "humane" practice of the American chain gang was not slavery would have sounded to James Davis as he lay dying in a pool of his own blood, chained to the man whose desperate attempt at avoiding an "unreasonable" whipping was the substantive cause of his biological death; or how such platitudes would have been received by the tens of thousands of black men, women, and children who laid chained to and stacked atop one another inside modern American barracoons such as the Tift County chain-gang cage at the very moment Justice Atkinson crafted his decision. What is at issue here is the necessity of our attending to the experiential as the substantive register of neoslavery and the degree to which the liberal white supremacist misogynist practice of post-1865 law rests at the very core of that experience, even when, or especially when, it attempts to deny that neoslavery exists. In fact, as mentioned briefly above, the most liberal legal document in U.S. history, the Thirteenth Amendment to the U.S. Constitution (1865), stands as the clearest example of the terroristic capacities of "humane" and "progressive" legal practice as levied against nominally free black bodies. In what follows, I uncover a largely untold legislative, statutory, and philosophical genealogy of this document of progressive dehumanization and the incantatory means by which the postbellum white supremacist state has used the emancipation amendment's exception clause to transmute countless precariously civil racialized subjects into publicly and privately terrorized slaves of the state.

"Except as Punishment for a Crime"

The Thirteenth Amendment and the
Rebirth of Chattel Imprisonment

Slavery was both the wet nurse and bastard offspring of liberty.

—Saidiya Hartman, *Scenes of Subjection*

It is true, that slavery cannot exist without law . . .

—Joseph Bradley, *The Civil Rights Cases*

ANYONE PERUSING THE advertisements section of local newspapers such as the *Annapolis Gazette* in Maryland, during December 1866, would have come across the following notices:

Public Sale—The undersigned will sell at the Court House Door in the city of Annapolis at 12 o'clock M., on Saturday 8th December, 1866, A Negro man named Richard Harris, for six months, convicted at the October term, 1866, of the Anne Arundel County Circuit Court for larceny and sentenced by the court to be sold as a slave.
Terms of sale—cash.
WM. Bryan,
Sheriff Anne Arundel County.
Dec. 8, 1866

Public Sale—The undersigned will offer for Sale, at the Court House Door, in the city of Annapolis, at eleven O'Clock A.M., on Saturday, 22d of December, a negro [*sic*] man named John Johnson, aged about Forty years. The said negro was convicted the October Term, 1866, of the Circuit Court for Anne Arundel county, for;

Larceny, and sentenced to be sold, in the State, for the term of one year, from the 12th of December, 1866.

Also a negro man convicted of aforesaid, named Gassaway Price, aged about Thirty years, to be sold for a term of one year in the State,

Also, a negro woman, convicted as aforesaid, named Harriet Purdy, aged about twenty-five years, to be sold for a term of one year in the State,

Also a negro woman, convicted as aforesaid, named Dilly Harris, aged about Thirty years, to be sold for a term of two years in the State.

Terms of sale—Cash.

WM. Bryan,

Sheriff Anne Arundel County

Dec. 26th, 1866.[1]

Congressional testimony and court dockets relating to these post–Civil War prison slave auctions reveal that each "negro" sold on the courthouse steps of Annapolis was actually charged with "petit larceny"—a small-scale property crime. In the men's cases, the list of alleged offenses included the theft of "6 barrels of corn," "1½ bushels of wheat," and "a hog"; and, in the cases of the women, it included taking "a pair of gaiter boots" and "stealing clothes from a lady." The docket also catalogues how the five black prisoners were sold for prices ranging from $27 to $50—and, while not including the names of each purchaser, does indicate that Harriet Purdy was "sold for $34.00 to Elijah L. Rockhold."[2] This small set of facts and figures, along with those contained in the advertisements placed in the local news by the county sheriff, represent the extent of information supplied by the historical archive in respect to the lives of these five "free" black people after being branded as *Negro criminal* by Maryland's legal system. Most of what we have in the way of any sort of encounter with their lives once they were converted into fungible black property for the alleged thieving of white property is the unspeakable conjecture allowed us by sonic, testimonial, and literary fragments of slaves and prison slaves—rememories gleaned from the wreckage of racial genocide as it piled over the mythological historical divide erected to convince us that scenes such as slave auctions had been forever vanquished with the culmination of the Civil War and the passage of the Thirteenth Amendment in 1865.[3]

However, as much as we do not know regarding the specific fate of one such as Harriet Purdy, who through her imputed theft of a pair of white "lady's" boots was literally sold, or at least *rented for a year*, to a white man on the steps of the Annapolis courthouse—the terror of what we do know, especially in terms of the "infinite uses" to which the chattelized black body had been subjected for well over two centuries leading up to her auction day, offers stark grounding for rumination. So far, my discussion of this element of recessed knowledge has mostly focused on the ways in which black writing, song, and testimony allow footholds of encounter with the terror, enormity, and unrepresentability of neoslavery. However, while doing so, I have also noted an equally important arena of neoslavery narration—that of the law. The various modes of legal discourse that allowed for the sale or lease of convicted bodies such as those of Purdy, Richard Harris, John Johnson, and Dilly Harris through criminal sanction supply a great deal of critical information insofar as they elucidate the conditions of possibility for the collective violence that black people have endured in the context of de jure freedom.

Indeed, as Joy James has pointed out, no discussion of neoslave narratives in the United States would be complete without centering the storytelling devices employed by the racial capitalist patriarchal state through the devastating fictive practices of the law.[4] This line of analysis is especially important given the law's dubious capacity to conjure the free black subject into a reenslaved object, a violent functionality that it had exhibited with all-too-efficient acumen well before December 1866. The border state of Maryland, where these courthouse auctionings of free black people occurred, is actually an illuminating political geography with which to begin such a discussion, since, because of its liminal physical and political positioning during the antebellum period, the state was home to easily the largest population of *free Negroes* in the country from the colonial period through the Civil War.[5] Therefore, when townspeople walking by the Annapolis County courthouse on December 8 and 26, 1866, bore witness to postemancipation auctions, the only novel aspect of the scene of a call for bids on "free" black bodies was the fact that it was occurring after the passage of the Thirteenth Amendment; for criminalized freepersons in the slave state had been the subject of disproportionate imprisonment and racially exclusive forms of punishment (both corporeal and capital) since its inception.[6] Such precariously free subjects had also been vulnerable to the spectacle of public auctioning since 1835, when, under its Black Code,

Maryland lawmakers passed the first of three statutory provisions that called for the sale or lease of criminally stigmatized free Africans.

The five auctioned black subjects mentioned above could very likely have resided in the state when the 1858 version of the code—that which led to their own public sale—was established by "an act to modify the punishment of free negroes, convicted of Larceny and other crimes against this State." The beginning of the legislation reads:

> SECTION 1. Be it enacted by the General Assembly of Maryland, That in all cases hereafter, where free negroes [sic] shall be convicted of the crime of simple larceny, to the value of five dollars and upwards, or accessory thereto before the fact, they shall be sentenced to be sold as slaves for the period of not less than two nor more than five years ... and every free negro who shall be convicted of robbery, may in the discretion of the court, be either sentenced to confinement in the penitentiary, as now provided by law, or be sold either within or beyond the limits of the State, as a slave for the period of ten years.[7]

Indicative of the politically and geographically liminal position of Maryland, Section 324 of its Slave/Black Code of 1858 embodies the disavowed intimacies of southern and northern white supremacist law insofar as it had nearly exact replicas, public auctioning included, within the racially restrictionist state constitutions of northern states such as Indiana, Ohio, and Illinois until as late as 1864.[8]

Furthermore, as I will discuss later in this chapter, its haunting reappearance in a particular branch of a seemingly infinite array of "color-blind" criminal statutes that catalyzed the nationally sanctioned and administered postemancipation trade in southern black convicts further illustrates the problematic historical cordoning of chattel slavery as a pre-1865 phenomenon. Relative to its pre-emancipation counterparts in the former Northwest Territories, however, Maryland's version came with an especially terroristic provision dealing with those free black persons who may have exhibited revolutionary inclinations:

> [I]f any free negro shall after the passage of this act, be convicted of willfully burning any ... Court House, county or public prison, or the penitentiary, poor house, warehouse or any building belonging

to the State . . . such free negro, his aiders or abettors and counsel-
ors, being free negroes, and each of them shall be sentenced to be
punished by hanging by the neck as now provided by law, or in the
discretion of the court to be sold either within or beyond the limits
of the State, as a slave for life.[9]

The discretionary power of the state to dispose of the would-be-free African body through either the public servitude of the penitentiary, the private servitude of chattel slavery, or capital punishment enacted by the
lynch rope dramatizes the gothic exchanges of civil, social, and premature
death that would continue to define black (and Indigenous) incarcerated
existence after collective emancipation. Whether rebirthed in the form of
the openly declared Black Codes of presidential Reconstruction, or those
administered under the color of color-blind laws that have reigned since
the late nineteenth century, the late antebellum white supremacist legal
codes stand as stark embodiments of the process of forward haunting that
I discussed in chapter 1 in reference to the chain-gang scene in *Beloved*. That
is, the three intimately connected and cross-fertilizing methodologies of
legally administered racial terror sanctioned in Maryland's statutory "modification" of its punishment of emancipated persons—imprisonment,
enslavement, and lynching—represented necropolitical precursors to legal
and extralegal formations of violence waged against countless free black
subjects for generations after the Civil War. This forward-haunting quality
of the Maryland Black Code and those of other southern states—along
with that of the "Negro Codes" and "Black Laws" of the northern United
States—disturbs a remark made by Republican senator John Creswell of
Maryland, who attempted to account for post-1865 public sales of free
black people by stating that the "law under which these decrees have been
passed . . . and these sales have been made is a relic of that code in its worst
aspect," a "vestige of [an] old spirit."[10]

As I will discuss at greater length below, the mix of public and private
mastery exhibited in the antebellum Black Code's handling of the problematic presence of the free "Negro" within the civil body was far from a
dead or flickering letter by the time of the public leasing of criminally
branded free persons. The state's wielding of the power to submit the black
subject to the official incarceration of the prison, the social incarceration
of the individual convict purchaser, or outright public extermination represented a chilling prefiguration, a statutory dress rehearsal, for the large-scale

state-administered public/private carceral hybrids that would come to define zero-degree black unfreedom after 1865: the convict lease camp, the chain-gang camp, the county farm, the peonage camp, the prison plantation, and the "modern" penitentiary. Stated differently, the auctioning, imprisonment, and lynching of nominally free black subjects under the law of slavery issued specters of chattelhood that would secrete across the fabled frontera of freedom as the state assumed full-fledged mastery over the always already criminalized "free" black body. Read in this light, the ritualized legal spectacle of the courthouse slave auction was not an episodic or anachronistic remnant of a soon-to-be completely vanquished system of legal violence and public profiteering: this apparition from chattel slavery

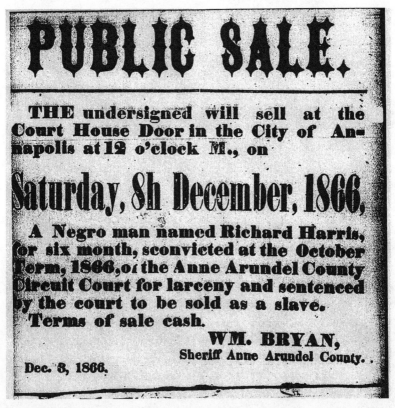

Figure 4. "Postslavery" prison slave advertisement from "Sale of Negroes in Maryland," a hearing of the U.S. House of Representatives Committee on the Judiciary, January 11, 1867, unpublished transcript.

was also a premonition of the state's primary role in the production, industrialization, and direct administration of spectacular and banal mechanisms of neoslavery from the chain gang to the prison–industrial complex.

But this line of argument in respect to the undead, or forward-haunting, propensities of late antebellum reenslavement statutes begs the vitally important question of method. That is, just how, in the context of the grand narrative of emancipation, were such documents of legal sorcery able to reanimate in the form of postbellum Black Codes and the racially motivated and administered "color-blind" statutes that replaced them, such as those dealing with vagrancy, breach of contract, public disorderliness, gambling, and petty larceny, socially manufactured "crimes" associated with structural black dispossession, landlessness, and vulnerability to legal and extralegal terror? What was the main legal channel whereby the public auctionings of black freepersons on courthouse steps in states ranging from South Carolina, to Maryland, to Illinois, would transfigure into the generalized courtroom and boardroom rentings of emancipated black bodies that defined postslavery imprisonment? How exactly was the statutory criminalization of black freedom that occurred in the antebellum period lawfully propelled into the future, producing various formations of neoslavery from the privatized public dominative regimes of convict leasing, peonage, and criminal-surety to the no less dominative and economically interested public systems of the county chain gang, the County Farm, and penitentiary plantation? How, for instance, was it possible for the poverty- and hunger-induced crime of hog-stealing to move so nimbly from being deemed "petty larceny" by Maryland's state legislature (a discursive gesture that proffered a rationale for the auctioning and reenslavement of Gassaway Price in Annapolis in 1866) to being dubbed "grand larceny" by Mississippi's state legislature after the supposed suspension of its Black Codes (supplying one of the key "color-blind" statutory pillars for the state's penal reenslavement and murder of thousands of black people after its passage in 1876)?[11] Put more directly, what was the legal conjuring method that allowed for *imprisoned slave auctioning* to seamlessly transition into both officially and customarily sanctioned *enslaved convict leasing*?

The central answer to these questions represents one of the most devastating documents of liberal legal sorcery ever produced under occidental modernity: the Thirteenth Amendment to the U.S. Constitution itself. As I briefly articulated earlier in reference to the primary legal mechanism by which the Middle Passage carceral model was able to lay hold to postemancipation black life, the very amendment to the Constitution that was to have performed the miraculous conversion of "chattel into man" actually facilitated his *and* her re-chattelization through imprisonment: "Neither slavery nor involuntary servitude, *except as punishment for a crime whereof the party shall have been duly convicted,* shall exist within the United States, or any place subject to their jurisdiction." The grandest emancipatory gesture in U.S. history contained a rhetorical trapdoor, a loophole of state repression, allowing for the continued cohabitation of liberal bourgeois law and racial capitalist terror; the interested invasion of "objective," "color-blind," and "duly" processed legality by summary justice and white supremacist custom; and the constitutional sanctioning of state-borne prison–industrial genocide.

That my attachment of such gravity and epochal meaning to the exception clause is no case of political hyperbole is registered by the publicly aired debate it caused, both at the time of its passage and in the years surrounding the implementation of the postbellum Black Codes. Carl Schurz spoke directly to the imminent reenslaving purposes to which postemancipation statutory law would be marshaled in filing a report on southern race relations just after the Civil War:

> The emancipation of the slaves is submitted to only in so far as chattel slavery in the old form could not be kept up. But although the freedman is no longer considered the property of the individual master, he is considered the slave of society, and all the independent state legislation will share the tendency to make him such. The ordinances abolishing slavery passed by the conventions under the pressure of circumstances will not be looked upon as barring the establishment of a new form of servitude.[12]

An explicit account of the primary role of the Thirteenth Amendment in the reenslavement of free black people was offered at the Joint Committee on Reconstruction in 1866, the same year that the neoslave auctions advertisements were posted in Maryland newspapers. In his testimony, a northern clergyman testified to having had a conversation with a white southern preacher who made a brazen declaration regarding the surreptitiously terroristic utility of the emancipation amendment, one that in its brutal accuracy expresses how the white supremacist opportunity afforded by the exception clause was a matter of southern common sense: "Alluding to the amendment to the Constitution that slavery should not prevail, except as punishment for a crime, [the southern preacher said] 'we must now make a code that will subject many crimes to the penalty of involuntary servitude, and so reduce the Negroes under such penalty again to practical slavery.'"[13]

While the southern minister's reference to a "code" of virtual reenslavement obviously refers to the openly racist Black Codes that would immediately begin to terrorize the black population after the war's cessation, in the remainder of this chapter I will explore the ways in which the exception clause had temporal reverberations that extended long after the apparent demise of openly racist statutory law, as well as a geographical reach that was in no way cordoned to points south of the Mason-Dixon line. Through my discussion of congressional debates, the peonage cases, and the hybrid formations of public/private neoslavery that placed free black people in a constant state of collective jeopardy, I underline the degree to which "color-blind" juridical, legislative, and penal law all played central roles in constructing an overall *code of reenslavement*—states of legalized and racialized exception made possible in large measure by the Thirteenth Amendment's punitive exception.

Aside from episodic interventions by prisoners, antiprison activists, and a small number of scholars in respect to its dominative effectivity, the exception clause has received very little in the way of sustained treatment within legal, social, and political histories of Reconstruction, southern neoslavery, and the national system of racial capitalist patriarchal punishment that continues to ravage black, brown, Indigenous, and poor people.[14] Legal histories that do not simply laud the amendment as a marker of liberal legal progress have focused almost entirely on some aspect of the shifting juridical interpretation of its prohibitory dimensions relative to slavery and its "badges." Read collectively, these discussions focus on the ways in which the amendment's common law construction during the first fifty years of emancipation vacillated from a relatively expansive view during Reconstruction (marked by cases upholding the constitutionality of the Civil Rights Act of 1866); to a restrictive view in keeping with Lochner-Era laissez-faire ideology and the liberal white supremacist sanctioning of Jim Crow apartheid (signaled most infamously with the *Civil Rights Cases* [1883]); to a moment of brief reexpansion in the early twentieth century with the Supreme Court's rulings in the peonage cases (*Bailey v. Alabama* [1911] and *U.S. v. Reynolds* [1914]).[15]

Centering the legislative and juridical treatment of the penal exception, and its ominously shrouded presence within moments of ostensible legal progressivism such as that exhibited in *Reynolds*, allows us to engage with counter-historical realities rendered largely invisible by this focus on the amendment's prohibitory function. It unveils the ways in which the Thirteenth Amendment offered legal cover and social acceptability for Jim Crow apartheid at its most abject and murderous degree within spaces such as the chain gang, the convict lease camp, and the peonage camp— how these public/private hybrids of neoslavery were enacted not through the emancipation amendment's juridical restriction but through its very deployment as a Janus-headed weapon of reenslavement. Again, I am concerned with the fact that the very act of liberal legality that registered de jure recognition of hard-won black Jubilee actually reinstituted enslavement through criminal sanction. Along these lines, I want to explore how a centering of the exception clause and the chattelized penal law that it produced allows for a critical disenchantment of the state's racialized, gendered, and class-coded discourses of "public safety," "law and order," and "penal reform." Just as important, in the remainder of the chapter I show how a centering of the exceptional loophole within the emancipation amendment exposes the legal, cultural, and penological channels whereby liberal bourgeois white supremacist law resuscitated both the badges *and* fetters—the incidents *and* fundaments—of chattel slavery and the Middle Passage carceral model.[16]

What's in a Name? *Involuntary Servitude* as Liberal Legal Euphemism

Troubled about the possible regressive consequences that could unfurl should the exception clause be allowed into the constitutional amendment outlawing slavery, Massachusetts senator Charles Sumner attempted to sound an alarm of opposition during the Senate's original debates on the amendment's wording. In fact, before waging his critique of what ended up being the final version of the legislation, Sumner submitted his own version, inspired by the French Declaration of Rights (1787), a joint resolution based on the liberal principles of "natural rights" and equality before the law: "Everywhere within the limits of the United States, and of each state of Territory thereof, all persons are equal before the law, so that no person can hold another as a slave." Realizing that his proposed version was a dead letter, the congressman focused on challenging the final version of the amendment coauthored by Senator John Henderson of Missouri, who was a slaveholder himself (at least until the Civil War). Sumner described how in its nearly exact repetition of the language of Article Six of Thomas Jefferson's Northwest Ordinance of 1787[17]—which in ostensibly outlawing slavery in the Northwest Territories also contained a provision for enslavement upon "due conviction" by law—Congress was in danger of resuscitating the very system it was purporting to cast into oblivion:

> There are words here . . . which are entirely inapplicable to our time. They are the limitation, "otherwise than in the punishment of crimes whereof the party shall have been duly convicted." Now, unless I err, there is an implication from those words that men may be enslaved as punishment of crimes whereof they shall have been duly convicted. There was a reason . . . for at that time . . . I understand it was the habit in certain parts of the country to convict persons or doom them as slaves for life as punishment for crime, and it was not proposed to prohibit this habit. *But slavery in our day is something distinct,* perfectly well known, requiring no words of distinction outside of itself.

In making his case against the exception clause, the abolitionist senator based his argument on the premise that there was a clearly discernible line of distinction between involuntary servitude and chattel slavery in 1864, a divergence that nullified the need to repeat the exception clause in an amendment attacking chattel slavery. His argument also rested on the fact that Jefferson's ordinance catered to the national "habit" in the late eighteenth century of submitting free and fugitive Africans to private slavery rather than public penal servitude as punishment for crimes associated with liberated blackness (a point also signified by Jefferson's unmentioned inclusion of a fugitive slave provision in the original language of the ordinance). Sumner concluded that the legislation relied on a "language that is not happy" insofar as it could be interpreted as a loophole for reenslavement. Other members of the judiciary committee, including fellow Republican Lyman Trumbull, who was acting chair, felt that Sumner's radicalist position on the wording amounted to nothing but a stubborn and misplaced grammatical fastidiousness: "I do not know that I should have adopted these words, but a majority of the committee thought they were the best words; they accomplish the object; and I cannot see why the senator from Massachusetts should be so pertinacious about particular words."[18]

Sumner felt that he had uncovered irrefutable proof that his supposed fit of grammatical nitpicking was actually based on a clear and present danger when, on January 3, 1867, nearly three years after originally posing his misgivings in respect to the exception clause, he opened a Senate debate on a congressional resolution calling for a "supplementary amendment" to the Thirteenth Amendment. He began the discussion by holding up the very advertisement for the courthouse auctioning of Richard Harris that is illustrated above (Figure 4), an event that had occurred in Annapolis just one month before Sumner's speech. After relaying the contents of the advertisement, he proceeded to read a transcription of the other public notice that I mentioned earlier for the sale of John Johnson, Gassaway Price, Harriet Purdy, and Dilly Harris, a group neoslave auction about which Sumner reported to have been informed by a personal "correspondent" who saw the black prisoners "sold in his presence, before his very eyes." Meant to arouse horror, disapprobation, and disbelief, Sumner's exposure of the odious scene of black bodies being sold at public auction nearly within site of the nation's capitol partook of a long-established abolitionist tropology that rested on unveiling the spectacular depravities of chattel slavery of which whips, chains, and auction blocks were essential symbols.[19] For him, it was not the fact of normalized arrest and imprisonment of free black persons that was the problem, but the unseemly manner in which it was conducted; the prisoner auction was proof positive that something beyond "normal" publicly administered involuntary servitude was functioning under the banner of the punitive exception, allowing for the institution of a revived form of private chattel slavery. "But I presume that the Senate, at the time they passed upon the amendment supposed that the phrase 'involuntary servitude, except for crime whereof the party has been duly convicted,' was simply applicable to *ordinary imprisonment.*" Sumner went on to recall that at the time of the amendment's passage he "feared that it was not exclusively applicable to *what we commonly understand by imprisonment,* and that it might be extended so as to cover some form of slavery."[20]

The Massachusetts congressman was joined in this dramatic unveiling of the Maryland advertisements by John Kasson, a Republican representative from Iowa, who held them aloft in the House of Representatives just five days after Sumner's speech. As in the Massachusetts senator's case, Kasson rested his arguments for revisiting the emancipation amendment on what he perceived to be a clear-cut boundary separating involuntary servitude to the state, as represented by "ordinary" imprisonment, and private servitude to an individual, as symbolized by the abhorrent spectacle of the courthouse auction block:

> I apprehend that few members of this House or of Congress, at the time of the passage of the amendment, supposed that in the very sentence abolishing slavery throughout the United States they had also made provision for its revival under another form and through the action of the courts of the country. The facts certified to us by the newspapers of the South, from week to week, show that the result of that action, as it is there construed, is to revive the institution of chattel slavery in all its odious characteristics; that free men ... are put upon the auction-block today and sold to the highest bidder into slavery.[21]

Kasson could feel so emboldened to strike at the exception clause partly because of a more definitive syntactical partitioning of "slavery" and "involuntary servitude" within his own state's constitution, in which the language of Jefferson's Northwest Ordinance was converted into a more overtly abolitionist phraseology: "Slavery, being incompatible with a free Government, is forever prohibited in the United States; and involuntary servitude shall be permitted only as a punishment for crime."[22]

In the spirit of this ostensibly definitive separation of two systems of punitive domination, Kasson introduced a bill (H.R. No. 956) that would have criminalized any

> *unofficial subjection to slavery* [of] persons who may be convicted of offenses against the law, by reason whereof certain inferior tribunals have adjudged free citizens of the United States to be so disposed of as to reestablish chattel slavery for life or for years, against the principles of the Christian religion, of civilization, and the Constitution ... which now recognizes no involuntary servitude except to the law and to the officers of its administration.

He concluded by positing what he considered to be a hermeneutical corrective in respect to the amendment's intended emancipatory function by stating that "no such thing as selling a man into slavery can possibly exist in the present condition of the Constitution and the laws of the country; that there must be a direct condemnation into that condition under the control of the officers of the law, like the sentence of a man to hard labor in the State prison in regular and ordinary course of law and that is the only kind of involuntary servitude known to the Constitution and the law."[23] For Kasson and Sumner, the auction block consequently operated as something of an abolitionist fetish, an emblem of an uncivilized, obsolete, and domestic modality of incarceration and unfreedom under a private master that would ineluctably make way for a more regulated, rational, and humane technique of human entombment: "Hard labor in the State prison."

The most cursory glance at such articulations lends itself immediately to a countering of the liberal abolitionist attempt at positing a definitive borderline between the auction block and the cellblock, between penal and chattel servitude. Even within its own terms, the logic of Sumner's and Kasson's self-assured statements in this regard fall apart at the seams, pointing toward an open secret lying at the core of their liberal vision and at the center of Euro-American carceral modernity as a whole. Kasson most clearly exhibits the untenable nature of the mythical private/public carceral binary when in the course of reenacting his own state constitution's syntactical severance of "slavery" and "involuntary servitude," he repeatedly performs their reunification. This first appears in the wording of his proposed bill to criminally sanction anyone taking part in the sale of "free" human beings, wherein he describes private servitude as an "unofficial subjection to slavery," a phrase that immediately signifies an unspoken Other working alongside such odiously unregulated private arrangements—that is, an "official" or properly public form of slavery issuing from the quotidian, predictable, and "humane" operation of the state police power. The specter of public penal enslavement then reappears in one of Kasson's most apparently self-certain assertions of the unconstitutionality of one person being held as chattel by another person, "that there must be *a direct condemnation into that condition under the control of officers of the law,* like the sentence of a man to hard labor in the State prison." Far from dislodging the rhetorically wedded terms *slavery* and *involuntary servitude,* liberal pronouncements of the putatively "ordinary" and "official" operation of juridical and penal law ultimately perform the absolute impossibility of their divorce. As noted in my earlier discussion of the North American chain gang, there are an untold number of disavowed stories of unfreedom, corporeal rupture, psychic terror, and chattelized entombment suggested in

Kasson's inadvertent discursive acknowledgment of the filiations of "ordinary imprisonment" and *that condition* known as slavery—historically sealed necropolitical experiences that underline the degree to which "involuntary servitude" works as a liberal legal euphemism shrouding long-standing intimacies of penal and chattel incarceration.[24]

Indeed, the methodological interconnections of the two ostensibly distinct systems are largely indexable within the history of the very ordinance for the Northwest Territories that occupied the center of the debate regarding the Thirteenth Amendment. This critically important genealogy points to the fact that in adopting the punishment exception in respect to *involuntary servitude*—that is, state enforced "hard labor" as punishment for a duly convicted offense—Jefferson replicated the reformatory logic of Cesare Beccaria, the influential Italian criminologist and penal reformer of the Enlightenment era whom the American slave-owning statesman held in extremely high esteem.[25] However, in offering his vision of what Foucault would come to describe as modernity's incremental movement away from the blood-ridden modalities of premodern feudal punishment to a "disciplinary" and "disembodied" penal philosophy, Beccaria unveils how liberal reform, modernization, and rationalization were founded upon the substitution of the convict's sanguinary death by something deemed more productively and pedagogically "grievous"—his literal enslavement. "If it be said that permanent penal servitude is as grievous as death, and therefore as cruel, I reply that, if we add up all the unhappy moments of slavery, perhaps it is even more so, but the latter are spread out over an entire life, whereas the former exerts its force at a single moment."[26]

For Beccaria, the "unhappy" civil death produced through penal enslavement would not only function as an intensification of biological death but would eclipse its counterpart as a more efficient technique of criminal deterrence through the terror of temporal indefiniteness: "It is not the intensity, but *the extent of punishment* which makes the greatest impression on the human soul. . . . It is not the terrible but fleeting sight of the felon's death which is the most powerful break on crime, but the long drawn-out example of a man deprived of freedom, who *having become a beast of burden*, repays the society he has offended with his labour."[27] The matter-of-fact aspect of Beccaria's argument for the pedagogical value of penal enslavement highlights the terror and domination that underlay what has been cast historically as "penal reform" from the Enlightenment through the birth of the "modern" penitentiary. Beccaria was nearly singular among his peers, however, in his open acknowledgment of the intimacies of penal and chattel servitude, a cross-fertilization that ranges at least as far back as the creation of the *servus-poeonae*—or criminally branded public slave—in Roman law,[28] and that continued into modernity with the transmission of plantation techniques of "labor management," surveillance, and corporeal rupture into European and U.S. prisons.[29]

Indeed, as David Brion Davis has pointed out, the penological ideas of Jeremy Bentham, the English penological theorist most closely associated with disciplinary carcerality, represented a "virtual caricature of the planter's ideal."[30] The inventor of the panopticon was incredulous, however, as to assertions that subjection to involuntary servitude amounted to any sort of transatlantic blowback of the colonial chattel principle of productive internment; but, as in Kasson's case, he raises the specter of the chattel moorings of modern imprisonment even while disavowing them:

> With regard to the popularity of this species of punishment in this country. Impatient spirits too easily kindled with the fire of independence have a word for it, which represents an idea singularly obnoxious to a people who pride themselves so much on their freedom. The word is slavery. Slavery they say is a punishment too degrading for an Englishman, even in ruins. This prejudice may be confuted by observing, 1st, that *public servitude is a different thing from slavery*. 2dly, That *if it were not, this would be no reason for dismissing this species of punishment without examination*. If then upon examination it is found not to be possessed, in requisite degree, of the properties to be wished for in a mode of punishment that, and not the name it happens to be called by, is a reason for its rejection: if it does not possess them, it is not any name that can be given to it that can change its nature.[31]

Leaving aside for the moment the tautological aspect of his claim that public servitude simply "is" a species of servitude distinct from slavery, I am interested in Bentham's depiction of an image of singularly "obnoxious degradation" arising in the mind of English commoners at the mere prospect of civil death. Notwithstanding the penal philosopher's initial words to the contrary, this grotesque social vision was based on the terrifying and utterly unthinkable prospect that criminal stigmatization would transmute the "white" convict into an ontological double of the most "degraded" not-quite-human being in the modern world—those units of enslaved African labor defined at law as objects of globalized commerce and localized sadism.[32] Equally important to note here is the manner in which Bentham's ruminations ultimately express a totalitarianist animus embedded within his utilitarianist vision. In the end, the social-engineering dream of producing a poor population in total conformity with the legal, political, and economic dictates of liberal bourgeois market culture justifies any method, including a penal version of that mentally and physically terrorizing thing that the targets of state sovereignty would "call" slavery. This is not to say that the white English commoner faced the same formations of chattelism in the prison that the African slaves faced in the barracoon, the slave ship, or the plantation, but to highlight the fact that the "whiteness" of the English commoner was placed in relative jeopardy through the stigmata of criminality. It is also to suggest a channel by which the feudal moorings of modern imprisonment would ultimately be ghosted into penal modernity on an unprecedented scale once the carceral state set its sights on those whose chattel enslavement laid at the foundation of white civil personhood.

The repressive aspects of the Benthamite philosophy would find their way into nineteenth-century prisons such as Auburn and Sing Sing, the latter of which was actually built through the "involuntary servitude" of prisoners transferred from the former. Elam Lynds, the warden who oversaw the contract labor and prisoner transfer project in the late 1820s, was unequivocal in his recognition of the affinities of his role and that of slave master: "According to my experience, it is necessary that the director of a prison . . . should be invested with an absolute and certain power. . . . My principle has always been, that in order to reform a prison, it is well to concentrate within the same individual, all power and all responsibility." For Lynds, such total disciplinary dominion was unthinkable without recourse to the most commonplace "seasoning" instrument of the plantation, the literal referent for what Bentham called *the lash of the law*: "I consider it impossible to govern a large prison without a whip. . . . If you have at once completely curbed the prisoner under the yoke of discipline you may without danger employ him in the labor which you think best."[33]

Not to be outdone by his transatlantic counterpart, Bentham himself once envisioned a "disciplinary" tool that has received a great deal less discussion than his panopticon. While his purportedly disembodied system of prisoner surveillance has risen to the level of a meta-symbol within critical treatments of modern carcerality, his idea for a slightly less subtle reform of feudal methods of publicly administered corporeal punishment (which again was to be reserved expressly for the English poor) speaks volumes for the parallel, intersectional, and mutually constitutive designs of "modern" punishment and "premodern" enslavement:

> A machine might be made, which should put in motion certain elastic rods of cane or whalebone, the number and size of which might be determined by law. The body of the delinquent might be subjected to strokes of these rods, and the force and rapidity with which they should be applied, prescribed by a Judge: [with] this everything which is arbitrary might be removed. A public officer . . . might preside over the infliction of punishment; and when there were many delinquents to be punished, his time might be saved, and the terror of the scene heightened, without increasing actual suffering, by increasing the number of machines, and subjecting all the offenders to punishment at the same time.[34]

That modern prison servitude originally amounted to a public simulation of the "private" practice of chattel slavery raises important questions in respect to Sumner's and Kasson's attempted abolitionist intervention on behalf of the emancipated. If at its outset modern state-borne penal servitude allowed for the white industrial worker to be subjected to some of the very mechanisms of corporeal rupture, private profiteering, dispossession, and social stigmatization that were essential to chattel carcerality (while also imagining innovations and calibrations of that terroristic modality such as the Benthamite whipping machine), then what were the legal or social grounds for challenging the state's wholesale auctioning of bodies whom white supremacist culture defined as metaphysically unproductive, incorrigible, atavistic, and whom liberal white supremacist law and custom had defined as undishonorable beings incapable of feeling the physical or psychic degradation of chattelhood? What was the logic of penal reform and criminal deterrence to do with the literal "beasts of burden" who were the objectified correlatives for Beccaria's metaphorics of civil death and who were thought incapable of either spiritual reformation or productive industrial discipline?[35] What were the limits of a liberal abolitionism that expressed horror at the site of free black people being auctioned on courthouse steps, but whose solution for such odious sites involved an enshrinement of more "ordinary" formations of involuntary servitude that began to entomb free black people in massive numbers immediately upon the passage of the Thirteenth Amendment? How did their narrow focus on isolated instances of what they considered to be an anachronistic holdover from chattel slavery obscure the larger state "public safety" project that would make the discursive link between "Negro" and "criminal" as inseparable after emancipation as "African" and "slave" had been before it? Finally, what did the long-standing infusion of private industrial interest into the putatively normal imprisonment of white bodies in the North mean for subjects who had been defined at law as nothing but fungible, culpable, and disposable since the Middle Passage?[36]

At issue here is what Hartman has described as the untenability of categorical distinctions between the public and private in respect to both chattel and penal servitude, and the degree to which in proffering such distinctions Sumner's and Kasson's challenge of the exception clause actually amounted to a reaffirmation of its most essential terms.[37] In other words, even were Congress to have passed the legislation that Kasson proposed to outlaw the sale of one individual by another—and had amended the Thirteenth Amendment to read closer to the more clearly articulated distinction between chattel and penal subjection in Iowa's constitution—the national state police power would still have involved the necropolitical right not only to kill free black people but to submit them to innumerable public/private carceral hybrids through the hypercriminalization of black being and the productive legal euphemism of "involuntary servitude."

As if to make perfectly clear that the security of the racial state rested on the sovereign right to terrorize the black subject in whatever form (and by whatever name) it deemed necessary, the Senate Judiciary Committee indefinitely postponed Kasson's bill after its passage in the House by claiming that any issues relating to the punitive reenslavement of "duly convicted" free persons were mitigated by the Civil Rights Act of 1866.[38] The outright cynical quality of this claim rests on the fact that, in its ostensible protection of southern black people against openly discriminatory postbellum Black Codes, the original Civil Rights Bill repeatedly invoked the very exception clause that Kasson and Sumner attempted to challenge. On its face, "An Act to Protect All Persons in the United States in Their Civil Rights, and Furnish the Means of Their Vindication" represented a positive affirmation and clarification of the citizenship rights granted by the Thirteenth Amendment and the legislative birthplace of liberal constructions of "color-blind" common law in reference to former slaves and other racially stigmatized persons. The first two sections of the bill read as follows:

> Be it enacted by the Senate and House of Representatives of the United States of America in Congress assembled, That all persons born in the United States and not subject to any foreign power, excluding Indians not taxed, are hereby declared to be citizens of the United States; and such citizens, of every race and color, without regard to any previous condition of slavery or involuntary servitude, *except as punishment for a crime whereof the party shall have been duly convicted,* shall have the same right, in every State and Territory . . . to make and enforce contracts, to sue, be parties, and give evidence, to inherit, purchase, lease or sell, hold, and convey real and personal property, and to full and equal benefit of the laws and proceedings for the security of person and property, as enjoyed by white citizens, and shall be subject to like punishments, pains, and penalties, and to none other, any law, statute, ordinance, regulation, or custom, to the contrary notwithstanding.
>
> Sec. 2. And be it further enacted, That any person, who under color of any law, statute, ordinance, regulation, or custom, shall subject, or cause to be subjected, any inhabitant of any State or Territory to the deprivation of any right secured or protected by this act, or to different punishment, pains, or penalties on account of such person having at one time been held in a condition of slavery or involuntary servitude, *except as punishment for a crime whereof the party shall have been duly convicted,* or by reason of his color or race, than is prescribed for the punishment of white persons, shall be deemed guilty of a misdemeanor, and, on conviction, shall be punished by a fine not exceeding one thousand dollars, or imprisonment not exceeding one year, or both, at the discretion of the court.[39]

What appears to function as a "vindication" of the full-blown positive power of the Thirteenth Amendment vis-à-vis its granting of citizenship and civil liberties to all persons born in the United States (besides untaxed "Indians") actually joins the emancipation amendment as an outright justification of the state's right to deploy criminal sanction as the most actionable and powerful means of dealing with the "problem" of the black (and Indigenous) presence within the national body. Note how an act that was to have put to rest the "whole subject" of black penal reenslavement—and more specifically the literal auctioning of black bodies—not only neglects to offer an outright ban on the sale or lease of human beings by the state, but actually reinforces that sovereign right by repeating the exception clause in both of its most important sections. The main reason that such an outright proscription against black fungibility could not occur was that the national government was busy inaugurating the wholesale renting-to-death of black bodies branded as both "felon" and "misdemeanant," otherwise know as convict leasing, at the very moment of the bill's crafting. This historical synergy has often been ignored in scholarly treatments of "southern" prison slavery during Reconstruction; or, when broached at all, it has been mystifyingly dismissed as a matter of "accidental" racism and political-economic expedience rather than a pivotal conjuncture based on the material force of white supremacy and the centrality of unfree black labor to the interconnected postbellum national projects of empire building and southern industrialization.[40]

In fact, the ease with which local and state regimes of racial apartheid would be able to maintain white supremacist legal practice under the color of color-blind law had already been made clear well before the act's passage with the proliferation of Black Codes that were racially nonspecific but teleologically white supremacist. As Donald Nieman has indicated, many of the most extremely racist statutes that were conducting thousands of black people into convict lease camps, chain gangs, and peonage at the time of this supposed "vindication" of black civil rights, immediately escaped any possibility of judicial scrutiny under the act's color-blind doctrine due to the removal of any mention of race from their wording: "Rather than being blatantly discriminatory, the black codes of 1866, while carefully designed to control the freedmen, were on their face non-discriminatory. Through contract and vagrancy laws that applied [formally] to whites and blacks alike, they gave state and local officials all the authority they need to provide planters with a cheap and dependable labor force."[41] Indeed, this loophole even made possible the renewal of the late antebellum slave code. Under the "color-blind" and "equal punishment" provisions of the bill, all the Maryland state legislature would have needed to do in order to resuscitate the slave code allowing for the sale or lease of free black subjects was to remove the word "Negro" from its wording and the odious scenes of free blacks being made into commodified objects on courthouse steps could have continued apace.

However, as the history of racialized neoslavery has exposed for over one hundred years after the passage of the act "protecting" black civil rights, the legal reproduction of black fungibility not only continued but actually expanded to alarming proportions through the liberal loopholes of the exception clause and the color-blind racial statutes that put the punitive exception into material motion. In an example of its ability to practice a certain amount of productive self-disciplining, the racial capitalist patriarchal state removed what for the liberal onlooker represented the unsightly scene of courthouse auctioning from public view while continuing a de facto neoslave trade inside courthouse chambers, a legal ritual of human commodification that subjected a swelling number of black prisoners to multiple varieties of *opus publicum* (public hard labor) and *vincula publica* (public chains) under the normalizing ostent of "due conviction."[42] That is, various forms of ignominious public unfree work and punishment that did ultimately begin to be cast into the ashbin of history for white subjects as far back as the late eighteenth century were reinvigorated and expanded through the banal operation of municipal, state, and national penal law— representing a legal prosecution of the national cultural mythos that framed such disreputable labor and bodily rupture as commensurate with the supposed inborn criminality, unbreachable joviality, and inhumanly high pain threshold of former slaves. In other words, the law exchanged the offensive site of the open-air neoslave auction for the no less abject, if socially acceptable, scene of black neoslave labor and terror on the chain gang, the convict lease camp, and the peon camp.

Again, when read in this light, the Maryland auctioning of the free is unveiled as a "post" slavery analogue of the various modalities of racial commodification that secreted across the fictive border of emancipation. It is also exposed as a futuristic relic of sorts, demonstrating the liberal legal channels whereby various modalities of spectacular and banal dehumanization essential to chattel slavery were reanimated and reconfigured through the birth of the convict lease system, peonage, the prison plantation, and the chain gang. This last point is vividly recalled by Richard Wright's boyhood persona in *Black Boy* (1945), who in mistaking a Mississippi chain-gang coffle for a herd of trunk-tied "elephants"—or stripe-clad "zebras"—disenchants the discourses of color-blind jurisprudence and public safety that crafted the social acceptance of neoslavery:

I saw that they were two lines of creatures that looked like men on either side of the road; that there were a few white faces and a great many black faces. I saw that the white faces were the faces of white men and they were dressed in ordinary clothing; but the black faces were men wearing what seemed to me to be elephants [or zebra] clothing. As the strange animals came abreast of me I saw the legs of the black animals were held together by irons and their arms were linked with heavy chains that clanked softly as their muscles moved.[43]

From the seemingly naive purview of childhood remembrance, we are allowed a momentary glimpse at unspeakable realities hovering at the periphery of the state's master narrations of law, order, and "Negro Problem" resolution. Such testimony supplies necessarily incomplete, contingent, and historically obscured entry into how the exception clause and the white supremacist ruse of color-blind statutory law represented not the cessation of black fungibility and dehumanization but their legalized transfer from courthouse steps into courtrooms, boardrooms, and "official" neo-slave coffles. As Hartman reminds us in respect to the productive amnesia of liberal legal color-blindness, "The refusal to see race neither diminishes that originary violence nor guarantees equality but merely enables this violence to be conducted under the guise of neutrality."[44]

For the remainder of this chapter, I will focus on largely obstructed and distorted legal and social conjunctures wherein black fungibility was transplanted from a slave code funneling free and fugitive African bodies into "private" chattelhood to a color-blind code of reenslavement that has disappeared countless free black people and other socially stigmatized persons into hybrid formations of public/private state-administered bondage.[45] This trajectory offers a mapping of the law's amoeba-like functionality in transposing the discursively open racial language of the Slave Codes and Black Codes into the decidedly more tenacious racist practice of color-blind provisions dealing with crimes of dispossession and basic black existence such as vagrancy, petit larceny, public drunkenness and disorderliness, gambling, and breach of contract (behaviors that often amounted to talking, walking, or breathing in the presence of the wrong white person). It also charts the process by which free black people were converted into commodifiable units of unfree labor and sadistic pleasure through banal courtroom bureaucratic rituals such as the bail or fine/fee hearing.[46] As noted above, the formations of neoslavery issuing from such legal violence ranged from the putatively regulated, ordinary, and nonpecuniary "involuntary servitude" found on the chain gang and prison plantation to zones of openly privatized penal slavery, such as convict leasing and the county-level consort of that genocidal system known as *criminal-surety*. By focusing mainly on the latter and lesser known of these two mechanisms of the black neo-slave trade, I will address the juridical mythmaking and color-blind statutory violence that gave an all-too-powerful and durable afterlife to Chapter 324 of Maryland's 1858–66 slave code, and that offered essential legal cover to the overall postbellum mass seizure, rupture, and terrorizing of free black men, women, and children doubly branded as *Negro* and *criminal*— two monikers of "ontological subordination" that have been as productively inseparable to U.S. empire as *slavery* and *involuntary servitude*.[47]

"Someone to Go My Bail": *US v. Reynolds* and the Ever-Turning Wheel of Neoslavery

The following surreal exchange and bit of early twentiety-century social commentary represents the opening of E. Stagg Whitin's *Penal Servitude* (1912):

> "Will you buy me, Sah?" asked a boy convict in an Alabama convict camp, when approached by the writer. "Won't you buy me out, Sah?" he reiterated to the rejoinder, "I'm not buying niggers." "It'll only cost you $20, Sah, an' I'll work fer you as long as you say. I'se fined $1.00, Sah, and got $75 costs. I'se worked off all but $20. Do buy me out, Sah, please do." The wail was raised by a small boy of fourteen years, with black skin, in a particular camp, yet the appeal is the appeal of many thousands who from want, disease, or evil environment have passed for a time out of our world into the hell on earth which we, in our wisdom, have prepared for them; the appeal recognized the economic status of our penal system.
>
> The status of the convict is that of one in penal servitude—the last surviving vestige of the old slave system.[48]

Whitin's text was a prison reformist work sponsored by the National Committee on Prison Labor, an organization that promoted a conversion of the profit-centered national penitentiary system into a wage-based, regulated, and uniform system of industrial training and redemptive individual reform. Notwithstanding its prominent placement at the head of the text, Whitin's exchange with the boy "with black skin"—along with a horrifying photo of a group of stripe-clad black men and a young boy shown seated, shackled, and long-chained to a tree at an unidentified chain-gang camp—represent the extent of the book's treatment of the racial dimensions of what the penal reformer describes as "the last vestige of the old slave system." Despite his attempted narrative evacuation from the site of southern neoslavery, however, the writer's brief interaction with the imprisoned adolescent child forces us to halt at the very moment he would have us depart along the main vectors of the text. Whitin's response to the unnamed boy's attempted marketing of his own body in the name of freeing himself from the convict camp—*I'm not buying niggers*—carries enough in the way of loaded meaning to demand that we stay with the young boy, at a place and time that a footnote to the encounter tersely informs us is "Banner Mine, Alabama, May 1911."

Indeed, the dateline alone carries a grim echo of the urgency heard in the unnamed prisoner's entreaty for the northern tourist to "buy" him out of the camp. That is, the "wail" he describes as emitting from a solitary *nigger boy* actually amounted to a chorus of haunting tones, the loudest of which were those still reverberating from the closely buried corpses of 111 of the child's fellow black male prison slaves who were killed in an explosion at the coal mine just days before Whitin's arrival.[49] With the absent presence of this revenant chorus in mind, I am concerned with how the white northern reformer's offhanded brandishing of the quintessential signifier of black subhumanity, fungibility, and zero-degree alterity actually bears critical significance in respect to the declared subject matter of his book insofar as it expresses in stark fashion the degree to which white supremacy—whether *southern-anachronistic* or *northern-progressive*—rested at the foundation of the system of national penal servitude that Whitin was hoping to fashion into a more "evolved" image. Along these lines, a more specific concern in respect to the scene has to do with the very fact that the white penal reformer could have actually purchased (or at least rented) a black neoslave child for $20 at a convict lease camp nearly fifty years after the Annapolis courthouse auctionings of Harriet Purdy, Richard Harris, and the other criminally branded "free" black bodies that I introduced at the beginning of this chapter. Notwithstanding Whitin's attempt at using the exchange as a representative point of departure for his discussion of industrialized punishment in northern penitentiaries, some-thing very particular was at work in the fact that the unnamed boy knew full well that the convict lease camp in which he and hundreds of other black males were entombed could be converted into a virtual auction block—that as a legally fungible body he could be subleased as easily as he was originally leased, thereby exchanging one form of privatized public neoslavery, the convict lease camp, for another, "criminal-surety."[50]

A variant of a widespread and nebulous state-profiteering apparatus of leasing public slaves to private planters and industrial concerns, the surety system was touted as a "humane" contractual avenue by which criminally branded black subjects could avoid the brutalities of the chain gang and convict lease camp through becoming party to a court-administered prison labor contract. Usually occurring while the black subject was literally sit-ting in a jail cell or standing before a local judge facing the possibility of being sent to a "hell on earth" such as Banner Mine, it involved a putatively consensual agreement whereby an individual white neoslave buyer, euphe-mistically described as the "surety," would post the exorbitant fees and costs associated with the black subject's alleged petty crime in exchange for his "confession of judgment." Upon signing a court-approved contract with the white bondholder, the black subject was legally conjured from a would-be public slave into a publicly borne private peon who was forced to sup-ply unfree labor—among various other unspoken and uneconomic forms of terror-ridden travail—to the surety until the amount posted had been "worked off." In Alabama and Georgia, where such arrangements were codified in state law, the state supplied a statutory guarantee that the indi-vidual convict-lessee would receive a return on his investment by making the prisoner's breach of contract with the surety a criminal offense. In such cases, the black subject could, at the discretion of the court, either be re-arrested and sent to the chain gang or rebound to a private master for an even longer period than stipulated in the original lease.[51]

The frequency of such neoslave contracts was so great in certain south-ern municipalities that their courthouses became de facto unfree labor agencies for local planters and industrialists. As historian Walter Wilson points out in an article published in *Harper's Monthly* in the early 1930s, the pecuniary gain associated with convict leasing, criminal-surety, and other customary "fee/cost" catalyzed systems of black prisoner trading was not limited to the near-absolute surplus value offered to private concerns; that is, just in the case of convict leasing, the submission of an untold number of black prisoners to criminal-surety and other racialized bail arrangements designed specifically for misdemeanants was based on a lucrative system of localized *public profiteering* that fed an overarching public/private neoslavery complex: "Aside from prison officials and private business men who profit from convict labor, there is another group of men who profit from convict slaves. Sheriffs, judges, clerks, and others serve as employment agents. . . . Under the notorious fee system law-and-order enforcement, officials are paid commission on the basis of the number of arrests and convictions they secure." After citing the very instance just discussed of the child at Banner Mine having to work off seventy-five dollars in "costs" for a petty offense that demanded only a one-dollar fine, Wilson goes on to describe the lucrative nature of the widespread local trade in black convicts for public officials in both Mississippi and Alabama—including the very county in which the young boy was likely convicted before being disappeared to Banner Mine: "According to leading citizens of Alabama, the sheriff of Jefferson county in 1912 was earning $50,000 to $80,000 a year in fees. A clerkship in the county seat was worth at least $25,000 in fees. Several sheriffs in Mississippi in 1930 earned over $20,000 each. The leading one made $24,350. The average for eighty-two counties was only slightly less than $6,000."[52] Adjusted for inflation, the $50,000 conservative estimate of the Jefferson county sheriff's bounty from the convict trade in 1912 would equal well over $1.1 million in today's dollars; and, even the $6,000 Depression-era average for sheriffs in the respective Mississippi counties cited in Wilson's poll would equate to a yearly neoslave trade commission of approximately $81,300.

This largely ignored public dimension of the overall profiteering on imprisoned southern black bodies throws into stark relief the earlier referenced productive hybridity and virtual indivisibility of public and private formations of terror and incarceration waged against the free black population as a whole since the passage of the Thirteenth Amendment. However, notwithstanding this incestuous interface of public and private interests in the project of black reenslavement, juridical interventions against the overall system of postbellum state-sanctioned "indebted servitude" defined peonage in general, and criminal-surety in particular, through the liberal frames of contract, individual obligation, and private hostility rather than as state-sanctioned neoslavery based on structural white supremacy.[53] In *US v. Reynolds* (1914), the first of the Supreme Court peonage cases dealing specifically with criminal-surety, this partitioning of the public and private was taken to its most absurd extreme given the state's central role as trader, broker, and neoslave patroller within that system. Indeed, as in the case of the supposed "vindication" of black citizenship found in the Civil Rights Act of 1866, the ostensible avenue of redress proffered in *Reynolds* against a particular form of involuntary servitude ultimately represented a further solidification of the state's sovereign right to reenslave the contaminating black presence within the national body.

The case involved a black man, Ed Rivers, who was arrested in Monroe County, Alabama, in May 1910, and charged with the crime of petty larceny. Just as in the circumstance of the young boy at Banner Mine, Rivers's poverty and dispossession were legally transmuted into the condition of possibility for his penal enslavement through the banal operation of inherently excessive bail. While the fine associated with his alleged petty theft amounted to $15.00, the fees that were levied by the court amounted to $43.75—an utterly unimaginable amount for a landless agrarian subject who most certainly would have never had anything close to that sum of cash on hand at any point in his life. At the inevitable acknowledgment of Rivers's inability to raise nearly $60, the law's swivel prerogative in respect to its handling of the criminalized black body swung into immediate and efficient motion. In order to recuperate Rivers's manufactured debt to society, the state's penal code allowed the court latitude either to transport him directly to the chain gang, thereby gleaning the money through his public neoslave labor, or lease him as a private "servant" (or peon), thereby retrieving the money in the form of the surety's bond payment. In order to avoid the protean forms of death that he knew he would face in at least sixty-eight days on a southern Alabama chain gang, Rivers elected to sign a surety contract with a white man, J. A. Reynolds, who, unlike Whitin, was indeed interested in "buying niggers" when he arrived at the Monroe County courthouse on a spring day in 1910.

Rivers ultimately signed a document with his surety, which read in part:

I . . . Ed Rivers, agree to work and labor for him, the said J. A.
Reynolds on his plantation in Monroe County, Alabama, and
under his direction as a farm hand to pay fine and costs for the
term of 9 months and 24 days, at the rate of $6.00 per month,
together with my board, lodging, and clothing during the said time
of hire, said time commencing on the 4th day of May, 1910, and
ending on the 28th day of Feby., 1911, provided said work is not
dangerous in character.[54]

Rivers would serve only a month's time on Reynolds's plantation before attempting to extricate himself from the court-administered peonage contract. Upon his escape, he was immediately rearrested under the provisions of Alabama criminal code (1907), section 6846, which called for the capture of any subject who "without good and sufficient excuse" failed "to do the act, or perform the service" owed to the surety. The code also allowed for an assessment of more fines and costs, and for the prisoner to be either sent to the chain gang or resold into peonage for an even longer duration. In Rivers's case, he was given a symbolic one-cent fine on top of what was left of the original $15.00, along with another $87.05 in phantom "costs." After the new bond was pronounced, Rivers once again attempted to avoid the chain gang by signing yet another surety contract with G. W. Broughton—a document that, according to the increased amount of fees levied after his first escape, called for Rivers to work as a peon for well over a year. The facts reported in the case culminated with Rivers again escaping his peon master, only to be rearrested once again.[55]

In offering the opinion for the case, Justice Day took pains to prove the rather astonishing thesis that criminal-surety represented a completely private affair between two freely contracting individuals, a portrayal that neglected to hold culpable the central state actors—the police, the court, and the general racist legal structure—without whom the surety "contract" would never have occurred in the first place. In spite of the state's central role in every step of the process, the court claimed that the moment Rivers's bond was paid and he walked out of the courthouse with Reynolds, he immediately ceased to be a prisoner and became party to a consensual contract between a *worker* and an *employer,* thereby making his labor under the threat of arrest for breach of contract a species of private involuntary servitude based on debt, or peonage:

> When thus at labor, *the convict is working under a contract* which he has made with his surety. He is to work until the amount which the surety has paid him—the sum of the fine and costs—is paid. The surety has paid the State and the service rendered is to reimburse him. This is the real substance of the transaction. The terms of the contract are agreed upon by the contracting parties, as the result of their own negotiations . . . in regard to which the State has not been consulted. (146)

The circumscription of the state-borne system of criminal-surety within the narrow parameters of "free" labor negotiation and exploitation was taken even further in John W. Davis's brief for the United States: "The terms, time, and character of service are matters of *purely private contract* between two parties, with which the state has no concern, notwithstanding the requirement of approval by the judge; and until the convict has in some way broken his agreement the State has *washed its hands of the whole transaction.*"[56]

In the clearest possible rendering of the law's absurd application of the liberal discourse of contractual "free will" to zones of racial apartheid, collective dispossession, and state domination, the court turned a blind eye to the actual circumstances of terror and physical jeopardy faced by the supposedly willful agent whom it unconsciously refers to as "the convict."[57] Moreover, in doing so, it also neglected to recognize the state's pecuniary interest in the postbellum reproduction of black alienability—how far from being disinterested referees of the surety arrangement, local municipalities, courts, police, lawyers, and clerks were actually awash in the money and power generated at every stage of this particular vector of the overall trade in criminalized southern black bodies.[58] Such considerations allow us to recognize that in submitting to work as Reynolds's peon, Rivers was not "agreeing" to a contract but hoping to avoid the zero-degree terror, natal alienation, and abjection that certainly awaited him on the chain gang. In this regard, his supposed freely negotiated "consent" to the surety arrangement actually amounted to a Hobson's choice—a sagacious blues reckoning with the gradient nature of civil, living, and premature death in carceral America. In other words, no one in a community ravaged by the genocidal operations of the chain gang and the system of convict leasing would ever choose *not* to avoid being coffled on a southern chain gang or at Banner coal mine even for a day, and even when such "choice" involved being transmuted into an object of liquid merchandise and submission to yet another horrifying species of neoslavery in the form of state-administered peonage.

Furthermore, any notion of a strictly private aspect to the surety arrangement is exploded by the fact that no white man would ever have agreed to supply the fees and costs associated with a black person's alleged petty crime were it not for the coercive threat of rearrest issued by the state, a fact that the court actually admits even as it attempts to reduce the surety system to a purely private affair: "This labor is performed under the constant threat of coercion and threat of another possible arrest and prosecution in case he violates the labor contract which he has made with the surety, and this form of coercion is as potent as it would have been had the law provided for the seizure and compulsory service of the convict" (146). As stated above, the spectrum of coercion under the "humane" systems of criminal-surety and peonage extended far beyond the threat of rearrest, however; in the thousands of complaints registered at the Department of Justice by black peonage prisoners, the range of violent repression includes but is not limited to rape, whipping, kidnapping, and mass murder.[59]

Day's construction of criminal-surety as a matter of exceptional private labor exploitation rather than a matter of banal public/private neoslavery culminates with his claim that the court-administered peonage contract actually submitted Rivers to a more painful brand of involuntary servitude than he would have faced on a chain gang—that is, the very space of abjection that he and countless other black people tried so desperately to avoid in electing to being sold in open court as peons. For the court, the fact that, under the terms of the original contract, Rivers faced a theoretically greater duration of labor at the hands of Reynolds than he would have while chained to other black men as an officially recognized slave of the state qualified the system of surety as decidedly worse than its public counterpart: "Under the Alabama Code, he might have been sentenced to hard labor for the county . . . for 68 days as his maximum sentence. . . . Under the contract now before us, he was required to labor for nine months and twenty-four days, thus being required to perform a much more onerous service than if he had been sentenced under the statute, and committed to hard labor." The court goes on to contend that the statutory allowance of the peon's rearrest and the ever-increasing debt owed to the surety for furnishing his bond further illustrate the relative heinous quality of this system of peonage in comparison to official involuntary servitude: "Under this statute, the surety may cause the arrest of the convict for violation of his labor contract. He may be sentenced again and punished for this new offense, and . . . the convict is thus *chained to an ever-turning wheel of servitude*" (146–47). Of course, given the court's strained attempt at describing Rivers's role in the surety arrangement as that of a willfully contracting free laborer, the question that immediately arises is why—given that he would have known infinitely more about the intricacies of the southern "wheel of servitude" than the honorable judge could ever imagine—would Rivers willfully assent to the surety arrangement if it were so much more arduous than the experience of official "hard labor"? In his concurring opinion, Oliver Wendell Holmes attempted to explain this contradiction within the court's deployment of the discourse of contractual free will by calling upon the time-honored racist mythos of black improvidence, ignorance, and irresponsibility: "There seems to me nothing in the Thirteenth Amendment or the Revised [peonage] Statutes that prevents a State from making breach of contract . . . a crime and punishing it as such. But impulsive people with little intelligence or foresight may be expected to lay hold of anything that affords a relief from present pain even though it will cause greater trouble by and by" (150).

Far from an aberrant moment of racial rhetoric within an otherwise progressive decision, Holmes's openly white supremacist comment actually represents a boldface expression of the liberal myopia and productive racial amnesia exhibited in the majority opinion itself, which remarkably attempts to use the facile and economically deterministic index of relative labor-time to isolate criminal surety as exceptionally onerous while normalizing two of the most brutal regimes of official punishment in U.S. history—the county chain gang and the state convict lease camp. The specter of these two public/private penal formations hovers over the entire decision, belying the apparent empirical certainty of Day's portrayal of criminal-surety as more arduous than its nominally public counterparts and unveiling a foundational element of state terror lying at the core of his performance of liberal legal progressivism. Indeed, the haunting presence of these dominative and profit-centered systems of public carceral terror is alluded to in documents pertaining to the case that the court neglects to include in its statement of "the facts." In correspondence with the U.S. attorney general in preparation of *Reynolds* as a test case of the constitutionality of criminal-surety, the U.S. attorney for the Southern District of Alabama, William H. Armbrecht, reveals a scene that is conveniently left out of the court's neat computations of the relatively humane, ordered, and temporally definite qualities of public involuntary servitude: "It does not appear in the indictment, but it is true that Rivers was sent to hard labor for the County for more than a year. In order to bring him before the Grand Jury I had to get an order from the Court directing that he be brought here. *He was brought here in chains with shackles riveted to his legs.* After he gave testimony to the Grand Jury, the Marshall took him back to the turpentine camp where he was performing hard labor for the County."[60]

It is not clear on which day of his "over a year" sentence Rivers was led from a county chain-gang camp situated deep in the woods of southern Alabama to the grand jury hearing in shackles and chains. His objectification and muzzling within the ritualized legal storytelling arena of the court opinion also disallows any discernible portal into the quotidian regiment of threatened death, chattelized internment, and unspeakable pain that he experienced with every passing minute as he was driven under a "red-heifer," a black-jack, or a rifle to the forest, coffled to other black men (and boys), and made to drive "cups" and "gutters" into trees to "catch resin that oozed from wounds opened by axe cuts through the bark."[61] We also are not given details as to exactly how much money was procured by those profit- and pleasure-seeking white men involved in every facet of the putatively public turpentine concern. Was the camp operated by the county itself or a private corporation that had successfully bid to lease the bodies of Rivers and his fellow neoslaves for "$11 a head"? How many of the camp prisoners were subjected to the turpentining coffle well after their official release date because of an escape attempt or because both their date and body had been obliterated from retrievable memory through the sorcery of racial state documentation? How many black captives were buried in unmarked graves in the middle of the woods after dying from "natural causes" at the age of twenty, or being "struck by lightning" on a bright sunny day? Did these burial mounds include the dishonored and dis(re)membered bodies of black women and girls interned at the camp just over a decade previously when women were still *mixed into the men* at such spaces of white supremacist misogynist horror? How many children of these women, born into this hell on earth as a result of their mothers having been raped by camp guards, were among the unremembered dead? Did the guards regularly cure fits of boredom on rare off-days by ordering prisoners to "strike it up lively" with a fiddle or dance the "buck and wing"?[62] What is clear from my earlier discussion of the terroristic operation of the chain gang, however, is that no matter whether he was shuttled to the courthouse on day one or day one hundred of his sentence, the terror and abjection that Rivers faced, as well as countless other black subjects who were literally chained to the "ever-turning wheel" of U.S. neoslavery, overflows the court's cynical reduction of the "onerous" qualities of imprisonment to the duration of involuntary labor supplied to the convict-slave master or even the amount of surplus value extracted from the entombed black body.

The example of juridical mythmaking offered in *Reynolds* bears a stark resemblance to the "progressive dehumanization" found in Kasson's and Sumner's earlier legislative call for the suspension of the courthouse auction block and the use of "normal" involuntary servitude as a more proper means of dealing with the problem of free incorrigible blackness. However, the mode of legal liberalism proffered in *Reynolds* represents an even more chilling exposition of the violent capacities of the law, since in offering a nominal check on a hyperpublic version of the supposedly hermetic system of peonage, the court did not even pretend to question the validity of the state's generalized leasing of black bodies; nor would it deign to acknowledge the publicly aired genocidal effects that the legal transposition of free black people into "duly convicted" commodified objects was producing at the very moment the decision was crafted. Like the peonage cases as a whole, *Reynolds* would offer only tepid reproof of what it constructed as an aberrant and improperly executed "private" branch of the general public/private trade in black convicts. The court's seeming blindness to the real effects of public neoslavery actually represented an interested liberal amnesia, a juridical accommodation and reproduction of the hugely profitable and socially edifying disappearance, sale, leasing, and subleasing of black people to places like the county turpentine camp and the chattelized industrial operations posing as "state penitentiaries" operated by companies such as U.S. Steel, Tennessee Coal and Iron (TCI), and Pratt Consolidated Coal Company. Again, according to the abhorrent color-blind racial logic of the court, Rivers's experience of being "chained" to the "wheel of servitude" would have been alleviated were he only to have been immediately disappeared to the purportedly more humane, regularized, and predictable living death he ended up enduring on the chain gang.

Far from challenging the fungible, disposable, and enslavable nature of emancipated blackness, *Reynolds* actually offered a backdoor affirmation of the genocidal state-administered trade in black bodies that began immediately after emancipation, the most obvious formation of which was convict leasing (a privatized system that was nothing if not a state-level version of the localized rental of black prisoners found in criminal-surety). This elephant in the white supremacist courtroom is openly acknowledged in Davis's brief for the United States: "We concede . . . that when a sentence to hard labor has been imposed it is entirely competent for the State either to employ the convict for itself or to hire him out for its profit. His time and labor have been confiscated by the State and, within Constitutional limits, *it may use them as it sees fit.*"[63]

As I noted above in my discussion of the euphemistic violence of the term "involuntary servitude," post-1865 law presented virtually no limit to the pain, terror, and physical/psychic rupture the racial state could visit upon the "duly" convicted "Negro." This dubiously constitutional fact is underlined at the very end of *Reynolds* with the truncated yet horrifyingly fatal appearance of the exception clause: "There can be no doubt that the State has the authority to impose involuntary servitude as a *punishment for a crime*. This fact is recognized in the Thirteenth Amendment." Indeed this unimpeachable sovereign right to reenslave the criminally and racially stigmatized body is actually repeated in every state and federal case dealing with peonage from *Clyatt v. United States* (1904) onward. The gothic reemergence of the penal exception in *Reynolds*, a decision that was to have offered the free black population a modicum of redress against what had been cast as a migration of various archaic forms of involuntary servitude and slavery into the twentieth century, underlines the national, structural, and public character of the apparently exceptional, episodic, and private brands of white supremacy found in the specific statutory practice of criminal-surety and the wider system of "southern" neoslavery. In fact, the backdoor allowance of public neoslavery in *Reynolds* through the court's matter-of-fact wielding of the exception clause has been replicated in U.S. common law up to our current moment of mass incarceration, since nearly every case in which a prisoner has attempted to lay claim to the emancipation amendment's supposed protections against slavery and involuntary servitude has been quashed, with the state repeatedly maintaining that the "Thirteenth Amendment has no application to a situation where a person is held to answer for violations of a penal statute."[64]

Read in this light, this relatively obscure case begins to take on a rather ominous gravity, connecting it to more commonly recognized moments of legal white supremacy such as *Plessy v. Ferguson* (1896), the *Civil Rights Cases* (1883), and *Dred Scott v. Sanford* (1857). Unlike these more well-known cases from the mid- to late nineteenth century, however, *Reynolds* and other decisions pertaining to peonage appearing in the early twentieth century represent something of a hidden but tenaciously present danger—especially when considered with respect to the current manifestation of America's centuries-old complex of industrialized chattel carcerality. Insofar as they offered apparent relief from one form of private servitude while simultaneously reaffirming the divine right of the law to treat the criminalized black body *as it sees fit*, such cases represent the ways in which color-blind liberal legality continues to function as an all-too-durable sanctuary for various modalities of racial capitalist patriarchal domination. They also signal how the genocidal practices of U.S. empire remain cloaked under the placebo-like discourses of liberal reform, rights recognition, and color-blind inclusion. Like the emancipation amendment itself, the progressive "protection" offered in *Reynolds* amounted to a liberal legal reproduction and entrenchment of the state's necropolitical right to publicly reenslave the black population and to make the penal enslavement of all bodies stigmatized as "criminal" a matter of public investment to the end of private profits (and sadistic pleasures) that both corporate interests and putatively disinterested purveyors of the law continue to enjoy.

CHAPTER 3

Angola Penitentiary

The Once and Future Slave Plantation

We charge genocide—not only of the past, but of the future.

—Ossie Davis, Preface to We Charge Genocide

The whip itself did not make slavery what it was. It was a legal system, it was a system of legality.... Slavery only took on another form: in prisons.

—Robert Hillary King

JOHN MCELROY IS UNKNOWN TO HISTORY. His name does not register among the ranks of black liberation fighters, musicians, and athletes whose images filled places like my college dormitory room in the early 1990s—when, like many of my peers in California's pre-209 era,[1] I placed posters of those such as Malcolm X, Billie Holiday, and The Coup on my walls, jigsaw style, in order to assert a budding political and social consciousness and to counter the historical erasure that barred even the icons of black political and artistic life from any serious consideration within U.S. mass media and educational curricula. Not even by the time that I began working on this book project in earnest, years later, and found myself being pulled northward along U.S. Highway 61 from Baton Rouge to Angola, Louisiana, did I have any notion of who John McElroy was, and how my ghostly encounters with him during this research trip would become so fundamental to my attempt at unearthing something of the untold and largely unrecoverable experiences of countless prison slaves who have been obliterated from memory once disappeared into domains of racial state terror such as Angola, Sugarland (Texas), Parchman (Mississippi), and Cummins (Arkansas). What was clear to me when I began the hour-long drive from the state capitol to the heart of West Feliciana Parish was that I had an irrepressible pitlike feeling in my stomach, a literal nausea

that grew stronger the closer I came to the front gates of the fully operational eighteen-thousand-acre slave plantation—a place that first began
converting black men, women, and children into chattel in the early nineteenth century—and a geography that to this day continues to perform
such mass (in)human conversion under its official name, Louisiana State
Penitentiary (LSP).

The pit in my stomach had a great deal to do with my recognition that
as I was heading toward the prison plantation, I was retracing a well-worn
groove in a road designated most often for young criminally branded black
men from places like the Lower Ninth Ward in New Orleans. I knew that
for them this ride must feel more like a plummeting to death as they sit
handcuffed in the back of countless prison buses and shuttled in modern-
day coffles through the picturesque Louisiana countryside, and added to
more than five thousand already entombed bodies—75 percent to 80 percent of whom are black—and many of whom can be found at the moment
I am writing these words, bent at the waist, picking cotton, soybeans, and
corn under armed guards on horseback, toiling as "two-cent men" in the
same fields in which black prisoners have been slaving for well over two
centuries (Figure 5).[2]

I asked myself how different a twenty-five-year-old from the Lower Ninth
Ward, or New Orleans East, or Shreveport, could feel while being driven
to "Angola" under a sentence of "natural life," than those such as Olaudah
Equiano, or countless (and nameless) others from Africa's west coast and
hinterland, who, as they approached the slave ship were sure they were to
be devoured by the crew or those awaiting them on the other side of the
Atlantic. Are not the innumerable blues soundings and stories that have
been passed down for generations within black communities about the
fate of those sent to the prison plantation disarmingly similar to the horror
tales shared among African commoners of what was to befall them should
they be coffled to the barracoon, shelved within the bowels of the slave
ship, and transported as fungible commodities to places such as the very
plantation I was steadily approaching on a beautiful summer's day in the
early twenty-first century?

Don't come to Angola, this is murder's home . . . This was the cautionary
refrain of the living dead testifying to America's seemingly interminable
Middle Passage that I heard echoing in my mind as I continued ineluctably
toward what is the largest expanse of official prison land in the country (if
not the world)—a revenant sound first emitted by black captives in the

early to mid-twentieth century, when they were still producing as much as twelve million pounds of refined sugarcane at Angola in a given year—a "hell factory in the fields" of West Feliciana Parish, which is greater in total area than the island of Manhattan.[3]

As I turned off the 61 and headed northwest along the "Tunica Trace," a road that begins some twenty-two miles from the front gates of the prison, I was struck by a nagging thought that had remained with me since the first time I wrote about Angola plantation, or "The Farm" (as the prison is euphemistically nicknamed). That is, I considered the absolute imponderability

Figure 5. "King Cotton," Angola Prison Plantation, 1999. Photograph by Wilbert Rideau. Courtesy of the artist.

of the fact that I could be driving toward more than five thousand bodies warehoused on an undead slave plantation—even if that mass captivity was performed under the national racialized and narcoticizing discourses of "corrections," "public safety," and state-sanctioned retribution. Another way to think of this is in the form of a hypothetical: What if, in modern-day Germany or Poland, a Jewish person convicted of a crime was sent to a fully operational Auschwitz or Buchenwald to pay his "debt to society"? What would the world's response be to such a scenario? Would the branding of a Jewish (or for that matter a Roma, Sinti, or communist) subject as "criminal" rationalize his disappearance onto a renovated concentration camp for the remainder of his "natural life"?[4] What is it about the social and ontological position of the black subject in the United States that makes his disappearance onto a modernized slave plantation both socially tolerable and experientially normal? Where was the outcry against this national atrocity? Why wasn't the twenty-two-mile stretch of road from St. Frances-ville to Angola riddled with banners and throngs of protestors from around the United States and the globe attempting to block the seemingly infinite procession of black, brown, and poor white bodies into an American prison slave camp that has never once been closed for business since the early nineteenth century, not even for a day? If there was no mass public outrage at the existence of a literal prison plantation, then what were the possibilities for inciting mass mobilizations against the entire prison–industrial complex that currently warehouses and terrorizes more than 2.3 million people, not just in the South but within northern and international spaces of U.S. neoslavery such as Chowchilla (California), Pelican Bay (California), Florence ADX (Colorado), Jackson (Michigan), Attica (New York), and Guantánamo Bay, Cuba?

At issue here is the transtemporal white supremacist social investment in blackness as uncivil, undishonorable, and uninjurable being, and how the liberal humanitarian allotments of public outrage and atrocity recognition are always already disqualified in respect to a collectivity whose penal slavery and civil death have been as central to the postbellum vision of white civil belonging as the African's chattel enslavement and social death were to white civil personhood before 1865.[5] When viewed in this manner, the sight of the black neoslave laboring in the plantation field at Angola becomes less of an exceptional scene of southern barbarism than a spectacular representation of a banal process of socially acceptable (and pleasurable) racial capitalist carceral genocide that continues to stretch across the mythological borderline of slavery and freedom. Indeed, as I discussed in chapter 2 in reference to the future haunting of the late nineteenth-century public spectacle of black prisoners auctioned as slaves on court-house steps in states such as Maryland and Illinois, to view Angola as an exception to the large-scale human cargoing taking place in the current stage of America's centuries-old complex of chattelized imprisonment would be to disengage from the reality that this structural modus operandi of American empire is defined not so much by the form in which mass racial-ized incarceration occurs but by the fact of mass racialized incarceration itself. Read in this light, Angola becomes less of a southern anachronism and more of a dubiously instructive living monument to the timeless national practices of human entombment and enslavement—a point reflected by Mumia Abu Jamal in his assessment of Louisiana's prison plantation: "If there ever was a question of *the slave parentage of the American prison sys-tem,* one glance at the massive penitentiary known as Angola . . . removes all doubt."[6]

However, as I continued along the road to Angola, there were no lib-eration banners or would-be neoslave liberators. What I did see was an assortment of highway billboards advertising romantic plantation bed-and-breakfast getaways aimed at capitalizing on tourists' well-ingrained visions of a pastoral, gallant, and "intriguing" antebellum South (Figure 6). With these visual emblems of the national tendency to screen the geno-cidal operation of the antebellum slave plantation as an idyllic country romance and a playground for national white supremacist fantasy and nos-talgia, I was given unsettling evidence of a racist cultural order that allows for no prison plantation protestors (and that produces an immediate dis-qualification of those who have indeed stood defiantly at the gates of Angola and other U.S. prisons). In fact, the other main explanation for the nau-seous feeling I had during the entirety of the journey from Baton Rouge was my knowledge that, aside from a smattering of family members com-ing to visit their loved ones, the only other civilian "freepersons" I was likely to encounter as I pulled up to the penitentiary would be a subset of the thousands of tourists that visit Angola every year from all over the United States and Europe.[7]

Like many other antebellum slave plantation sites in Louisiana and elsewhere in the South, LSP has successfully transformed itself into a tour-ist attraction that treats the (un)hallowed ground of racial genocide as an occasion for fun, relaxation, and the reproduction of white supremacist

Figure 6. Billboard along the road to Angola. Photograph by the author.

historical mythology—except in the case of Angola plantation, the horrors of slavery are successfully evacuated, muted, and contorted in spite of and through the ever-presence of prison slaves.[8] Instead of being recognized as embodiments of the accretion of slavery into the present, the imprisoned body on the living plantation is deployed as a resource for public amusement, white self-definition, and the normalization of racial capitalist atrocity, a fact symbolized most infamously by the prison's annual rodeo and hobby-craft fair—otherwise known as "The Wildest Show in the South"—in which tens of thousands of people converge on Angola during two months of the year to witness untrained prisoner "rodeo cowboys" perform in events such as "Convict Poker" and "Guts and Glory." In the first event, a clown places a card table in the middle of the six-thousand-person rodeo arena, around which four prisoners sit and pretend to play a game of cards. A modest monetary prize is awarded to the man who remains seated the longest as a bull attempts to gorge all four contestants. For the second event, a large number of stripe-clad men attempt to remove a poker chip tied between the horns of a bull. Prisoners are regularly tossed over twenty feet in the air by the two-thousand-pound animals. They also routinely suffer from broken bones, deep lacerations, and concussions as a result of this spectacle. One prisoner is known to have ultimately died from a heart attack resulting from his participation in one of the events.

Those who have engaged critically with such scenes of perverse amusement, performative dehumanization, and spectatorial punishment at Angola have correctly drawn allusion to their similarity with the ancient Roman practice of forcing slaves to fight with animals and one another in the gladiatorial arena.[9] That recent opening ceremonies of the rodeo have culminated with the prison's current warden entering Angola's arena in a horse-drawn chariot driven around its perimeter by prisoners does much to corroborate this comparison. However, upon my arrival at the prison museum parking lot situated just outside the penitentiary's front gate and directly across the road from the visitor's parking area, I was focused on the connection between the rodeo and formations of chattel entertainment that are much closer to home, both temporally and geographically, than ancient Rome. Indeed, the main reason for my visit to Angola was to try to locate a set of photographs in a box at the museum that ranged as far back as the early to mid-twentieth century—a period when plantation entertainments such as the prison-sponsored blackface minstrel show were being held on Angola's grounds and in various "free" communities in and around West Feliciana.[10] In fact, I hoped that I might come across an image of one of these blackface troupes, a visual representation of the degree to which spectacles of neoslavery such as the prison rodeo draw upon a long history of prison plantation entertainment. The modern genealogical roots of these spectacles go as far back as the Middle Passage and antebellum plantation, when, as Saidiya Hartman suggests, slaves were forced to simulate consent to bondage through song, dance, and other less public forms of ritualized "unproductive" travail that were as essential to the formation of white mastery as their "productive" labor in cotton, rice, tobacco, and sugarcane fields.[11]

Immediately upon entering the prison plantation museum, the dread I had felt during the entire drive to Angola was confirmed. I was confronted with the patently absurd nature of attempting to conduct "archival work" in a space of mass living death—namely, one that doubles as a staging ground of amusement and identificatory fantasy for the free civil subject. On my way to find the staff member who was to help me locate the photographs, I walked through the gift shop, which is the first room one sees upon entering the museum site. Here, in easily the largest area within what is generally a rather small building, one can choose between an array of prison-plantation–themed objects intended to elicit chuckles and dollars from patrons, including handcuff key chains, replicas of the striped shirts that Angola prisoners were made to wear until the mid-twentieth century, sweatshirts emblazoned with the words "Angola: A Gated Community," stuffed animals in the likeness of the bloodhounds that have been used to terrorize fugitive prisoners at Angola since (at least) the late nineteenth century, and a fruit spread called "Strawberry Fields," which is made with produce that current prisoners have planted and picked in slave plantation fields. I looked on as dozens of visitors nonchalantly perused these items, and while one mother took advantage of a photo opportunity in a section of the museum adjacent to the gift shop that involved placing her two young children—the older of whom was wearing his brand-new prison-striped shirt—into a mock prison cell. The scene of white tourists indulging in comedic recreation, consumptive pleasure, and familial bonding through what, after its sadistic Roman counterpart, might be called a *prison planta-tion holiday,* stood in stark contrast to the feelings of dispossession, broken-ness, and injury expressed on the faces of the mournful procession of black people I saw on the other side of the road leading to Angola's front gate—those who had made long treks from Louisiana's urban centers in order to visit their disappeared sons, fathers, brothers, uncles, cousins, and friends, and who did not, for a moment, look across the Tunica Trace toward the museum before crossing the threshold of the neoplantation.

The disparity between the scene of gothic amusement and consumer fulfillment inside the museum and the scene of mourning and natal alien-ation just across the road was exacerbated by my knowledge that, as I walked through the "historical site" in search of the living dead of Angola's past, there were more than five thousand living dead of the plantation's present just across the razor-wire gates that separated me from the prison. This reality worked at odds with the museum's narrative framing as a space wherein the abject violence of Angola's past has been successfully artifacted as an emblem of the modern, "reformatory" nature of the current penal order. The museum's brochure encapsulates its narrative of the obsoles-cence of repressive plantation management and the prison's supposed com-pleted passage into the oxymoronic liberal repressive echelon of "humane" mass entombment: "Once known as the 'bloodiest prison in America,' the Louisiana State Penitentiary at Angola has emerged as one of the most progressive and well managed prisons in the country. In order to fully appreciate the accomplishments of this prison, one must first visit its past." While walking through the museum space one is asked to bear witness to the veracity of the state's claims to progressive modernization, to the death of "old Angola," and the prison's conversion into an arena of "well-managed" human cargoing. This conjuration is performed by way of exhibits displaying various torture devices that have been used against prisoners over the years, including whips, guns, bats, and ax handles. Juxtaposed with these exhibitions of the putatively embalmed practice of repressive punishment at the prison are displays intended to show the ostensibly humane, rehabilitative, and recreational brand of modern imprisonment at Angola, such as rodeo posters, a seemingly infinite variety of evangelical reeducation programs, and memorabilia from the many films that have been shot at the plantation, including an actor's chair autographed by Billy Bob Thornton when Angola was used as a set for the filming of *Monster's Ball*.

Conspicuously absent from the museum's installations dedicated to the theme of penal progress are some of LSP's most prototypically modern and postmodern architectural and repressive apparatuses. To invoke Aimé Césaire once again, penological advancement at the prison plantation has translated into a system of "progressive dehumanization" whereby the real measure of the facility's ascension to "northern" standards of mass human disappearance is the degree to which it has successfully exchanged putatively anachronistic brutalization techniques, such as the whip, "bat," and "sweatbox," for more "humane" ones, such as four-point restraint tables, the "body sheet," tear gas, "black box" handcuffs, and modernized punishment units in which prisoners are subjected to indefinite solitary confinement and other forms of legally sanctioned torture.[12] The importation and sedimentation of such state-of-the-art mechanisms of entombment and physical/psychic terror marks the prison plantation as an illuminating spatial symbol of the mutually constitutive and cross-fertilizing relationship of southern and northern white supremacist penal law. And as I will discuss below, the easy cohabitability and effective indistinguishability of past, present, and futuristic modes of terror at the neoplantation expose the degree to which the progressive path of penal modernity has remained tightly bound to its moorings in chattel slavery.

Aerial photographs of the largest maximum-security prison in the country offer stark evidence of the dynamic and interdependent fusion of "old" and "new" at the prison plantation through views of LSP's assortment of postmodern "telephone-pole"–style cell-block camps as they have been grafted onto its thousands of acres of slave plantation fields.[13] As I sat outside the front gates, I considered that perhaps the most horrifying aspects of imprisonment at Angola occur not in its cotton, corn, and soybean rows but inside its most modern, and supposedly postslavery, punitive architectures—spaces such as the CCR "dungeon" and Camp J punishment cells, wherein Albert Woodfox and the late Herman Wallace of the Angola 3 (have) spent more than forty-one years, or about fifteen thousand days, in solitary confinement.[14] If the experience of eight years of political imprisonment and indefinite solitary confinement in Soledad and San Quentin made their fellow Black Panther George Jackson feel that he had been shuttled into a permanent Middle Passage with "cotton and corn growing out of [his] chest," then, as two of the longest-standing political prisoners in the world, Woodfox and Wallace must feel (and have felt) as if they have been buried even further within the bowels of the land-based slave ship, especially given the literal cotton and corn crops that continue to be grown and picked by their fellow prison slaves just outside their "modern" solitary cells.

Wallace attempts to give words to the unspeakable treatment that "freemen" levied against political prisoners, the mentally ill, and those branded as "gang members" or "the worst of the worst" within what is euphemistically described as *administrative segregation*:

> I have witnessed guards from 2002 to 2004 while I was in Angola's . . . [most] restrictive punishment unit, who have thrown buckets of ice water (in winter) on men who were on 4-point restraint, wearing only paper gowns. I've seen guards snatch food trays out of [a] prisoner's cell bars and throw the tray against the wall, then call SWAT teams to gas and beat the prisoner for throwing the food. After SWAT team is done with the prisoner, they take him to the infirmary and then the prisoner goes to [internal prison] court, is found guilty, sentenced to begin the punitive program from the beginning . . . as well as pay for his medical treatment and restitution for damaging the paint on the wall.[15]

Given the quotidian occurrence of such modernized terror methodologies at the neoplantation, the museum's narrative of progressivism actually serves to throw the undead nature of its regressive "past" into more palpable relief. Far from successfully disassembling its rootedness in chattel slavery, the convict lease system, and the early prison plantation, the state's framing of penal progress through the lenses of punitive performance, public enjoyment, and repressive lenience actually serves to express the impossible severance of the *now* of "modern" penal entombment from the *then* of "premodern" carceral enslavement. When read in combination with LSP's more apparently overt repressive practices, punitive spectacles such as the rodeo, the use of the prison plantation as movie studio, and the ritual of tourists donning stripes and posing for photos in mock prison cells suggest how the history and present of state terror at Angola (and throughout the rest of America's archipelago of neoslavery) are written both in corporeal rupture and terror-ridden pleasure. That rodeos, film crews, and museum visitors function to convert the site of neo-enslavement into a staging ground for public enjoyment and *criminal minstrelsy*[16]—with the burnt cork of the minstrel show being replaced by the faux handcuffs, bars, and prison stripes of the neoplantation tour—expresses the degree to which racial terror, living death, and chattelized imprisonment have most often been accompanied by and performed through painfully fraught amusement, the ruse of enslaved prisoner contentment, the instrumental bestowal of punitive "privilege," and the obscene public display and spectatorial consumption of human state property.

While waiting at a table in a corner of one of the museum's rooms for the photographs that I hoped would contain evidence of Angola's blackface troupe of the early to mid-twentieth century, I considered how the sight of twenty-first-century plantation tourists modeling striped shirts and laughing as they took photos of one another inside mock prison cells represented a disturbingly fitting contemporary accompaniment for my attempt at a counter-historical unburial of the practice of punitive performance at the plantation. The tableau of free civil bodies immersing themselves in "convict" drag at the very site wherein mass civil death was being simultaneously visited upon thousands of prisoners represented a grotesque modern-day analogue of the long-standing intimacies of (neo)slave abjection and public pleasure, prisoner dehumanization and free white self-definition, and captive performance and the enactment of racialized violence within sites of chattel carcerality.[17] As the only other black man present in the museum approached me, dressed in all white, with a dolly holding four dusty boxes he had plucked from one of the museum's closets, I was further disabused of any notion that what I was conducting at the

plantation that day could in any way be mistaken for a backward looking "archival" journey into a completed or dead history. As I stood up to
greet this man and he quickly shook my hand and then rather nervously
attempted to refuse my aid in moving the boxes to the table, I was immediately hit with a shudder of awareness as to his station. This man was not
a "worker" at the museum: he was in fact a prisoner, a man whose laboring presence signified his status as "trusty," that is, one whose officially
recognized adherence to the penal sovereign's decrees of proper captive
comportment allowed him a channel away from plantation fields and the
solitary cell while affording him the "privilege" of performing the role of
all-purpose servant to the museum staff.

The trusty's presence at the site of my attempted encounter with the
past was suggestive of the extreme difficulty, or absolute inapplicability, of
the word "archive" in reference to the study of Angola and other political
geographies of neoslavery. The word "archive" pronounces and reenacts
the death of the object of analysis—namely, when that "object" is actually
a human being who has been literally objectified by the law.[18] Beholding
this man as he was ordered to perform a seemingly endless litany of tasks
(including serving my needs as researcher), and mindful of the infinite
routines of labor, pain, and rupture being suffered at that very moment
by thousands of other plantation captives not afforded the privilege of
working as museum servant, I asked myself how I could properly engage
with a past that has never died. When I began to look through the boxes,
I knew that I was embarking on a process of mnemonic encounter with
present-day racial genocide as much as an archival search for subterranean
elements of a forgotten or grossly distorted past. This again is the epistemic and experiential purchase of Toni Morrison's concept of rememory;
it is also what Jamaica Kincaid meant in describing the black subaltern's
position as being caught by and in history, whereby the past is experienced
not as an object of intellectual inquiry but is felt as an "open wound" that
keeps reopening with every breath.[19] In this light, the question is not simply what historical antecedents have led us to our current perilous predicament, but why the "now" is so reminiscent, reflective, and painfully
resonant with the genocidal "then."

From this perspective, the ubiquitous and unavoidable presences that
emit from the historical and continued manufacture of the civilly, natally,
and socially dead at the American neoplantation represent dubious and
unspeakable resolution to what, in *Lose Your Mother*, Hartman presents as

the nearly impossible task of recovering the ghosts of chattel slavery within the barracoon-like enclosures of the master archive and the desolate and long inoperative slave dungeons of Elmina and Cape Coast Castles in Ghana. As I sat down to work at the precipice of America's "Angola," and what stands as the longest operating slave fortress in the Western hemisphere, if not the world, my frustration was not that there were no dead "revenants lurking in the dungeon" to reclaim, it was with the reality that among the modern-day barracoons of the prison–industrial complex there are far too many living revenants to count. Indeed, the living plantation represents an all-too-literal embodiment of Hartman's contention that if "the ghost of slavery still haunts our present, it is because we are still looking for an exit from the prison."[20]

Minstrel Show at Camp A:
The Excesses of Neoplantation Management

> *The photograph . . . takes its place in this contest of haunting.*
>
> —Avery Gordon, *Ghostly Matters*

It did not take long at all. After stealing a surreptitious bit of conversation with the Angola "trusty," who had unearthed four boxes from a backroom in the museum—a hushed exchange in which he let me know with his eyes as much as his words that his body and soul knew more than I could ever conceive in my mind about neoslavery—I had only to flip through three photos before I saw John McElroy without knowing that I was seeing him and that he was also (literally) seeing me. There he was/is, standing on crutches, with a dismembered right leg, in a prison-striped version of a tuxedo jacket, positioned front and center of the prison plantation's "Negro orchestra" and eighteen fellow members of Angola's blackface minstrel troupe (Figures 7 and 8). Before I discovered that it was Camp A prisoner number "37708" staring out resolutely from the center of a photograph intended to stage black contentment with and inurement to the predicament of penal chattelhood, and days prior to the moment that he would reach out directly from the grave and make me aware of what he had to tell me (and everyone else within striking distance of these words), I was fully convinced that in snatching this *unhistorical event* from the well-fortified oblivion of official history, I had completed a research task of my own choosing.[21]

Figure 7. Camp A minstrel troupe, Angola Prison Plantation, c. 1947. John McElroy, the troupe leader, is shown front and center with crutches. Courtesy Angola Museum, Louisiana State Penitentiary.

Figure 8. Close-up of John McElroy, the minstrel troupe leader at Angola.

The haunting quality of the photograph was not lost on me before I was approached by its most prominent unquiet presence. For instance, I knew that the costumed prison uniforms worn in the shot—including the tuxedo jackets, the vertically striped pants and shirts, the striped hat bands, and the horizontally striped socks worn by one of the three performers in drag— had been patterned and sewn by black women at "the Willows," the mellifluous "Sweet Home"-sounding name given to the section of Angola's eighteen thousand acres allotted to the entombment of women, the overwhelming majority of whom were black. I knew that, along with slaving in the plantation's cotton fields under armed guard, working as nannies to children of white prison employees, and other traditionally unspoken forms of rupturous labor, they most certainly would have suffered as domestic neoslaves in the homes of white men, these women were tasked with making all of Louisiana's prison uniforms from the early twentieth century until they were eventually transported to a women's penal "farm" at St. Gabriel in 1962.[22]

With the absent presence of these women in mind, I first sat looking at the group of blackfaced, cross-dressed, and prison-striped men posing on a plantation house concrete porch made to double as a minstrel stage with what Fred Moten describes as a sonic "interior exteriority of the photograph" emanating in my ears in the form of the voice of Odea Mathews.[23] The image emitted a ghostly reverb of a sorrow/survival song that this particular black woman prisoner once delivered into the microphone of a white folkloric tourist to the neoplantation while she sat, her hands and feet bound to their daily manipulation of a sewing machine, positioned in physical proximity to the place I was now sitting and on a day not far removed from the one upon which the photograph was taken.

> There's somethin' within me, Oh Lord,
> That holds in the rain (yes it is).
> Somethin' within me,
> Oh child I cannot explain (yes it is).
> Somethin' within me,
> Oh Lord I cannot explain (oh yes),
> All I can say, praise God, somethin' within.
>
> Have you somethin' within you (Oh yes),
> That's burnin' inside? (Yes it is),
> Somethin' within you, Oh child, you know it never gets tired.

> Somethin' within you, Oh Lord it never gets tired,
> And all I can say, praise God, somethin' within.[24]

With an enthralling vibrato that sounds eerily similar to the Dinah Washington of "This Bitter Earth," Mathews gestures toward, longs for, and produces an unnamable, unlocatable, and inexplicable loophole of (dis)embodied retreat that is situated deep within her reified, ruptured, and ruled body.[25] Through an act of spiritual marronage that could just as easily have been rendered during Angola's birth-time as an antebellum plantation more than 120 years before the recording, the incarcerated, natally alienated, and chattelized subject testifies to and re-creates an unfungible somethin' within and beyond the publicly owned and physically exhausted corporeal self that has been mechanized, criminalized, and colonized by the state. However, insofar as her attempted self-reclamation depends on and is performed through the detachment of her "tireless" spirit from her imprisoned body, Mathews's act of sonic redress expresses the burdened, dispossessed, and terrorized collective predicament of the living dead through the very act of sounding claim to a modicum of individual freedom. After all, what is the necessary severance of the would-be-free spirit from the physically tortured body if not a nearly exact simulation of the untimely termination of life?[26]

Somethin' within me, Oh Lord, that holds in the rain—The redressive disintegration of the spiritual self from the pained black body, bound in the rain (or reign) of a literal hell on earth, seemed a fitting sonic accompaniment for my first contact with a photograph in which the bodies of Mathews's fellow prisoners are captured in a moment of prison plantation "downtime," performing in the quintessential white supremacist cultural modality of spectatorial dehumanization and black disfigurement. The grotesque penal resurfacing of the blackface mask beckons us to the photo's centrally positioned subject and the historically voided captive experiences registered by his carceral dismemberment. Indeed, nothing shown in the minstrel troupe photograph more clearly signifies the punitive dimensions of black captive performance and the terroristic terms under which the prison slave would have elected to perform in blackface more than the redolent onstage absent presence of his amputation. As I sat at the foot of the very place where the photograph was shot, with Mathews's haunting refrain reverberating in my ears, I considered how the black prisoner's missing right leg signals the fact that the redressive spirit-body detachment of the neoslave is most often coupled with and deployed in response to what Hortense Spillers describes as the ritualized tearing apart or mortification of black captive flesh—a routine of sadistic state violence that in this instance has more than likely led to the permanent detachment of the imprisoned body from one of its main parts.[27]

As I pulled away from Angola's front gate, I knew that I would return to this anonymous figure (and his disappeared limb) when I returned home from Louisiana. But I also knew that, in doing so, I would have to conduct an act of counter-historical imagination since the leader of Angola's minstrel troupe had been obliterated from history, along with countless other black prisoners who had been enslaved on the plantation since the early nineteenth century.[28] There was no pathway for recovering this particular buried story—or so I thought. Three days after I returned to Baton Rouge, I found myself sitting at the Louisiana State Archives, scanning a rather unforthcoming microform reel of correspondence pertaining to the Louisiana State Penitentiary. I had hoped that the file of letters written to and from the State Attorney General's office from the late 1940s to the 1950s would contain clemency statements written by Angola prisoners— testimony that, however mediated, would at least give a measure of "blood to the scraps" that I had been able to recover to that point.[29] As I heard the voice of one of the archive's staff address patrons over the intercom informing us that the facility would soon be closing, I had found next to nothing.

On a whim, I decided to scan the reel again, turning the advance knob clockwise as far as it would go. With the images flashing over the screen at the highest speed, I stopped the reel and landed squarely on the following letter:

Angola LA Camp A
March 3—49
Dear Sir Mr Kimp,
    I hav recive a few Letters from you. And as yet I haven't got any one to help me as you have sent word for them to help me. As I have already told you that I have life here. On sircumstance everdence I am a one leg man. And I do not have any one to help me at all. But you. So will you try to Get Some one to Get me out on a pertinal pardon are they serch law as that So if you will please sir write me at once

Yours Truly Sir
From John McElroy 37708
Camp A Angola La
Answer Soon.[30]

I knew the words were significant. But I also knew that there was no way I could possibly be hearing the voice of the same "one leg man" I had first seen at Angola three days before in the minstrel show photograph. No way. I was not prepared to receive the spectral summons contained in the desperate refrain, *help me . . . sent word . . . to help me . . . I am a one leg man . . . I don't have anyone to help me at all. But you.* I quickly printed the letter and moved on to the next image (Figure 9):

John McElroy is unknown to history. Indeed, he was imprisoned, enslaved, and dis(re)membered by a living history that kills—that contorts, disqualifies, and annihilates the experiences and the truths uttered by the untold millions who make up the desecrated and unquiet dead of American racial genocide. Both his name and his life were to have been forever eradicated through the legal stigmata of black criminalization and neo-enslavement. They were to have been stenciled over by the punitive mark of "37708"—a branding that represents a twentieth-century penal reinscription of the very dis-naming and cataloguing practices that began in Euro-American modernity's original racial capitalist misogynist prisons: the barracoons, "factories," holds, pens, and plantations of the Middle Passage and antebellum chattel slavery.[31]

But there he was/is. The very "one leg man" I thought I had found buried in a box at Angola had actually found me. At this moment I had to reckon not only with a literal ghost, or zombie, of the master archive but also with the fact that the task I thought I had been engineering on my own, of searching out the remnants of punitive performance at the prison plantation, had actually been conducted all along by one of its living revenants—the leader of Camp A's "colored" minstrel troupe—a man whose repeated call for liberation had been muted for decades within Angola's slave plantation fields (and performance stages) and by the enclosures of the master archive, but who nonetheless had continued wailing an incarcerated blues refrain that had finally been heard: *Help me . . . help me . . . I am a one leg man . . . I don't have anyone to help me at all. But you. I am. John McElroy . . .* And there I was. He was calling out to me (and everyone within striking distance of these words) from an unlocatable grave to un-desecrate his death, to remember his stolen and dishonored name and body, and to listen to his unaccounted-for ghostly encounter with a structure of necropolitical terror that continues to denigrate his memory and that of his fellow captives through the mass production and consumption of neoslaves, such as the "natural lifer" who had delivered the minstrel

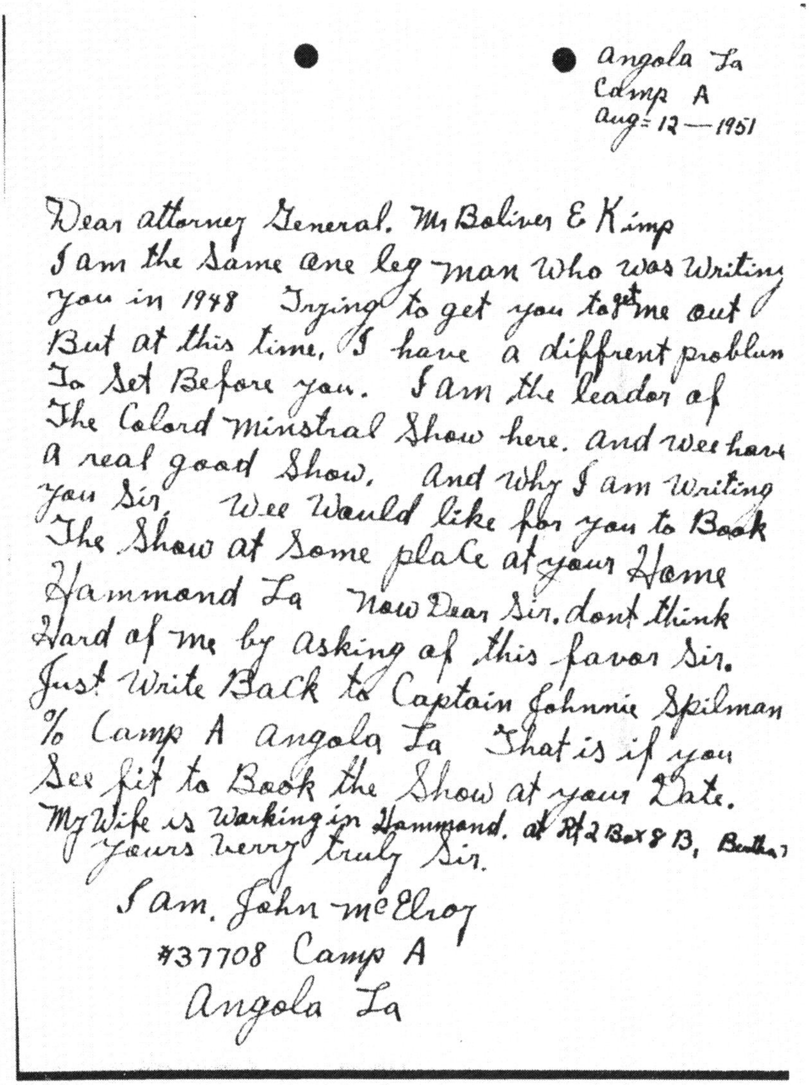

angola La
Camp A
aug 12 — 1951

Dear attorney General. Mr Boliver E Kimp
I am the Same one leg man Who was Writing
you in 1948 Trying to get you to get me out
But at this time, I have a diffrent problum
To Set Before you. I am the leader of
The Colord Minstral Show here. and Wee have
a real good Show, And Why I am Writing
you Sir Wee Would like for you to Book
The Show at Some place at your Home
Hammond La Now Dear Sir. dont think
Hard of me by asking of this favor Sir.
Just Write Back to Captain Johnnie Spilman
% Camp A angola La That is if you
See fit to Book the Show at your Date.
My Wife is Warking in Hammond. at Rf 2 Box 8 13, Bertha
Yours verry truly Sir.

    I am, John mcElroy
    #37708 Camp A
    angola La

Figure. 9. John McElroy to Louisiana Attorney General, Bolivar Kemp Jr., Louisiana State Penitentiary, General Correspondence (microform), 1951–52. Louisiana State Archives, Baton Rouge.

show image to me in a box three days before at Angola. Indeed this was the very sort of moment Avery Gordon, in conversation with Derrida, had spoken of in suggesting that if "the ghost is alive," we "are in relation to it and it has designs on us such that we must reckon with it graciously, attempting to offer it hospitable memory *out of a concern for justice.* Out of a concern for justice would be the only reason to bother."[32]

However, as I began the work of respectfully and hospitably attending to one who, out of his own posthumous concern for a counter-juridical variety of justice, had literally reached out from the inhospitable tomb of official history, I was aware that, in many respects, my task was as impossible as it was necessary. The first and most obvious thing that must be said along these lines is that no amount of attentive engagement with John McElroy's spectral presence will do anything to repair the breach inflicted upon his life, that of his entire family, and those of other racially and criminally stigmatized persons who have been subjected to neoslavery in mass numbers at places such as Angola, Parchman, Sugarland, Cummins, Banner Mine, and Attica since the passage of the Thirteenth Amendment. Aside from this, one must respectfully acknowledge the chasm between our desire to welcome one such as McElroy into rememory and the epistemic erasure and seizure that constitute the unhistorical positionality of the neoslave. Indeed there was enough in the way of unavailable and inaccessible knowledge accompanying the ghostly resurfacing of the Angola blackface minstrel photograph, and two last-ditch missives from the troupe's "one leg" leader, as to make the imperative duty of careful listening seem vexing at best. For instance, what exactly was the alleged crime for which John McElroy received a life term of civil death? Were his mother and father still alive when he attempted to convince Attorney General Bolivar Kemp Jr. to allow his minstrel troupe the "favor" of resurrecting the antebellum "darky" for the citizens of Hammond, Louisiana? By what surreptitious and surprisingly bold expressive means did he and his fellow black prison slaves incorporate the blues voice that inhabits his letters into their stage performances of neoslave joviality, subhumanity, and contentment? How many children did he and his wife, "Bertha," have before he was disappeared to the neoslave plantation, and how many of these children would ultimately find themselves imprisoned at Angola, a local "County Farm," a chain gang, or a northern penitentiary? Just how long had McElroy been enslaved in West Feliciana before writing his first letters to Kemp (he mentions that correspondence began in 1948)? Do these unrecoverable letters contain details of the exact manner by which he became dispossessed of his right leg?

But here we are met with an equally important question: How can one enter into a reckoning with the ghostly presences of neoslavery with any expectation of historical, experiential, or expressive transparency on the part of one of its revenants, even one that approaches us with the head-on (and leg-off) intensity of John McElroy? As Hartman (following Edouard Glissant) advises us, anyone taking on such a task must respect "the right to obscurity" of those who have endured the unsayable, the unthinkable, and the irreparable.[33] A desire for transparency, clarity, and full semantic disclosure on the part of even the most unquiet revenant of the chattelized carceral disrespects and disregards the magnitude of the very unavowed atrocity we are attempting to honor through our careful listening. As Sethe's "crawling already" baby and ghostly survivor of the Middle Passage reminds us throughout *Beloved*—but with most arresting intensity in the antigrammatical monologue I discussed in chapter 1—those who emerge from oblivion hungry for rememory do not and cannot speak, write, sing, wail, or scream in complete sentences (or sounds). Rather, it is the very incomplete, cut-off, broken, and incomprehensible nature of the aural, written, and visual remainders of the socially and civilly dead that qualify their semantic depth and social urgency, and that signal the counter-historical, counter-epistemological, and counter-pedagogical value of their muzzled and submerged transmissions from the many unmarked graves of American racial genocide. Here we might think of the ellipses and silences of both the Angola minstrel show photograph and McElroy's two "kites" from Camp A as bearing a gravity akin to the echo-laden silences and caesuras that accompany John Coltrane's tenor saxophone in "Alabama" (his dirge to Addie Mae Collins, Denise McNair, Carole Robertson, and Cynthia Wesley); or what Frederick Douglass describes as the incomprehensible but inestimably "deep meaning" of the slave songs he first heard in boyhood, whose mere mnemonic recurrence was enough to bring tears to his eyes as he wrote his autobiography of 1845; or the unspeakable thing that Stamp Paid felt in his hand and spirit during the travestied "freedom" time of 1874, when he reached into the Ohio River and pulled out what he thought was a cardinal feather but was actually a "red ribbon knotted around a curl of wet wooly hair, clinging still to a bit of [a black girl's] scalp."[34]

Like a ribboned bit of hair and scalp retrieved from the watery grave cutting Kentucky from Ohio, the muted, fragmented, and subterranean transmissions of the neoslave are resoundingly clear in their expression of the terror, dispossession, and rupture that have underpinned the predicament of liberal de jure freedom for black people in the United States. And, like a vestige of an anonymously murdered black girl in 1874 (or a publicly slain black boy in 2012),[35] John McElroy's phantom right leg—or rather his phantasmal reassertion of it—disassembles dominant historical, cultural, and legal truths that have attended the cross-generational punitive violation of the criminalized, dehumanized, and dishonored black subject from chattel slavery to prison slavery. McElroy's spectralized counter-deployment of his dismembered body both in his letters and on the neoplantation stage suggests how at the zero degree of chattelized entombment the only acts of "resistance" often made available to the captive involve an embrace, exhibition, and even a furtherance of one's very condition of brokenness, rupture, and dispossession.[36] In other words, when keeping in mind that he likely never achieved freedom, and that his only method of getting beyond Angola's gates may have been through the perverse privilege of performing the "darky's" cheerful acceptance of the very condition of enslavement that he tried so desperately to escape, McElroy's apparitional body and voice present less of a claim for reparation than a demand for attuned acknowledgment of the enormity of the unhistorical crime of state slavery and the irreparable pain associated with unachieved liberation.

Here we might think of the historically anonymous neoslave's performative and written redeployment of his captive body as an unrecognized and unromantic analogue of other embodied acts of injurious resistance, such as the hunger strike, that have been performed by "radical" or "political" prisoners. By openly declaring the reality of his punitive rupture, brandishing it onstage, and discursively fusing it to his identity under civil death in his repeated letters to the state's preeminent purveyor of the law (and to us)—*I am a one leg man . . . I am the same one leg man*—the undead social and political presence who is John McElroy transmutes the dismembered part of his body into a painfully eloquent and "radical" absence that disenchants the white supremacist mythos surrounding the torturous spectacle of black captive performance, including the minstrel show that he sought to book to a space *anywhere* outside the confines of the prison plantation after his repeated calls for actual deliverance received no answer.

Indeed, whereas none of prisoner number 37708's letters imploring the state's attorney general to offer him a pardon from "life" at Angola received any real attention, his presentation of the idea of directing a prison-striped blackface show in the official's hometown elicited an immediate and congenial response.

Dear John—I was very glad to get your letter and to learn that activities such as minstrel shows, etc. are being organized and carried on by the inmates. Things of this kind not only make a stay at the institution more bearable but are bound to be a help in preparing you for the ordeals of life when you are discharged. Right at the present I do not know how booking of your minstrel show could be accomplished, but I expect to be at Angola shortly and will discuss your letter with the officials there.

> With Regards, I am
> Sincerely Yours,
> Bolivar E. Kemp, Jr.
> Attorney General[37]

For Kemp, the "gladness"-inspiring image of black prisoners performing the resurrection of the contented-to-be-enslaved "darky" at the prison plantation must have seemed like a well-timed and normalizing palliative for the momentous public relations problem the state was facing in respect to Angola at the very moment he received "John's" bid to bring Camp A's minstrel troupe to Hammond, Louisiana, in August 1951. In fact, the upcoming visit to the plantation he mentions in his letter more than likely had to do with another collective prisoner performance that had occurred in February of the same year, an act of desperate and injurious resistance taken by a group of prisoners from Angola's only white "dormitory," Camp E, who became known as the "Heel-String Gang." In an action that led to the biggest prison scandal in state history, and that gave Angola the dubious distinction of "bloodiest prison in America," thirty-seven white men used razor blades to sever their Achilles tendons in protest against LSP's ritualized violence and "can't to can't see" field labor[38]—the very dominative regime that countless black prisoners had endured without an iota of public outrage since Louisiana reclaimed its privately leased "Negro" prison slaves from the estate of Samuel Lawrence James in 1901.

By the time of the heel-string incident, Angola's black captives had long resorted to acts of last-ditch protest and bodily endangerment that received scarce coverage in local or national newspapers. These actions included but were not limited to self-mutilation, violent self-defense, the destruction of tools, poisoning guard families' food, and escape attempts whose least horrifying conclusion often consisted of an encounter with the plantation's bloodhounds followed by a hiding from a five-foot club or black-snake whip.[39] But a reading of this history in concert with the unheeded call that continues to emanate from McElroy's letters and an unburied photograph of the Camp A minstrel ensemble forces some important questions into view. For instance, does not the black captive's last-resort effort at securing a tenuous and always already incomplete reprieve from the penitentiary's innumerable other staging grounds of punitive terror through painting on the mask of black self-immolation represent an act as desperate, injurious, and vexing as self-mutilation? Can we not discern the state of legalized exception as readily in the outline of the prison minstrel's smile as in the contours of the whip-scars, bite marks, knife wounds, and bullet holes that covered many of the troupe members' bodies?[40] Such questions force into view those who are present at the minstrel show but who are not caught within the frame of the photograph—the penitentiary employees and visitors who are situated at the windows of the plantation house and on the other side of the plantation surveillance camera. The harrowing unseen dimensions of the photograph leave us wondering just how many members of the Angola minstrel troupe were forcibly removed from slaving in the fields or the plantation house and made to perform in front of employee families and white visitors under the pain of being whipped, bludgeoned with the "line pusher," or killed by a gun-toting prisoner trusty;[41] or how many of them had previously been shot with bullets issuing from the shotgun of the same "Captain" or "Sergeant" who was in charge of shooting the minstrel photo. From Kemp's perspective, however, such realities were imponderable, or at least unactionable. The urgent plea that he confronted in McElroy's earlier letters was always already muzzled and shuttled through the comforting image of Sambo's return, even if the conjuration of that image depended on the interested elision of prisoner number 37708's previous communications from memory and a willful suspension of acknowledgment of the fact that this particular criminally branded "Sambo" was appearing on the neoplantation stage not as a contented prison slave but as a *one-leg man* whose apparent smile screamed out for *help*.

From the perspective of Kemp, and those free white people who did have the opportunity to reap enjoyment from interested mis-hearings of the "reels," blues, jazz, "work songs," and spirituals of those such as McElroy and Mathews over the years, the spectacle of picaresque "niggers" playing the "happy-go-lucky" slave represented stark visual opposition to the unruly white prisoner's enactment of pained resistance and overt defiance in the face of civil death—a dichotomy that secured the ontological partitioning of whiteness and blackness notwithstanding the criminal stigmatization of the white prisoner. The ontological, pedagogical, and literal currency that attached to the prison slave's performative and domestic neoslave labor at Angola functioned in dialectical interface with the economic returns associated with his use as "productive" laborer in plantation fields.[42] For many white working-class employees and their families who resided in the de facto free municipality that grew within the borders of the prison, the sense of racial superiority derived from the fungible black body served as a critical psychological and material supplement for the relatively modest monetary wages offered to many prison guards and administrators of an industrialized public neoslavery concern that operated at a technical loss through most years of its existence. Patsy Dreher, the daughter of an Angola guard captain, expresses this dynamic through a nostalgic recall of an idyllic childhood at the neoplantation when a steady supply of *all-purpose black men* were placed at the disposal of her family and those of other white employees: "Angola was a pleasant place to live back then. A vegetable cart came by every morning. What you didn't get in pay, you got in benefits. You . . . could get inmates as cooks, yard boys, house boys; you could have two or three of them if you wanted. We had an old cook named Leon who cried like a baby when he got paroled; he said ours was the only home he had known in a long time."[43] The seemingly limitless public/private utility and status-augmenting efficacy of the trustworthy and faithfully imprisoned "Negro boy" was also enjoyed within the socially incarcerating structures of Angola's surrounding communities, not simply through occasional free-world concerts such as the one McElroy hoped to book to Hammond but also through an informal convict lend/lease system whereby black trusties were dispensed to local white families as field-, house-, and *musical slaves*: "The adjacent parishes and few small communities in *the area greatly benefited from the labor and talents of the inmates.* Inmates were unofficially 'loaned as skilled laborers, skilled workers, and even entertainers.'"[44]

The liberal utilization and public dissemination of the postbellum "Negro" prisoner as either field slave, house slave, or musical slave underlines the inseparability of "productive" forms of market-oriented labor and "unproductive" forms of labor, terror, and dishonor within spaces of neoslavery, and the degree to which geographies such as Angola plantation have been built as much on the reproduction of white supremacist pleasure and domination as on the production of cash crops and monetary profits. Here we are reminded of William Goodell's earlier statement from the early 1850s regarding the fungibility, or seemingly limitless economic and social utility, of the black captive—that "Slaves, as Property, may be *used*, absolutely by their owners at will, for their own profit or pleasure."[45] Read in this light, what I have described above as the "unhistorical" aspect of captive performance at Angola not only refers to the occlusion of those such as John McElroy and Odea Mathews from the master archive, but to the virtual absence of their experiences of neoslavery within liberal and "radical" historiographic treatments of the subject of postbellum convict labor—many of which either downplay the connection between that dominative system and chattel slavery or describe penal neoslavery as something that only happened "down there" or "back then."[46] Such discussions have tended to reduce the repressive scope of racialized imprisonment either to the liberal humanitarian terms of relative death rates, or to the "radical" economistic terms of production and labor exploitation without accounting for the ways in which (1) black postbellum imprisonment is itself a formation of mass civil and living death grounded in the mass social death of chattel slavery; (2) how, far from operating simply as an "economic" system, racialized incarceration (and by this term I am again referring to the necropolitical order of gendered, economic, spatial, and racial terror that began under the Middle Passage) has represented a mode of "cultural imposition," ontological subordination, and legal domination fundamental to free/white collective self-imagining and to the overall material structuring of American empire.[47] The atrocities of slavery and neoslavery cannot be fully contemplated within the narrow economistic indices of production and labor exploitation, namely when we attempt to approach them from the nearly impossible-to-recover position of the corporeally and psychically terrorized black captive. In other words, the unhistorical experiences of those such as McElroy and Mathews unveil how chattel carcerality is not simply a mode of economic production: it is also a process of ontological, corporeal, spatial, legal, and cultural domination residing in the DNA of occidental modernity.

Along with registering the unhistorical import of black neoslave performance as a modality of white supremacist cultural reproduction and
communal self-fabrication, Kemp's allusion to the way in which the recreational privilege of minstrelsy successfully made the black neoslave's experience of plantation imprisonment "more bearable" represents a mid-
twentieth-century redeployment of the racialized carceral discourses of
natural "Negro" contentment, submissiveness, and slave-worthiness that
had been part and parcel of the chattelization of black being and the con-
solidation of whiteness since the Middle Passage. From its beginnings on
the decks of slave ships, the coffles that herded Africans to the auction
block, and with the weekend and holiday "frolics" of the antebellum slave
plantation, the staging of captive amusement had been implemented as a
primary mechanism of managing the enslaved and imprisoned black body,
of cultivating the psychic well-being, social dominion, and pleasure-drives
of the white civil subject, and of normalizing the collective rupture, terror,
and abjection black captives faced under centuries of chattelized incarceration.[48] As Hartman suggests in her seminal theorization of the instrumental deployment of the black performative body in the antebellum period,
the orchestration of captive gaiety, musicality, and docility during ostensibly "unproductive" off-times laid at the fulcrum of plantation relations,
registering the degree to which the "hours of sundown to sunup were as
important as those spent in the field in cultivating the productivity of the
plantation household and maintaining social control." She adds that during
the mid-nineteenth century,

> such diversions were an important element in plantation manage-
> ment, as the internalization of discipline and reward was consid-
> ered essential to the good order of the plantation. . . . Prizewinning
> essays on the ideals of management held that 'industry and good
> conduct should be encouraged [and] the taste for innocent amuse-
> ments gratified.' These designs for mastery *troubled the distinctions
> between leisure and labor* and employed an extensive notion of dis-
> cipline that included everything from the task system to the modes
> of singing allowed. . . . According to the planter, the whip used
> sparingly, the fiddle, and the Bible formed the holy trinity.

As if copying its design for state mastery directly from one of these prize-
winning antebellum essays, Angola's administration of the early 1940s

described its ideal philosophy for managing "Negro" prison slaves as a perfectly balanced apportionment of *physical* repression and *spiritual* hegemony:

> To keep the convict separate from society is partly a physical and partly a spiritual problem. As a physical problem it involves iron fences, bars of steel, leather straps, clubs, and guns. As a spiritual problem it involves humane treatment; a friendly attitude, tasks suited to the strength and talents, trusts and loyalties, work and recreation. The spiritual factors are the most promising and reliable though the physical factors are a necessary last resort. Therefore we rely on kind and just treatment of the prisoners . . . [their] life should be made as happy as possible.[49]

That black prisoners are known to have suffered from well over ten thousand *reported* whippings during the decade leading up to this statement represents the quotidian functionality of so-called last-resort terror apparatuses within the pseudohegemonic arena of racialized civil death and the degree to which labor, leisure, and terror have been as virtually indistinguishable and mutually constitutive under the slavery of prison as during the prison of slavery.[50] Far from representing an anachronistic remnant of premodern mechanisms of terror, dishonor, and perverse captor pleasure, the "fun" side of the Middle Passage model of imprisonment came to represent a foundational element of carceral modernity as a whole—not only in the American chain gang, prison plantation, and penitentiary but in other racialized necropolitical spaces such as Auschwitz and Birkenau wherein certain prison slaves were allotted the "privilege" of acting as musical and athletic entertainers in the concentration camp version of the afore-mentioned *plantation holiday*.[51] If the teleology of antebellum mastery called for the creation of a kind of genocidal equilibrium based upon the calibrated application and fusion of "productive" and "unproductive" forms of captive travail ranging from field/house work, to corporeal rupture, to "innocent" and/or "spiritual" diversions such as singing, dancing, and the Bible, then the practice of captive performance at Angola and other U.S. prisons, County Farms, and chain gangs registers the degree to which this terroristic matrix of chattel incarceration haunted its way into the experiential reality of black people for generations after the Civil War.

The centrality of weapons of recreational diversion and ostensibly unproductive forms of labor to the project of neo-enslavement can be gleaned even among the most apparently prosaic descriptions of black captive "work" on the "state penal farm." For instance, in an article that appeared in the *Louisiana Municipal Review* in 1943, what is intended to be a straightforward cataloguing of Angola's industrial capacities ends up producing a neoplantation pastoral scene in which the time-honored southern planter and northern "romantic racialist" mythos of master-slave harmony and reciprocity is resuscitated through the evocation of the plantation holiday and the euphemistic introduction of the World War II edition of the Camp A minstrels:

> A combination of mule and tractor power is used. Forty miles of railroad traverse the cane fields, from which two trains transport cane to the sugar refinery which can handle 1,400 tons of cane

Figure 10. The terror/labor of neoslave "leisure." Atchafalaya River Levee Camp section of Louisiana State Penitentiary, c. 1900—just four years after the camp death rate had reached 20 percent. The original caption for the photograph, which appeared in the annual report of the Board of Control for the state penitentiary for 1901, read, "Fun in levee camp." Henry L. Fuqua Jr. Lytle Photograph Collection and Papers, Louisiana and Lower Mississippi Valley Collections, LSU Libraries, Baton Rouge.

daily. The 30 miles of gravel roads intersecting the plantation make it convenient to supplement the hauling of cane with tractors and cane buggies. The refinery is operated continuously on a 24-hour basis through the cane season, which in 1942 lasted 65 days.

The men work through the harvest regardless of weather, for much of the success of a cane crop depends upon the speed with which it is gathered. After the harvest, there is a celebration period during which turkeys raised on the farm and other delicacies grown at the penitentiary are combined for festive dinners at the camp. The prisoners are allowed the privilege of putting on a vaudevill [sic] show with a cast composed exclusively of inmates. With their pent-up emotions released in healthy laughter, they usually enjoy one night and two afternoon performances of the show. Warden Bazer is generously helpful in making provisions for and directing the show.

The sugar refinery is supplemented by a railroad shop and foundry, light plant, and a machine electrical shop. There [is] also a leather shop.[52]

The intrusion of the prison plantation harvest festival and "vaudevill[e] show" into an otherwise routine outline of sugarcane production and other forms of industrialized neoslavery at Angola illustrates the degree to which the round-the-clock labor regiment of the neoplantation was in no way limited to the sixty-five-day cane-processing season—how the painful "work" of prison slavery was felt on a twenty-four-hour basis even in moments of apparent reprieve. Nothing signals the imbrications of penal recreation and corporeal repression—of managerial lenience and carceral surveillance—more than the warden's tripartite role as industrial planta-tion field commander, bestower of performative privilege, and "director" of the very break from productive slave labor that he grants the black pris-oner. Accordingly, the narrative bears striking resonance with numerous accounts offered by former slaves that expose the vital function of such "celebration periods" in the attempted scientific management of the chat-telized body, psyche, and spirit before 1865. Compare the perverse notion proffered here that the prison master's benevolent conferral and directorial orchestration of punitive privilege in the form of the blackface show offered the state slave a moment in which the "emotions" associated with bond-age could be "released in healthy laughter" to Douglass's deconstruction of

similar holiday entertainments he personally experienced while incarcerated as a chattel slave in Maryland: "From what I know of the effect of
these holidays upon the slave, I believe them to be among the most effective means in the hands of the slaveholder in keeping down the spirit of
insurrection. . . . These holidays serve as conductors, or safety-valves, to
carry off the rebellious spirit of enslaved humanity."[53]

While Douglass's recollection of the plantation holiday offers an integral demystification of the malevolent designs that underpinned the staging of prison master benevolence and captive performance, it does so
without accounting for the ways in which "the rebellious spirit of enslaved
humanity" often maneuvered its way into the very festive events the master attempted to employ as weapons of punitive pacification and perverse
pleasure. However, as discussed above in reference to McElroy's spectral
image and voice, the rupturous lower-frequency practices of resistance employed by the prison slave will most often leave one grossly unsatisfied if in
considering them one implements a framing of the "insurrectionary" similar to that which Douglass himself offers immediately prior to his description of the plantation holiday—that is, his epic, exceptional, and "manly"
overcoming of Edward Covey.[54] Indeed, before closing this chapter, I want
to introduce how the critical suspension of a presupposed normative man-
liness and a self-possessed heroic model of resistance in respect to the hyper-
circumscribed positionality of the dominated represents an apposite point
of entry into another spectral element of the Camp A minstrel photograph.

If we return for a moment to the close-up of the photograph, we see a
person standing to John McElroy's far right, clapping her hands, wearing
a floral print skirt and blouse and a neatly tied scarf on her head. In drawing attention to this unknown subject, I want to be clear that my usage
of the gender-specific pronoun "her" represents an act of (un)historically
informed imagination rather than a desire to "narrow down" or reify this
person's gender or sexual identity. The prisoner could just as easily have
identified as a gay man, as bi or questioning, or as a hetero male who happened to perform on the plantation minstrel stage in drag.[55] Any discern-
ment of the prison slave's gender or sexual identity is made all the more
vexing when posed in relation to a chattelized punitive apparatus in which
sexual violence and domination have always represented de facto elements
of the prison sentence and wherein many are coerced into assuming certain
gender and sexual roles as a means of avoiding an intensification of corporeal rupture or of preserving their biological life.[56] The reified, fungible,

and object status of the slave of the state exposes the limits of the concept of self-identification within spaces of legalized rape, torture, and civil murder of the "self." Moreover, the historical mediations I have spoken of in reference to McElroy and other neoslaves are that much more prohibitive in respect to this imprisoned figure and others captured in the photograph—persons for whom we have no unburied letters to offer us even a peripheral glimpse into their personal biography or their particular experience of neo-enslavement. Fully aware of these crucial concerns, I have chosen to enact the imaginative leap of isolating this tall and slender "woman" out of a strong feeling that this could quite possibly be a pictorial vestige of an Angola trusty named James Bruce, a person who would have featured regularly as a drag queen in McElroy's minstrel troupe in the mid- to late 1940s, and who, as a longtime domestic and performative neoslave at Angola, represents a haunting internal extremity of the photograph made no less powerful by our inability to verify if s/he is indeed the one standing behind McElroy in the image. Furthermore, I do so with the conviction that even if the person is not who I think s/he may be, that my uncovering of a sliver of Bruce's story via the channeling accompaniment of the Camp A minstrel troupe image may limn important aspects of the unspeakable, unspoken, and unclaimed ordeals of chattelized captivity, incarcerated performance, and neoslave resistance specific to the experience of the legally disappeared and historically anonymous black queer/trans prison slave.[57]

McElroy actually enables our reckoning with Bruce's apparitional presence within the minstrel photograph in his second letter to Kemp, in which he identifies Captain "Johnnie" Spillman as the "care of" addressee for what he hopes will be the attorney general's affirmative response to his bid to book the Camp A show to Hammond, Louisiana. John Spillman was a second-generation Angola guard who began his apprenticeship in the overseeing, driving, and virtual ownership of criminalized black bodies at the prison plantation in 1916 as a teenager, and who, by the time of McElroy's initial clemency letters in 1948, would have long been in charge of Camp A, one of three sectors of the sprawling penitentiary that were known in the local white supremacist parlance as "Jungle Camps." For McElroy, Bruce, and their fellow prison slaves, a more appropriate name for this space of racialized living death and others like it on the neoslave plantation would have been—to resound George Jackson's terminology, an *American concentration camp*—one in which what I defined earlier as the Middle Passage carceral model was executed in a manner that represented a state-level simulation of the hyperconstricted, suffocating, and scatological spatial arrangements of the county chain-gang's portable cage.

One of the more clear-cut examples of the "land-based slave ship" model of human entombment at Angola came in the form of Camp A's "sweatbox," an architecture Spillman and other administrators deployed to punish, segregate, and torture those deemed "unruly" or "lazy" for decades leading up to the heel-string incident, and one reserved exclusively for the black neoslave. Indeed, as in the case of the sepulcher-fashioned boxcars in which chain-gang prisoners throughout the southern United States were long-chained and stacked atop one another, the sweatbox represented a dubious actuation of the "box" within which Paul D and his forty-five fellow chain-gang prisoners were buried underground in *Beloved*. Edward Stagg offered this description of the Camp A isolation/punishment unit after he and a group of fellow journalists conducted a surprise visit to Angola following the Camp E heel-string action:

> One of the peculiarities we came upon appeared to be a solid block of concrete. Three iron pipes stuck up from the top like periscopes.
>
> On closer examination, we discovered three steel doors on one side of the block. Each was of solid metal, except for a small louvered rectangle near the bottom, similar to the draft vent beneath the grate of a furnace.
>
> We banged on the door with our fists. A man's voice answered from within! We saw that the door was locked, and that there was no one around who could open it. We asked the man inside if he was all right, and he said he was. We saw that the second door was locked, and we assumed there was a man behind it, too. When we came to the third door, we found it to be unlocked and swung it open.
>
> The walls and ceiling were painted black. There were no windows. The only sources of light or air were seven-inch wide, down-tilted slits in the bottom of the door and a two-inch hole in the ceiling. The hole led into a pipe on the roof that was bent in the opposite direction of the prevailing wind.
>
> A bed stood along the wall. In an opposite corner was a concrete box for a toilet. The entire cubicle was the size of a small clothes closet. Into this stifling space as many as seven men were jammed at a time. At least one man had been removed in a state just short of roasting.[58]

Those of Captain Spillman's "Negroes" who managed to avoid being buried alive and roasted within the sweatbox were subjected to *can't to can't see* field labor under rifle, whip, and bat—and were then herded into a wooden shack in which they were stacked on top of one another in triple-bunk formation, and where no more than four toilets were allocated to nearly three hundred men. It was in the same article from 1952 that an indirectly quoted and anonymous prisoner from Camp A captured in a single truncated phrase what volumes of history on the subject of imprisonment in the United States had not: according to him, the "dormitory" in which he was held emitted a *"stink like the hold of a slave ship."*[59]

Angola's implementation of the Middle Passage carceral model represented an essential contributing factor to the neoslave's desperate attempts at securing any channel of possible reprieve from the most physically brutal conditions found at the prison plantation. Indeed, the home of Captain "Johnnie" Spillman himself—like those of other guard captains and numerous white men and women outside Angola who were given the opportunity to rent or borrow its domestic neoslaves—represented one such zone of relative and rupturous respite from the zero-degree death rehearsals found in the sugarcane and cotton fields, the neofeudal stocks, the Camp A stockade, and the sweatbox. It therefore comes as no surprise that shortly following his disappearance into Camp A in 1935 on a burglary conviction, a young black New Orleanian named James Bruce seized upon the chance of working for Spillman as a domestic neoslave. S/he would end up doing so for approximately thirteen years, functioning variously as cook, "yard-boy," and "houseboy"—positions that, along with the more often discussed role of convict guard, represented the most common stations occupied by those prisoners who were branded as *Trusty Negroes*. Here the state's use of the letter "y" instead of today's more familiar "ee" at the end of the signifier denoting a captive of putative privilege, illustrates the degree to which in spaces such as Angola, Parchman, Cummins, and Sugarland, the "trusty" neoslave was conceived of as a post-1865 reincarnation of the ever-faithful, ever-dutiful, antebellum "house slave"—the "Mammies" and "Uncles" of the white supremacist cultural imaginary who were cast as maintaining an unbreachable fidelity to the master, a selfless and boundless loyalty, that was offered as evidence of the paternal benevolence of the plantation, and the infantilism, atavism, and natural slave-worthiness of the collectivity of "niggers" held prisoner within it.[60]

The dubiously literal possessive investment in such stock images by white residents of Angola's free township is rendered graphically in the photo albums of Spillman and other guard captains, which are replete with portraits of "trusty" black prisoners captured in chattelized pastoral tableau alongside head of cattle, horses, dogs, various crops produced at the neoplantation, and young white children for whom the trusties acted as "Uncles," "Mammies," and atavised playmates (Figure 11).[61] In fact, it was through the childhood remembrance of Spillman's own daughter, JoAn, who was raised at the penitentiary from birth, that I was first made aware of James Bruce. Much of what the guard captain's daughter has to say in respect to the "sort of chocolate colored . . . tall, skinny, mulatto man"[62] she recalls from her childhood at Angola reads like a perfectly synchronized narrative accompaniment for the portraiture of domestic tranquillity, (un)productive abundance, and black subservience on the neoplantation. Bruce is described as having acted as a perfectly domesticated prison slave who went about his interminable duties with a joyful exuberance. Whether he was busy

Figure 11. Black prison slave with white child standing on a load of seed cotton, Louisiana State Penitentiary, Angola Prison Plantation, c. 1901. Henry L. Fuqua Jr. Lytle Photograph Collection and Papers, Louisiana and Lower Mississippi Valley Collections, LSU Libraries, Baton Rouge.

cooking the family's meals, "moving their dirt from one place to the other,"[63] tending to (other) livestock, or cranking the handle of a homemade ice-cream maker in preparation for one of JoAn's yearly backyard birthday celebrations she hosted for neighboring white children, Bruce is remembered as a happy-go-lucky sort of trusty Negro. According to JoAn, he was "a very good worker, kept the house immaculate, cooked good food and everything" and was "always whistling or singing; you'd have thought he was the happiest person in the world." The state's gothic transmutation of Bruce and other black incarcerated subjects into the personal accoutrement, or *human produce*, of white guard families gave JoAn the sense that time had frozen, or plunged backward, during her plantation upbringing—that, along with her mother and father, she had lived a real-world production of an idyllic and aristocratic country romance: "It was wonderful. I was the princess and my daddy and mother were the king and queen, and we had servants, and we didn't want for anything. And I was Little Miss Jo, or [the trusties] called me Curly or Shirley Temple, because I had curly hair. And it was just a storybook childhood."[64]

If the youngest member of the Spillman household was envisioned as Angola's version of America's "little curly top"—Shirley Temple—then James Bruce functioned as an incarcerated double for Bill "Bojangles" Robinson, whose famous staircase dance performance with Temple in *The Little Colonel* (1935) appeared in U.S. movie houses in the very same year that Bruce was first entombed at Camp A. Indeed, as in the case of Robinson's character in the depression-era romanticized and sanitized portrayal of 1870s Kentucky plantation life, Bruce's all-too-real role as mid-twentieth-century imprisoned "houseboy" was not restricted to cooking, butlering, and cleaning for the Spillmans. He, like many other black men and women at Angola, also served in the capacity of musical slave; specifically, as mentioned above, Bruce was one of the featured performers in McElroy's minstrel troupe during most of his thirteen years at the penitentiary. Furthermore, while Warden D. D. Bazer was credited in the piece from the *Louisiana Municipal Review* as being the troupe's administrative sponsor and director, it was in fact JoAn's father, Captain "Johnnie," who acted as de facto manager of the Camp A minstrels. Not only did Spillman oversee those of his neoslaves who performed for fellow inmates, honored guests, and tourists to the state plantation, but he also supervised the transportation of McElroy, Bruce, and other members of the troupe well beyond Angola's borders where they performed for white audiences in towns such as Jackson and Pineville, Louisiana, the latter of which is situated more than 120 miles from the front gates of the prison. While these tours likely generated a bit of unofficial revenue for Spillman and other members of Angola's administration, they also served as family outings for the guard captain and his young daughter, whom he often brought along so that she could witness the family's collection of musical Negro trusties perform in distant "free-world" environments.[65]

We have no way of knowing what specific song-and-dance numbers the Camp A minstrel ensemble used as temporary tickets outside Angola's grounds. However, a deep recess in the historical archive does inform us that Bruce did not don the "burnt cork" for these shows as did many of his fellow troupe members—that as one of the stars of McElroy's ensemble s/he performed exclusively in drag. Again, as stated above, the fact that s/he performed at Angola and surrounding towns as an imprisoned drag queen does nothing to clarify how Bruce actually lived in terms of gender or sexuality. The severely circumscribed range of information that we are offered in respect to the experiences of the neoslave most often precludes definitive assessment of any aspect of "selfhood," let alone her gender identity and chosen bonds of intimacy. Even on the rare occasions in which we are allowed thin strands of detail in respect to Bruce's "personal" or "social" world, such information is rendered vexing at best when read in relation to the objectified, ventriloquized, and violated postsocial position of those whom the law has morphed into fungible state property. This problematic is that much more salient in respect to racialized bodies also labeled abnormal in respect to gender and/or sexuality, and whose carceral subjection thereby includes zero-degree vulnerability to the "invisible punishments" associated with sexually and gendered civil death.[66] Whether instigated by state actors or other slaves of the state, such predations include but are not limited to rape, sexual auctioning, the punitive severance of any *relatively* consensual intimate attachment, and homophobic and transphobic brutality.[67]

Along with the elision of the prison slave's terror-ridden experience after being disappeared to a place like Angola, racial capitalist patriarchal criminalization also works to produce a retroactive erasure of the neoslave's personal history before conviction, especially when targeting one such as Bruce whose official imprisonment was predicated on the socially incarcerating structure of Jim Crow apartheid—and who, upon legalized disappearance, was subjected to a predicament of state-borne natal alienation that forestalls any systematic gathering of "facts" as to personal or familial history. In fact, if Bruce was indeed a transgender or gay black person, then the historical enclosures I referenced earlier in respect to the carceral experience of those such as John McElroy and Odea Mathews are even more insurmountable given the nearly total absence of any substantive discussion of black queer/trans bodies within histories of Jim Crow "convict labor" and neoslavery. This context of historical erasure certainly leaves us with more in the way of interested questions than clarifying answers vis-à-vis the experience of the criminalized and invisible black trans/queer subject. For instance, what can an (un)historically informed engagement with the social context in which s/he was arrested in New Orleans in the early 1940s tell us about the conditions of possibility for Bruce's domestic and musical enslavement? If Bruce did see herself as a trans black woman or gay black male, then was her incarceration a direct outcome of the social isolation and economic dispossession that would have befallen a body branded as both "Negro" and sexually "freakish"?[68] Does this combination of racial, gender, and "sexual eccentricity" help explain why Bruce had to resort to breaking the terms of her initial parole from Angola by stealing $200 from her roommate in a New Orleans housing project in 1945?[69]

If s/he did indeed hone the performative talents that made her one of the stars of McElroy's minstrels before s/he was disappeared for a second time onto the prison plantation, then Bruce's final arrest could well have occurred in the Magnolia Housing Project—a structure of urban apartheid that sat directly across from Lasalle Street's famous Dew Drop Inn.[70] As a regular audience member and/or performer at this uptown cabaret, Bruce would have been able to develop an expansive repertoire of black vaudeville, tent show, minstrel, and rhythm and blues numbers by watching the likes of Irving Ale, aka Patsy Valdalia, the well-known drag queen who sang, danced, and emceed at the venue and who also hosted its annual "Gay Ball"—the interracial and thereby illegal affair that began to take place between Bruce's first and second terms at the prison plantation.[71] In fact, if s/he did have regular opportunities to watch stage shows at the Dew Drop, Bruce also would have been able to enhance her apprenticeship in drag performance by taking note of the incomparable technique of another talented drag artist named Princess Lavonne, who, just before her discovery at the Dew Drop, changed her name to "Little Richard."[72] Finally, and most important, if Bruce was a regular performer and/or audience member in this relatively trans/queer friendly space, s/he would have experienced repeated violent encounters with the law that went unreported on her official criminal record. Specifically, s/he would have been among those targeted and arrested in the regular police raids that occurred at the club—a systematic profiling that occurred as a result of the city's adherence to the national practice of gendered racial apartheid calling for the restriction of *public* race-mixing and *public* displays of nonheteronormative behavior to black neighborhoods, or "vice districts."[73]

Conjectural assertions of Bruce's possible social incarceration and criminalization as a black trans or gay subject before her second disappearance to Angola represent a great deal more than trivial speculation. At the risk of belaboring the point, it must be repeated that the stakes involved in reclaiming the "woman" shown standing at McElroy's far right in the Camp A minstrel show image are extremely high given the near complete silence of even the most self-consciously radical and culturally attentive historical and literary scholarship in respect to the black queer/trans subject's experience of slavery and Jim Crow prison slavery.[74] In fact, it is this very archival and historiographic silence in respect to the black queer (neo)slave experience that forces upon us the responsibility of engaging the ghostly traces of that experience with a kind of politically interested unhistorical imagination. Moreover, even if Bruce did not identify as a transgender person, one of the other two other cross-dressed troupe performers captured in the photograph may well have; and, at the least, even if none of the bodies shown in drag behind that of McElroy were actually trans or queer, then the black male's deployment of performative gender-transgression on the porch of a neoplantation house offers symbolically illuminating expression of the importance of attending to the stigmatized, criminalized, and historically disqualified predicament of the queer/trans black captive—unhistorical experiences that most certainly *did (and do) happen* even if they remain unclaimed, unaccounted for, and historically unavailable. In Bruce's case, her possible sexual and/or gender alterity would have certainly marked her as a prime target for the sort of ritualized physical trauma and sexual predation that is associated with the imprisonment of queer/trans bodies. In fact, the black neoslave's vulnerability to such violent encounters with guards and other slaves of the state in places like the Camp A stockade further elucidates the horrifying terms under which Bruce would have chosen to avoid contact with Angola's general population as much as possible by submitting herself to the peculiar terrors associated with acting as the Spillman's yard-boy, houseboy, and musical "boy."

If, as I have suggested, Bruce is indeed the apparently trans black person to McElroy's far right in the minstrel photograph, then the fact that s/he is shown wearing a floral print skirt and blouse on the Spillman house porch represents a haunting visual signal of why this historically invisible subject enters into the archive at all beyond the small number of legal documents pertaining to her arrests in 1935 in Baton Rouge for burglary, and for her alleged theft of $200 in New Orleans. It was just this sort of flowered print that JoAn's mother, Rubye Spillman, was known to have been fond of wearing in and around the family home and while attending formal social gatherings outside Angola.[75] Bruce would have known of this penchant for floral prints on the part of the "Queen" of Camp A. In fact, over the course of thirteen years of domestic neoslavery, the trusty would have developed an acute awareness of most of Rubye's personal preferences, particularly those relating to plantation household management. Bruce's knowledge in this vein would have ranged from the more general, such as the manner in which Mrs. Spillman's trusties were expected to conduct the laundering, babysitting, housekeeping, and meal preparation, to the more minute, such as which doors they were allowed to walk through (and at what time of day); exactly which songs she asked her house prisoners to perform for houseguests on muggy summer evenings before they had to hurriedly trace the wafting scent of shit back to the Camp A stockade in time for the 8 p.m. head count; and the precise amount of water she liked her "niggers" to pour onto the sweet-smelling gladiolas and chrysanthemums she regularly carried to market in Baton Rouge in order to make extra spending money.[76]

In a manner akin to his fellow neoslaves who toiled daily under armed guard in Angola's cane and cotton fields, Bruce's keen awareness of Rubye Spillman's specific requirements for her workday was honed through a liberal application of what the above-quoted Angola administrator euphemistically describes as the "physical factor" of neoslave management. Along with being shot, beaten, and tortured by the prison's official staff and administrators during her time at LSP, Bruce was subjected to quotidian physical and psychic terror by the "Queen," or de facto "mistress," of the Spillman house. In a moment that undercuts her overall portrayal of life at Angola as an edenic pastoral scene in which her family and its "whistling and singing" domestic neoslaves coexisted in picturesque white supremacist harmony, JoAn discusses how she ultimately learned details of Bruce's horrifying treatment under her mother from other white subjects at *The*

Farm: "From what I gather from other people and family members, she was mean to him. . . . I don't have any first-hand knowledge of it, because all I know was how she treated me. . . . But she used to hit him with a broomstick when he didn't do something that she wanted."[77]

Notwithstanding its hypermediated form, such statements regarding the predicament of domestic neoslavery at Angola signal how, as in the case of its chattel slavery counterpart, the white supremacist order of the neo-plantation household was predicated on a repressive pedagogy that linked grueling physical labor, psychological terror, and serialized corporeal rupture. Bruce's experience in this regard recalls that of Mary Prince, who, in her autobiographical rendering of her ordeals as a domestic slave in Barbados in the early 1800s, speaks in graphic detail about the dubious epistemology of chattel domesticity. In one such instance, the nineteenth-century slave gives voice to Bruce's submerged, sanitized, and ventriloquized experience of twentieth-century neoslavery through recollection of her first full day of *hands-on instruction* under one of her own white mistresses:

> The next morning [she] set about instructing me in my tasks. She taught me to do all sorts of household work; to wash and bake, pick cotton and wool, and wash floors, and cook. And she taught me (how can I ever forget it!) more things than these; she caused me to know the exact difference between the smart of the rope, the cart-whip, and the cow-skin, when applied to my naked body by her own cruel hand. And there was scarcely any punishment more dreadful than the blows I received on my face and head from her hard heavy fist. She was a fearful woman, and a savage mistress to her slaves.[78]

Such testimony disturbs any attempt at delineating a clear line of separation between the private/unproductive sphere of captive "privilege" and the public/productive domain of captive terror on the plantation; and, insofar as they give language to experiences that Bruce was never able to utter in public, Prince's words offer an instructive counter-narrative to the discourses of savagery, incorrigibility, and sexual monstrosity that would surround the circumstances of Bruce's final escape from Angola on the first day of cane cutting, October 19, 1948.

When s/he awakened at sunrise on that clear autumn day to the putrid smell of shit, sweat, semen, and blood, the Spillman houseboy felt for the brush that rested within a little braided straw basket s/he had tied beside her vermin-filled mattress. After leaping down from her slot in one of the innumerable triple-bunks old-time neoslaves had been forced to wedge inside the Camp A stockade, Bruce hurriedly ran her hands over her short-cropped hair as s/he did every other day before s/he was expected at that lady's house. And, as always, s/he could feel the brush bristles slide easily over the steel plate situated just above her right temple—a piece of metal that had been implanted (just in time) two days after they had first tried to murder her some years back.[79] Bruce replaced the brush, exited the stockade (because s/he never attempted to use *that* "toilet" unless s/he could not help it), and began retracing the well-worn groove s/he and countless other houseboys had trudged into the long dirt trail leading directly from the Jungle Camp to Captain Johnnie's house. Adjusting her neatly tied head scarf, s/he dragged her right leg behind the rest of her body as fast as s/he could, passing a line of "Big Stripe" sugarcane men whose whistles accompanied her entrance onto the path leading to her designated starting position on that lady's back porch. S/he was made even more breathless than usual by the effort because it was imperative that s/he arrived at her post a little early on that particular Tuesday morning.

According to Baton Rouge newspapers, the houseboy did not need to employ the Spillmans' ice pick after she had fallen. In paraphrasing the deputy coroner's autopsy, the reports indicated that she had already died from a broken neck sustained from a severe blow to the chin before her "trusty" Negro raised the weapon. The half-dozen stab wounds were believed to have been inflicted postmortem because of the "comparative lack of blood" found at the scene at which Rubye Spillman's body was found slumped over, in her nightgown, hidden behind an armoire in her daughter's bedroom, at 2:30 a.m., Wednesday, October 20, 1948.[80] Over the next eleven days, the newspapers would offer daily coverage of the killing along with updates on the three-hundred-person manhunt that ensued once the guard captain's wife was found dead in JoAn's room. We are informed that Camp A guards became alarmed several hours before the discovery of Rubye's corpse by the fact that the family's "prison houseboy" did not show up at the stockade for head-count and lockdown the night of the killing—that they searched for Bruce throughout the penitentiary grounds until they arrived at the Spillman residence and located Rubye's body. We are also made aware that much of what occurred on the day of the incident seemed to fit into the banal routine of domestic slavery and mastery that had taken place for decades at the Camp A plantation house—that Bruce busied himself preparing morning breakfast for the family, answering phone calls, offering JoAn assistance as she prepared for an overnight stay at the home of a young cousin who resided at Camp H, and preparing late afternoon dinner for John Spillman after he had returned from overseeing the first day of the sugarcane harvest.[81] For her part, the guard captain's wife spent her time early that day giving her trusty neoslave *detailed instruction* as to the tasks she wanted completed ahead of her departure for one of the most important social engagements of that calendar year in Louisiana. The local coverage chronicles how she and other Angola wives were scheduled to attend an "afternoon tea" in honor of Mrs. Earl K. Long, the wife of the state's governor—a society-page function held at "Afton Villa," a forty-room French-Gothic mansion on the outskirts of St. Francesville that was originally built by the hands of slaves in 1849.[82]

The local reports then relate how, after killing the neoplantation mistress (and somehow managing to conceal her dead body from her husband for a number of hours), Bruce shed her "bloody prison uniform," disguised herself in the high-heeled shoes, white gloves, and new *dark-colored dress with big flowers* Rubye had planned to wear to Afton Villa, and escaped through the Angola cane fields toward the Mississippi River under cover of darkness. In reading the accounts of the "female impersonating" trusty, one is immediately reminded of a parallel use of fugitive cross-dressing in William Craft's *Running a Thousand Miles to Freedom* (1860), in which a slave woman, Craft's wife, Ellen, uses the fact of her light complexion to disguise herself as a white "invalid gentleman" traveling with a slave attendant (William), and successfully shuttles herself and her husband away from Georgia to the "free" city of Boston, Massachusetts.[83] Indeed, as in the case of the Crafts' theft of their own bodies in the late 1850s, rebellious agency on the part of the Spillmans' domestic and musical neoslave could only be cast as culpability within the racist cultural and legal imagination of the late 1940s.

However, the similarities between the acts of radical black fugitivity on the part of Ellen Craft and James Bruce evacuate almost as quickly as they arise. The first thing that must be said here is that, unlike her "passing" counterpart from the nineteenth century, no amount of cross-dressing could have disguised the phenotypical blackness that marked Bruce and every other black body in Louisiana and surrounding states as both naturally suspect and (extra)legally disposable—namely, when this legalized branding and hunting process was invoked in response to the unimaginable occurrence of a white "lady" being killed by her "Negro houseboy." Second, given the dual nature of Bruce's transgression of her status as slave of the state—that is, her theft of her own body and its accompanying act of violence against the body of the guard captain's wife—the escaped black neoslave would have been devoid of any social equivalent to the white abolitionist community of the late nineteenth century that helped the Crafts reach the relatively safe physical geography of the northern United States. In other words, given the broad-based social consensus in post-bellum America regarding both the ostensible denouement of slavery and the "natural" criminality of the freed black subject—as well as Bruce's radical violation of the national taboo against violent self-defense and self-reclamation on the part of the imprisoned—there would have been no modern equivalent to the Underground Railroad for the neoslave fugitive to seek out as s/he made her way through the woods surrounding Angola plantation.[84] Nor would there have been a relatively secure physical space anywhere in the United States to which her socially and legally stigmatized body could be spirited away in the event that such a network did indeed exist. The final and most important distinction to be made between Bruce's fugitive action and that of Ellen Craft has to do with our knowledge that the act of male impersonation on the part of the nineteenth-century black woman represented a temporary moment of gender-bending in the service of an attempt at laying claim to something of the heteronormative prerogative of legal marriage between a "man and a woman"—a racialized patriarchal status that was precluded by fiat for chattelized bodies, and that subsequently represented a comforting image of normative conjugal aspiration befitting the expectations of the white liberal Christian audience to which the slave narrative was directed.

While we are given nothing in the way of personal testimony or reliable documentation in respect to James Bruce's gender or sexual identity, the hypermediated and demonizing perspectives offered by white Angola residents and in newspaper accounts following Rubye Spillman's death underline the degree to which the escaped "houseboy" was publicly interpellated as the very antithesis of white heteronormative masculinity. While the first report describes Bruce's utilization of Spillman's flower-print dress as a "clumsy but apparently successful disguise attempt," subsequent coverage would use the fact of her regular performances in drag as proof-positive that the escaped neoslave's tactical outward disguise was actually expressive of a perverse inner ontological reality. In the language of one such piece, Bruce came to be defined as a "feminine type"—one who had not simply worn women's clothing in an isolated instance of desperate rebellion, but who actually "*delighted in playing female parts* in amateur theatricals at the prison."[85] The projection of ontological aberrance onto the neoslave's apparent queerness is also registered in the childhood recollections of JoAn Spillman, who, while defining Bruce as a happy-go-lucky houseboy, also recalled that s/he was both "a little strange" and "a little prissy."[86] Even if s/he did actually identify as a straight man at the time of her desperate attempt at escaping the prison plantation, the interpellating voices of white Angola residents and local media classified Bruce as among the collectivity of criminalized subjects banished to LSP and other U.S. prisons whose criminalization and predicament of civil death had been accentuated with and exacerbated by the stigmatic tags of sexual *perversion* and *degeneracy*. Offered in lieu of any discussion of her actual motives for killing the guard captain's wife (or any official evidentiary proceeding or trial), Bruce's imputed gender and sexual aberrance served to ascribe a second level of alterity and abnormality onto a body that had already been preappointed as expendable due to the biometaphysical affliction of blackness.[87] When deployed in combination with her racial difference, Bruce's imputed gender/sexual deviance represented a priori social adjudication of the unquestionable guilt of the erstwhile "Trusty" Negro, and her utter disposability as the target of the three-hundred-man "posse" that hunted her with bloodhounds, guns, shackles, and (legal lynch) ropes through Louisiana's woods and urban centers after the discovery of Spillman's dead body.[88]

Indeed, her unseemly "prissiness" was repeatedly asserted in the last appearance Bruce would make in the local press, on October 31, 1948—a day after her dead body was allegedly discovered floating facedown in the Mississippi River with buzzards circling overhead. "Those seeing the body immediately suspected it was Bruce's because of the female clothing. Bruce was wearing women's' undergarments, silk hosiery, a blue dress, a green sweater and a woman's wig. The wig, it was said, belonged to the prison. Bruce had used it when playing the part of a woman in prison theatricals." In an attempt to dispel the notion that immediately circulated among the prisoner population at Angola that the "feminine type" fugitive had been lynched by John Spillman or another of the three hundred prison slave catchers that stalked her along the river's path, officials asserted that Bruce's death was the result of an "accidental drowning." To legitimize this narrative, Angola officials and state police ordered that the medical inquest be performed at an unquestionably "Negro" site. "The jury, impaneled in a negro [sic] funeral home, brought in a verdict of death by accidental drowning. Dr. Roberts declared that Bruce definitely drowned. 'I examined him from tip to tip,' he said, 'and there was not a single mark of violence or a perforation on the body.'" Claims to the unviolated and "un-perforated" state of the neoslave's corpse are immediately subverted in the very next section of the article in which a local sheriff nonchalantly explains why he was able to offer positive identification of the partially decomposed and supposedly drowned prisoner: "Martin stated that he could identify the body by a bullet wound he himself had inflicted in 1936 when Bruce had tried to escape [from Angola] but was found two days later."[89] The contradictory nature of official claims to a lack of violent encounter with Bruce's chronically ruptured body had already been made clear in earlier coverage of her escape when officials were quoted as having found the fugitive's tracks based on a disability s/he had incurred on the neoplantation; they intimated how the main reason Angola's trusty "Negro dog-boy" and his pack of Cuban and English bloodhounds were able to overcome Bruce's use of a scent-covering mixture of turpentine and garlic was the definitive nature of the tracks left by a "convict [who] dragged one foot as he walked."[90] Unmentioned in any of the reports, however, was the other permanent disfigurement Bruce likely suffered as a house slave—the skull fracture that led to the insertion of a metal plate into her head.

Notwithstanding the factual murkiness that surrounds her ultimate loss of biological life, the declared and undeclared state-inflicted injuries to her entombed and preyed-upon body underscore how the predicament of racialized, gendered, and sexualized neoslavery was the substantive cause of James Bruce's (and Rubye Spillman's) premature death. Indeed, given the patent absurdity of the state's claims of innocence in respect to a subject whom it had transmuted into a fungible public/private object, one can imagine that John McElroy would have been incredulous as to the official narrative that accompanied the loss of one of the stars of his Camp A minstrel show. The necessary opacity of the unhistorical experience of neo-enslavement forces us to speculate regarding what ran through the mind of the "one-legged man" when he heard the news of the horrifying conclusion to Bruce's freedom bid from within the camp stockade, a guard captain's kitchen, or while offering musical entertainment to one of the neoplantation's young white children. Did the prison grapevine offer

him a clear vision of the specific ordeals that his leading performer faced
in her last hours as s/he was stalked by members of nearly every sector
of Louisiana's law-and-order apparatus? More specifically, did McElroy or
one of his fellow black prison slaves work as a domestic in the home of the
Angola guard who was known to openly display a set of photographs of
Bruce's corpse for the pleasure of white houseguests—images depicting
her hunted and tortured body as it rested prone on a Mississippi River
sandbar after s/he had purportedly "drowned"?[91] What significant details
appear in these images that were never allowed to reach the daily news? Did
they show some of Louisiana's neoslave patrollers posing behind Bruce's
remains after their fugitive hunt had reached successful climax? If so, what
looks appeared on their faces? And were these photos taken with the very
surveillance camera that had once captured McElroy, Bruce(?), and their
fellow imprisoned minstrels performing on the steps of Captain Johnnie
Spillman's plantation house? Were any of Bruce's fellow prisoners forced
to act as grave diggers for her corpse when no family member or loved
one would or could show up at the front gates of "murder's home" to claim
her body? And, finally, what sort of blues-laden notes could be heard emanating through the Tunica hills as the Camp A minstrel troupe appeared
at the Angola sugarcane harvest "celebration" of 1948? Was one of those
onstage or in attendance actually a lover still in mourning?

The fact is that we will likely never be allowed to attain definitive
answers to most of our questions concerning Bruce's death. However, the
pain of what we do know in respect to the quotidian horrors that s/he,
John McElroy, Odea Mathews, the Angola 3, and an incalculable number
of others have faced while enduring "life" at LSP allows us to recognize
how thirteen years of domestic and musical slavery was enough to drive
the star of the Camp A minstrel troupe to a last-ditch act of radical black
suicide. In fact, as stated above in reference to the one-legged leader of
the troupe, Bruce's desperate attempt at securing freedom registers the fact
that the mask of black contentment and happy-go-lucky "trusty-ness"
often contained a militant desire for self-possession—a cloaked neoslave
insurrectionist impulse that, in Bruce's case, found expression in a form of
individualized radical violence that recalls the collectivized revolutionary
black abolitionism of Nat Turner. But even as her desperate act of self-
reclamation may be read as "heroic" on a certain level, Bruce's embodied
awareness that her escape attempt would most certainly end in more bullet
scars and bite marks, if not the complete cessation of her life, suggests how

this heretofore untold story of prison slavery can in no way be mistaken for the sort of triumphalist, exceptional, and morally admissible model of resistance and freedom acquisition offered in many nineteenth-century slave narratives. In fact, Bruce's hypercriminalization as an apparently transgender black person who was said to have committed a grisly act of violence against a white woman's body would have precluded attainment of "hero" status even were s/he to have eluded her human and canine pursuers along the Mississippi River and achieved "successful" fugitivity within the socially incarcerating landscape of post–World War II America. Nor has a story such as Bruce's yet been allowed entry into the current register of black prison narratives or prison-centered "neo-slave narratives"—generic spaces that have generally been reserved for publicly acknowledged "radical" political prisoners of the post–civil rights era.[92] In fact, the historical present of U.S. racial genocide continues to disallow academic, social, or legal recognition of neoslavery as an actual lived experience, let alone any kind of celebratory consideration of the resistive capacities of a long-buried and unknown prison "houseboy" from uptown New Orleans who had been poly-stigmatized as a "feminine type," "Negro," "killer," "convict."

However, it is the very unheroic, "immoral," and inassimilable aspect of Bruce's experience of civil, living, and premature death that demands that we finally bring our attentive focus to her experience of neoslavery and to that of people such as Mathews, McElroy, the Angola 3, and the anonymous twenty-first-century black "museum trusty" who handed me a box containing a long-forgotten photograph while I sat bearing witness at the site of neoplantation tourism and terrorism. Indeed, it is the very failure of the freedom bids of McElroy and Bruce that qualify their experiences as dubiously representative of past ordeals of neoplantation incarceration and the unspeakable present-day realities faced by the more than 2.3 million bodies currently held captive in the generalized slavery of U.S. domestic and global imprisonment. The very fact that the living plantation continues to feed on millions of human bodies—whether in a bend of Louisiana's section of the Mississippi, the "hell-factory" fields of California's Central Valley, or a "Salt Pit" just outside Kabul, Afghanistan[93]—demands that we do much more than "attend" to the civilly dead predicament of the millions and more of today's prison–industrial genocide. In the spirit of prisoner number 37708 and his most talented troupe member, we must write, sing, wail, organize (and more) for complete abolition even when unhistorical failure seems to be the only foreseeable reward.

CHAPTER 4

The Warfare of Northern Neoslavery in Chester Himes's *Yesterday Will Make You Cry*

If you're black, you were born in jail, in the North as well as the South. Stop talking about the South! Long as you're south of the Canadian border, you're south.

—Malcolm X, "The Ballot or the Bullet"

When I was 14 I got busted for "joy-riding" . . . and sentenced to a year at [a reform school]. The first day there I was put into a dorm and one of the dudes . . . beat me badly in front of the other guys. He topped his beating off by raping me and established my identity as a "nigger punk." I spent that year servicing the boys in the dorm and any of their friends that wanted sex. . . . That was when I realized that my position wasn't too different from my ancestors and that for the rest of the year I wasn't any different from a plantation slave.

—Anonymous, "The Story of a Black Punk"

IN THE CLIMACTIC SCENE OF *Yesterday Will Make You Cry* (1998), Chester Himes offers a horrifying account of a prison fire that takes place at the Ohio State Penitentiary in 1930. Describing the scene as "a page torn from Dante's inferno," the narrator offers remembrance of the fire through the eyes of the novel's protagonist, Jimmy Monroe, who runs into the prison yard in a state of shock as hundreds of charred bodies are being carried out of the "Idle House" cell block by his fellow prisoners: "And he was running . . . across the yard, with a high-stepping sense of being too tall to stay on the ground. He ran harder, lifted his feet higher, until he was churning with motion, going nowhere. He stepped into something and looked down at it and saw that he had stepped into a burnt-up convict's stomach and had pushed out huge globules of vomit through the tight-clenched teeth and over the black-burnt face." Monroe's tumult into the abject is punctuated by the smell of burning flesh and the screams of those whom he can hear being incinerated in their cells as he continues to run atop the bodies of the dead. In a manner akin to Henry Fleming in Stephen Crane's *The Red Badge of Courage* (1895), Monroe's role in the fire scene is that of antiheroic spectator more than active participant. While he stands watching "living convicts lugging the dead" and "working overtime at being heroes," he can only chide himself for being unable to perform according to his epic vision of "manly" valor: "All his life he wanted to be a hero. Ever since he had first read the *Iliad* and became a worshipper of Achilles. All his life! And now was his chance. He felt his lips twitching as a wave of nausea swept over him."[1]

The narrator's allusion to the Homeric Trojan War legend ends up carrying an extrametaphorical valence in the scene as the survivors of the prison fire are branded as enemy combatants by the state. Contending that the warden and certain prison guards had actually allowed hundreds of their fellow prisoners to "burn to death in their cells like rats," a large number of prisoners stage a protest, demanding a new warden and to be treated as "human beings."[2] Led by a core group of men calling themselves the "Committee of Twelve," the fire survivors organize a program of "passive resistance" that includes breaking the locks of their cells and refusing to accede to the warden's order for them to leave the prison yard. The warden responds to the resistance by immediately declaring martial law, issuing a shoot-to-kill order, and calling in hundreds of local and state police, Navy reserve, and National Guard troops, who construct a makeshift prison within a prison to hold those deemed to have participated in the resistance. Having missed the first installment of the uprising because of injuries to his eyes that he sustained from excessive smoke exposure, Monroe is alerted to the military incursion by a friend after exiting the prison hospital: "Blocker took him down to the ball diamond and showed him the wire-enclosed stockade with machine guns mounted at each corner and armed soldiers marching in pairs up and down each side." Jimmy quickly learns that this spectacular performance of state domination will have immediate and deadly consequences. While partaking in a bit of gallows humor with Blocker and an unnamed "colored convict," the latter's head is blown off by machine gun fire: "[T]he top of the convict's head flew up into the air. He had been making his bunk, and now, on the white sheet which his hands still held, a gooey mass of brains appeared. [Jimmy and Blocker] were still looking at him, and his mouth was still grinning as it had been before he lost the top half of his head, but his eyes were gone and blood was coming out of the edges of his skull."[3]

While Jimmy spends much of the action in *Yesterday Will Make You Cry* attempting to repress his memory of the holocaust and its terroristic aftermath, he is brought into total "post" traumatic recall much later in the text by a series of photographs he encounters in a local newspaper—images that are based on actual documentary photographs taken by Laurence Stallings and that appeared in his late Depression work, *Photographic History of the First World War* (1933). In *Yesterday*, the narrator describes how these "pictures touched Jimmy that spring. There was one, a careless scatter of corpses on a patch of utter desolation, captioned, 'No More Parades.'" Immediately upon viewing the scene of official warfare, Jimmy's repressed memory of the scene of de facto warfare that had occurred with the prison fire is revivified in the form of the charred bodies of his fellow prisoners: "He could see those burnt-up convicts lying on the prison yard . . . he could see all those convicts dying and dead. *And he could see himself dead and rotting* in the oblivion of a grave, never having been anything but a number on a board in a prison having in the end lived and died for nothing and was nothing in the end but worms in the ground."[4] Jimmy's struggle with punitive abjection is not simply a matter of a too-close physical proximity *to* the dead; rather, the oblivion of prolonged encagement—of being transformed from a living being into a number on a prison board—has brought him into perilous experiential identification *with* the dead.

As one of Chester Himes's lesser-known literary works, and as one of the first northern focused black (written) narratives of neoslavery, *Yesterday Will Make You Cry* supplies a chilling example of how the reality of life and death under U.S. state terrorism, mass entombment, and neoslavery is often more horrific than gothic fiction.[5] This posthumously published work represents a late twentieth-century archival rescue of the original manuscript version of Himes's post–World War II prison narrative, *Cast the First Stone* (1952), and is actually a fictionalized autobiography based on Himes's own experience as prisoner No. 59623 in the Ohio State Penitentiary from 1928 to 1936. Jimmy's rememories of the holocaust are in fact based upon Himes's experiences as a twenty-one-year-old survivor of the most deadly prison fire in U.S. history—the "Easter Monday Fire" of 1930, which killed 322 of the 4,900 human beings who were tight-packed into their cages on a spring evening in Columbus, Ohio, at the height of the Depression.[6] Indeed, Jimmy's traumatic remembrances of the blaze and the subsequent militarization of the prison are matched nearly item for item in local and national newspaper coverage that occurred contemporaneously to the event. In one such article, entitled "Mutinous Convicts in Ohio Shot Down by Prison Guards," a reporter details how penitentiary guards unleashed "a rain of bullets" on a group of prisoners who were leaders of the postfire uprising, seriously wounding two of the so-called mutineers. In a piece entitled "Tunnel to Home of Warden Found by Guards," another reporter relates how members of the prison resistance—which was led by a group called the "Committee of 40," upon which Himes's "Committee of Twelve" is based in *Yesterday*—managed to cut through a six-inch concrete wall in their cell and began digging toward Warden P. E. Thomas's home, which was situated adjacent to their cell block. Another article, "Machine Gun Kills Two Ohio Convicts," details the incident in which Jimmy and Blocker witness a black prisoner's head getting blown off. The piece describes how "Albert Freeman, Negro, and Frank Ross [presumably a white man] ... were killed as they slept in the dormitory, where the better element of prisoners were confined." It chronicles how "their heads [were] pierced by machine gun bullets, accidentally discharged by an Ohio National Guardsman," but assures readers that the prison guard captain who led the investigation into the purported "accidental" shooting claimed that such events "cannot be helped."[7] In total, the state would end up marshaling at least one thousand state troopers, local and state police, and Navy reserve personnel (along with a group of ROTC students from Ohio State University), who periodically opened fire on prisoners with machine guns, rifles, and tear-gas bombs at different moments of the prison insurgency—a campaign of repression that represented an ominous presaging of later moments of spectacular state terrorism and fascism in U.S. prisons such as Attica in western New York State in September 1971.[8]

While the mass media portrayed the penitentiary holocaust through the individualizing liberal bourgeois framework of "tragedy"—as an unfortunate but aberrational moment of administrative negligence within an otherwise orderly and necessary formation of social control, human warehousing, and involuntary servitude—Himes's autobiographical prison novel exposes the degree to which the Depression-era northern prison, like its more notorious southern counterpart, amounted to what Mutulu Shakur, Cedric Robinson, Ruth Wilson Gilmore, and others have described as a regime of *domestic warfare* against those branded as contaminating elements within the U.S. national body.[9] While I have thus far focused attention primarily on geographies of neoslavery situated in the southern United States, such as the chain gang and prison plantation, the depiction in *Yesterday Will Make You Cry* of spectacular and banal forms of dominative violence that suffused the putatively modern, progressive, and "disciplinary" regimes of northern penal law underlines the fact that the perennially reerected binary of southern white supremacist exceptionalism and northern racial progressivism represents a deadly false dichotomy—a tenaciously productive ideological mythos that has played a foundational role in the reproduction and social acceptance of the mass chattelized entombment of black, Indigenous, brown, and poor bodies from Emancipation through today's prison–industrial complex. In this chapter, I focus on how the practices of racialized, classed, and homo/transphobic state violence as exhibited throughout Himes's prison autobiography underline the degree to which the horrifying events surrounding the Ohio Penitentiary fire were but spectacular analogues of a quotidian system of living, civil, and biological death reproduction, which, in its devastating accretion into our current moment of prison–industrial genocide, explodes categorical distinctions between northern and southern violence, carcerality, and neoslavery. Ultimately I want to explore the ways in which, as a structural modality of U.S. heteromisogynist racial capitalism, the material practice of white supremacist ideology is presented in *Yesterday Will Make You Cry* as a foundational, if unavowed, aspect of the pre–World War II northern prison—an institution that by 1930 had already begun to be packed more and more with members of a black southern migrant population whose northern exposure inaugurated the state's increasingly repressive bearing toward bodies branded *criminally deviant and ontologically degenerate* along articulating vectors of race, class, gender, and sexuality.[10]

To those familiar with *Yesterday Will Make You Cry*, its de facto literary prequel, *Cast the First Stone*, or the relatively sparse amount of critical treatments of Himes's autobiographical prison writings, my assertion of the primacy of racial domination to their contents may come as something of a surprise. Indeed, one of the main contributing factors to the relative lack of critical attention given to both books, as well as the series of short stories upon which Himes's autobiographical prison manuscripts were based, is the fact that all of his fictive portrayals of his experience of imprisonment are told through the eyes of a white protagonist. That there can be no doubt that "Jimmy," the white southern migrant from Mississippi featured in *Yesterday Will Make You Cry* and *Cast the First Stone*, is based directly on his own experience of imprisonment is indicated within Himes's interviews, personal correspondence, and officially autobiographical writings. For instance, when asked about his prison writings in an interview with Michel Fabre in 1983, Himes replied: "Just open *Cast the First Stone* and you'll realize the kind of material I found in the penitentiary. This is one of my most autobiographical novels, although the publishers cut a lot of it [i.e., the material that reappears in *Yesterday*]."[11] In *The Quality of Hurt* (1971), the first installment of his two-volume official autobiography, Himes again asserts the fact that Jimmy is based on himself: "I . . . made the protagonist of my prison story a Mississippi white boy; that ought to tell me something, but I don't know what—but obviously it was the story of my own prison experiences."[12] And, in a letter he wrote to his longtime friend and adviser, Carl Van Vechten (or "Carlo," as the writer/photographer is affectionately addressed in their correspondence), Himes even details the degree to which Jimmy's forays into writing in *Yesterday Will Make You Cry* (a plot element that was completely expurgated from *Cast the First Stone* by its editors) are representative of the fact that Himes began his own career as a writer inside a prison cage in Ohio:

> I have Jimmy develop an ambition to write and reveal the growth of emotional motivations for various short stories which he writes during that time. Which, of course, is more or less autobiographical. *That is when I began writing* and during that time I wrote a great number of prison stories, two of which were published in the then budding *Esquire*, "Crazy in the Stir" in the August 1934 issue, "To What Red Hell" (the chapter on the fire) in the October 1934 issue.[13]

Critics who have dealt with Himes's autobiographical prison writings have consequently been largely befuddled by his choice of articulating his story of imprisonment in virtual "white face." Indeed, one critic went as far as labeling *Cast the First Stone* as "raceless," or "assimilationist," arguing that it was among a series of novels produced by black authors in the mid-1940s to the 1950s that purposely eschewed the sort of racially oriented protest fiction that was being produced by authors such as Richard Wright, Ann Petry, and Himes himself in the 1940s.[14]

However, this explanation for an ostensible lack of blackness in Himes's autobiographical prison novel fails to account for the fact that, as pointed out in his letter to Van Vechten, his fictionalized portrait of his experience of imprisonment actually began in the 1930s (while Himes sat in a prison cage), not in the early 1950s, when *Cast the First Stone* finally appeared in print after a long series of galling encounters with a decidedly racist—and, as we shall see, overtly homophobic—U.S. publishing establishment. Indeed, Himes's series of short stories represented the scaffolding for a number of manuscript versions of what ultimately would be published as *Cast the First Stone* in 1952, versions with titles including *Present Tense, The Way It Was, Black Sheep, Debt of Time, Solitary, Day After Day,* and *Yesterday Will Make You Cry*—all of which drew, sometimes word for word, from 1930s short stories such as "To What Red Hell," "Crazy in the Stir," and "Prison Mass."[15]

Along these lines, one of the simplest answers to the riddle of racial characterization in both *Cast the First Stone* and *Yesterday Will Make You Cry* comes at the outset of the interview with Michel Fabre when Himes speaks directly to his choice of cloaking the story of his imprisonment in the habits of a "Mississippi white boy" at a time well before the "protesting Negro" was in vogue for U.S. publishers:

> In my early prison stories, I wrote about white characters. *It made publication possible,* or at least easier, in big magazines like *Esquire.* When I started writing in the U.S. in the early thirties, a black writer had a hard time getting published. For a long time no one realized that I was a Negro. *I wrote about white men because their problems were the problems of convicts, no matter what color they were.* They experienced the same emotions, whether they were black or white.[16]

One interpretation of Himes's statement here about feeling pressed into portraying his prison experience through a white fictive persona would actually give credence to the view that Himes's autobiographical prison novel represents a universalist depiction of the U.S. carceral experience, a "color-blind" mode of narration that stands in opposition to his more apparently black-centered works such as *If He Hollers Let Him Go* (1945) and *Lonely Crusade* (1947). Indeed, the opening of "Prison Mass," one of the short stories that served as a building block for the prison novel, seems to further indicate that Himes took a nonracial approach to the condition of penal entombment: "The convicts shuffled up the worn, wooden stairs.... *Just convicts.* Some were white, some red, some brown, some black, some yellow. Some were Americans, some were Europeans, some Indians, some Mexicans, some Malays, some Chinese, some mongrels, a little of each. *Just convicts.*"[17] However, what Himes's repetition of the word "convict" signifies here, and in the interview, is less of a testament to a lack of racial identity formation, or "blackness," in his autobiographical prison series, than an experientially informed awareness that the state's branding of socially taxonimized bodies as "just convicts" performs a relative racial deconstruction of the universal "white" citizen subject—a perilous fall *toward* blackness.

Here I am alluding to the way in which the state's homogenization of criminalized bodies into a "prison mass" through the stigmata of civil death initiates a punitive suspension of a great portion of the property of whiteness for the Depression-era "native" white working-class and/or European immigrant prisoner. In doing so, it renders the would-be-normative racial body vulnerable to formations of violence, dispossession, natal alienation, and (in)human cargoing that, by the time of Himes's imprisonment, had most often been the peculiar province of always-already racialized subjects such as Chinese immigrants, "Indians," Mexicans, and black people. Furthermore, this relative deconstruction of whiteness is also catalyzed by the social degradation that would have accrued to criminalized white bodies brought into repressive social (and sexual) intercourse with criminalized black, brown, Indigenous, and Asian bodies—a forced racial integration that, for the white prisoner, represents a de facto element of punishment marking him as *déclassé* relative to normative whiteness. When read in this way, the state's ascription of the brand "convict" onto an otherwise ethnically diverse racial population does indeed produce a universalizing effect; except, rather than constructing a "nonracial" sphere, racial capitalist heteromisogynist criminalization functions in a manner not dissimilar to racial stigmatization as waged against subjugated nonwhite peoples both in the prison world and the socially incarcerating structures of the white supremacist "free-world." In other words, it represents a dynamic of punitive homogenization grounded in a commonly endured state of carceral terror, familial dislocation, legalized dispossession, and collectivized abjection. Here Colin Dayan's historicizing of the intersections of the social death of chattel slavery and the civil death of penal neoslavery is instructive. She cites William

Blackstone's *Commentaries on the Laws of England* (vol. 4, 1790), in which he defines the felon as metaphysically tainted at the level of blood—and, as such, the felon is defined as a "monster and a bane to society, [and] the law sets a note of infamy on him, puts him out of its protection, and takes no further care of him barely to see him executed. He is then called attaint, *attinctus*, stained or <u>blackened</u>.'"[18] The indistinguishable quality of those rotting in their prison cells, and the scatter of corpses lying in the prison yard after the fire, is predicated on the law's branding of the 4,900 criminally stigmatized bodies inside the Ohio Penitentiary as exceptions to the rule of "normal," law-abiding, white-hetero-bourgeois humanity—a transfiguration of a previously diverse grouping of "free" civil subjects into criminally "blackened" slaves of the state, who could, in the words of Giorgio Agamben, be "killed without the committal of homicide."[19]

However, if the punitive practices of criminal stigmatization and civil death represent dynamics of quasi-racialization, a plummeting toward the social (no)thing status of blackness for the white prisoner, then what do these processes of state terror represent for the already black (brown and/or Indigenous)—for those whose social, cultural, political, and legal stigmatization are outcomes of *the crime of nonwhite birth* rather than consequences of any court-adjudicated "criminal act"?[20] Many antiprison autobiographies and manifestos of incarcerated black radicals of the black and Third World movement era—the 1950s and 1970s—make reference to the degree to which, notwithstanding the homogenizing effects of imprisonment, the northern penitentiary refabricates and intensifies dynamics of spatial apartheid and white supremacist violence that pervade outside U.S. prison walls, creating a racialized prison within a prison for black, brown, and Indigenous captives through practices such as race-based segregation, solitary confinement, disciplinary infraction, ritualized verbal and physical abuse, torture, and outright murder.[21] For instance, in *Soledad Brother,* George Jackson describes the processes by which California penal law enacts a radically unequal distribution of violence whereby the fatal punitive technique of "justifiable homicide" is most often reserved for black captives. After relating how his fellow black prisoner, Fred Billingslea, was teargassed to death inside a prison cell in the "B" section (the segregated black range) of San Quentin in 1970, he describes how white supremacist racial difference was also repressively reaffirmed in integrated "public" zones of punitive surveillance such as the recreation yard, "where any type of minor mistake could result not in merely a bad conduct report and placement in the Adjustment Center [punitive segregation], but death. A fistfight, a temporary, trivial loss of temper will bring *a fusillade of bullets down on the darker of the two men fighting.*"[22]

While Himes describes himself as having told the story of captivity in a manner expressive of the "problems" and "emotions" that all prisoners faced, whether "black or white," the action of *Yesterday Will Make You Cry* continually highlights the degree to which the Depression-era northern penitentiary exposed the "Negro" prisoner to a brand of white supremacist penology that represented a haunting reemergence of "southern" modalities of punishment, as well as a forward-haunting methodological precursor for regimes of racist penal law that Jackson, Assata Shakur, Angela Davis, and millions of anonymous others from the movement era through today's prison–industrial complex have experienced on a regular basis. In one particular instance that occurs well before the Easter Monday Fire in *Yesterday*, a black prisoner, who like many of those currently entombed in U.S. jails and penitentiaries, suffers from a form of mental illness, is murdered at the hands of two white prison guards.[23] In elucidating the events that led to the execution, the narrator recalls how a "crazy" prisoner named Perry was initially paid a nighttime visit by one of the guards in range 1-I, otherwise known as the "Black Bottom," the tier to which all of the Ohio Penitentiary's mostly southern migrant black captives (including Himes) were immediately segregated upon their arrival.

> "What the hell's the matter with you black bastards?" Jimmy heard the guard snarl. "Every goddamn night you get into an argument."
> "It's him," the . . . voice accused. "He walks and talks to hisself."
> *"What's the matter with you nigger?"* the guard asked.
> There was no reply.
> *"Smart nigger,* eh? Come on out of there!" the guard asked.
> There was no reply.
> *"Smart nigger,* eh? Come on out of there!" Jimmy heard the click of the lock, the crack of the door as it was opened. Then the guard's voice again, "Come on out or I'll blow you out!"
> "Aw, let that poor bastard alone, he's crazy," a voice called from Jimmy's range.

After beating Perry in front of his fellow black prisoners, the guard takes him out of the Black Bottom to one of the prison's (other) punishment units. Soon after the cell extraction, prisoners on multiple tiers are startled by the echoing staccato of gunfire. Jimmy and his fellow prisoners quickly learn through the penitentiary grapevine that two white guards murdered Perry inside the punishment corridor. In a northern version of a long-standing sadistic penal recreation ritual that, as discussed in chapter 3, is most often associated with southern chain gangs, prison plantations, and zones of "private" neoslavery, the Ohio prison guards turn Perry into hunting game: they beat him repeatedly with a lead pipe in front of his solitary-confinement cell with the intent of causing him to run so that they would be justified in using his body for target practice; except, rather than using a bloodhound to aid in the capture of a runaway "crazy nigger," the modernized northern version of the black neoslave hunt involves the two white northern guards simply "cut[ting] loose at him with a Tommy Gun."[24]

Here I am as interested in the initial exchange between Perry and his white assailant in the prison's Black Bottom as in the unbearable fact of his killing inside the solitary-confinement corridor. Thus I want to return to the moment that Perry sits silently in his cage in the Black Bottom while being repeatedly hailed with what amounts to a transgenerational racist incantation—*you nigger . . . smart nigger . . . smart nigger*—a ritualized refrain of black fungibility, inhumanity, and disposability that in its horrifying repetition serves as discursive double for and ideological catalyst of the series of bullets that are ultimately emptied into his tortured body. To reinvoke Sylvia Wynter, the "figure of the nigger" has functioned within Euro-American liberal white supremacist humanist thought as the "negative signifier of the mode of being embodied in the bourgeois 'figure of man,'" and has thereby been crafted to signify a "primal human nature whose differentiation from *a lurking bestiality* [is] so dangerously imprecise and uncertain . . . as to call for a question mark to be placed with respect to the humanity of this zero degree category."[25] In the case of the legalized torture and murder scene at hand, any questions as to the humanity of the mentally ill black prisoner were settled by way of the guard's thrice-uttered exclamatory declaration of reified black subhumanity. The sign of the prisoner's human being, "Perry," was automatically nullified by the sign of collectivized black object being, "nigger"—an overdetermined nominative erasure that served as authenticating prelude to justifiable murder.[26] Notwithstanding Himes's earlier allusion to the experiential leveling effect produced by the state's branding of all prisoners as *convict*, the racist and sadistic theatrics of Perry's murder are illustrative of the differential quality of civil death as executed in the modern penitentiary in reference to the *nigger convict*—how northern neoslavery, like its more vilified southern counterpart, was endured at its zero degree by those whose humanhood had been a matter up for philosophical conjecture and chattelized violent suspension for centuries leading up to Perry's arrest, imprisonment, and legal lynching.

Wynter's reference to how blackness came to be cultivated within the liberal bourgeois imaginary as an ontological threat—*a lurking bestiality*—resonates directly with the historical period in which Himes and thousands of other black bodies were disappeared into Ohio's penitentiary, jails, and reformatories. The northern entombment (and execution) of black bodies in spaces such as the state prison in the 1920s and early 1930s occurred in the context of an unprecedented mass movement of black southern migrants into northern cities popularly known as the Great Migration—an exodus that saw more than a million black people leaving the South between 1910 and 1930.[27] As in the case of other northern urban localities, those black migrants who settled in cities such as Cleveland, Cincinnati, and Columbus were immediately perceived as a collective menace by a white population that imagined that America's own lurking beast of a people had arrived in the flesh. The discourses of black migrant "shiftlessness," "idleness," immorality, and criminality represented a public and intellectual consensus reflected in both the white and black press, and within dominant U.S. sociology and criminology—a consensus that amounted to nothing if not a self-fulfilling prophecy of the white supremacist state whereby black migrant subjects were blamed for living the predictable outcomes of U.S. social apartheid.[28] The perilous predicament of new black urbanity under northern Jim Crow included structural poverty, white supremacist legal violence, geographical hyperisolation into cramped and overpriced housing, and a northern segregationist labor (and union) system that restricted a majority of black migrant men and women to unskilled factory work and domestic service, and that led to regular unemployment for many migrant subjects.

By creating what amounts to a narrative aperture for the submerged spectral voices of black migrants who experienced northern neoslavery, Himes treaded on familiar personal territory. Although he was born in the sectionally liminal "border state" location of Jefferson City, Missouri, in 1909, Himes spent the greater part of his childhood in southern states such as Arkansas, South Carolina, and Mississippi (the home of his white fictive persona in *Yesterday Will Make You Cry*) as his father attempted to forge a career as a professor at a number of black land-grant and A&M (Agricultural and Mechanical) colleges. In 1925, the Himes family moved to Cleveland. But unlike the majority of other black southern migrants to Cleveland who were segregated into the Scovill/Central district, the ghetto in which 90 percent of the city's black population lived in overpriced tenements, crammed boarding houses, abandoned buildings, and tent encampments,[29] the Himes's were able to purchase a house in Cleveland's Glenville section, a middle-class Jewish neighborhood that was also home to a small number of black families.[30]

Much to the chagrin of Himes's mother, whom the writer often described as maintaining overtly elitist and "color-struck" perceptions based in part on what she claimed as a noble, white, paternal ancestry, Himes frequently trespassed the internal class divide within Cleveland's black community, spending a great deal of time in the Scovill/Central district prior to his arrest for armed robbery in 1928. It was in this "vice district" that a teenage Himes would frequent prohibition-era black gambling and music clubs, such as Bunch Boy's and Elks' Cabaret, the latter in the basement of a house owned by the Cleveland chapter of black Elks, and in which Himes remembered hearing bands such as Bud Jenkins's Cotton Pickers play to a mostly southern migrant crowd. While Himes would frame his time in the Scovill/Central district as a kind of coming of age in terms of his sexuality and his self-proclaimed street hustler's mentality—telling of how Scovill was the site of his first sexual experience with a black prostitute at the age of sixteen and his first involvement with gambling, drinking, and acts of petty crime— his description of the people of Cleveland's ghetto underlines how Himes absorbed a great deal of the black middle-class aversion to working-class and jobless black migrants. This class-based intraracial antipathy expresses itself in Himes's recollections of Scovill by way of an internalized racism and a boldface misogynist depiction of the district's black women:

> Scovil [sic] Avenue ran from Fifty-fifth street to Fourteenth Street on the edge of the black ghetto and was the most degraded slum street I had ever seen. The police once estimated that there were fifteen hundred black prostitutes cruising the forty blocks of Scovil Avenue at one time. The black whores on Scovil for the most part were past their thirties, vulgar, scarred, dimwitted, in many instances without teeth, diseased, and poverty-stricken.

This brutal characterization of black women on Scovill is matched by an equally mortifying internalized white supremacist description of the black southern migrant men Himes encountered in prison: "The advantage that I had over the other black convicts was that I knew my own mind. I could influence them to do things the reason for which they didn't understand. Most of the black convicts in the Ohio State Penitentiary were dull-witted, stupid, uneducated, practically illiterate, *slightly above animals*."[31]

Such galling moments within Himes's official autobiography signal the hegemonic nature of anti-black southern migrant white supremacist and misogynist ideology in the Depression era, and how, notwithstanding his status as a fellow southern migrant, the writer saw himself as being *among but not of* the black migrant population of Scovill and the penitentiary—a fact that adds another level of complexity to his decision to portray himself as a "white boy" in his prison autobiography. This elitist self-perception is represented clearly in *Yesterday* by the fact that most of the novel's black migrant characters amount to a kind of sonic background tapestry, or apparitional chorus, rather than fully rendered subjects with any sort of an individualized or complicated interiority. However, it is the very ghostliness of the black southern migrant voice in *Yesterday* that is the novel's most powerful signal of the haunting symmetries of northern and southern neoslavery. This is represented most clearly in a moment well into the text when Jimmy enters the Black Bottom and is confronted with a ghostly black sound: "A wail rose, poignant, stirring—'Allll night lo-o-ooo-OOONG Ah set 'n mah cell an' mo—o-aaaOAAAAAAAAAnnn!'" Indeed, this black apparitional sound becomes so intense at one point in the novel that an exasperated guard yells into the Black Bottom: "Pipe down! Pipe down! What the hell do you think this is, a levee camp?" When considered in the context of Himes's dehumanizing portrait of black southern migrant women and men in his official autobiography, this moaning presence from southern levee camps, chain-gang camps, and neoslave plantations in his prison autobiography suggests how *Yesterday* represents less of an ideologically clean rendering of the black southern migrant experience than a kind of unconscious narrative portal for the ghostly emergence of a submerged incarcerated black sound—an unhistorical access and excess point—that offers a wailing, moaning, and melancholic reverb of the disavowed filiations of "northern" and "southern" white supremacist ideology, racial state terror, and legally remanufactured black unfreedom.[32]

While the black southern migrants who were rounded up in "vice districts" such as Scovill and entombed within the Ohio prison's Black Bottom do not supply much in the way of spoken lines in *Yesterday Will Make You Cry* (with the exception of a rather butchered version of black vernacular speech), their voices continue to call out to us both from within the novel itself and from its previously unclaimed *exterior interiority*.[33] In redeploying Fred Moten's provocative term for the spectral moan that still emits from Emmett Till's lynching photograph, I am gesturing toward an unhistorical figure that has reemerged during the course of this book's research from beneath the official accounts of the Ohio Penitentiary holocaust. While completely unknown to history, Himes would most certainly have come to know a man named Joe Sweet while he was a prisoner. Hailing from the rural town of Many, in western Louisiana, close to the border with Texas, Sweet came north at the height of the Great Migration only to land in prison on a bootlegging charge. The only way that I have been able to rescue Joe Sweet's name and the other scraps of his personal biography that I have just related is that he also happened to be one of the several black men who were killed in the Easter Monday prison fire. True to Benjamin's characterization of the wedded relationship of civilizational documentation and civilizational barbarism, to my knowledge all that is left in the public record of this black southern migrant's *life* is the state's accounting of his untimely death—his death certificate (Figure 12).[34] The spectral reemergence of this document-image of U.S. neoslavery, state terror, and legal lynching demands that we approach its contents in the same manner that Moten instructs us to bear witness to the continued resurfacing of Emmett Till by way of Mamie Till Mobley's black radical brandishment of her son's extralegally lynched body. That is, as in the case of the image of Emmett Till's lynching, the bureaucratic trace-image of Joe Sweet's de facto legal lynching hails us with a wailing, moaning entreaty, from one who was disappeared into the Ohio Penitentiary and left to burn alive in his cell, that we "listen to (and touch, taste, and smell) a photograph . . . to attune [ourselves] to a moan or shout that animates the photograph with an intentionality of the outside . . . that structures and ruptures the photograph . . . with a piercing historicality."[35]

A main element of the piercing historicity, or ghostly unhistoricity, supplied by Sweet's death certificate has to do with what it omits as much as what it includes. Unlike many of his white counterparts who were murdered

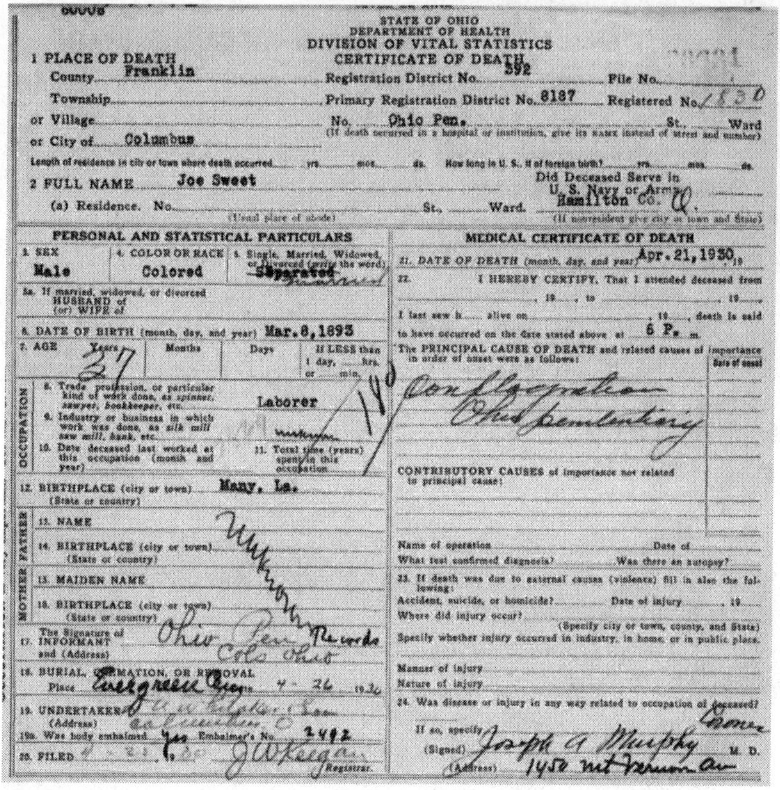
STATE OF OHIO
DEPARTMENT OF HEALTH
DIVISION OF VITAL STATISTICS
CERTIFICATE OF DEATH

1 PLACE OF DEATH
County Franklin Registration District No. 392 File No.
Township Primary Registration District No. 8187 Registered No. 1830
or Village No. Ohio Pen. St., Ward
or City of Columbus (If death occurred in a hospital or institution, give its NAME instead of street and number)
Length of residence in city or town where death occurred yrs. mos. ds. How long in U. S., if of foreign birth? yrs. mos. ds.
2 FULL NAME Joe Sweet Did Deceased Serve in U. S. Navy or Army?
(a) Residence. No. St., Ward. (Usual place of abode) Hamilton Co. O. (If nonresident give city or town and State)

PERSONAL AND STATISTICAL PARTICULARS
3. SEX Male
4. COLOR OR RACE Colored
5. Single, Married, Widowed, or Divorced (write the word) Separated
5a. If married, widowed, or divorced HUSBAND of (or) WIFE of
6. DATE OF BIRTH (month, day, and year) Mar. 8, 1893
7. AGE Years 37 Months Days If LESS than 1 day, hrs. or min.
OCCUPATION
8. Trade, profession, or particular kind of work done, as spinner, sawyer, bookkeeper, etc. Laborer
9. Industry or business in which work was done, as silk mill, saw mill, bank, etc. unknown
10. Date deceased last worked at this occupation (month and year)
11. Total time (years) spent in this occupation
12. BIRTHPLACE (city or town) (State or country) Many, La.
FATHER
13. NAME Unknown
14. BIRTHPLACE (city or town) (State or country)
MOTHER
15. MAIDEN NAME
16. BIRTHPLACE (city or town) (State or country)
17. The Signature of INFORMANT (Address) Ohio Pen Records Cols Ohio
18. BURIAL, CREMATION, OR REMOVAL Place Evergreen Cem. 4-26 1930
19. UNDERTAKER (Address) Columbus O
19a. Was body embalmed yes Embalmer's No. 2492
20. FILED 4-21 1930 J W Keegan Registrar.

MEDICAL CERTIFICATE OF DEATH
21. DATE OF DEATH (month, day, and year) Apr. 21, 1930
22. I HEREBY CERTIFY, That I attended deceased from , 19 , to , 19 .
I last saw h alive on , 19 , death is said to have occurred on the date stated above at 6 P. m.
The PRINCIPAL CAUSE OF DEATH and related causes of importance in order of onset were as follows: Date of onset
Conflagration
Ohio Penitentiary
CONTRIBUTORY CAUSES of importance not related to principal cause:
Name of operation Date of
What test confirmed diagnosis? Was there an autopsy?
23. If death was due to external causes (violence) fill in also the following:
Accident, suicide, or homicide? Date of injury , 19
Where did injury occur? (Specify city or town, county, and State)
Specify whether injury occurred in industry, in home, or in public place.
Manner of injury
Nature of injury
24. Was disease or injury in any way related to occupation of deceased?
If so, specify Coroner
(Signed) Joseph A Murphy M. D.
(Address) 1450 Mt Vernon Av

Figure 12. Joe Sweet, Certificate of Death, Franklin County Public Health Department, Columbus, Ohio.

in the fire, the lines next to the "mother" and "father" section of Sweet's death certificate are met only with the word "unknown." Along with signaling Sweet's natally alienated unsocial position, the document also draws attention to the circumscribed positionality of the black migrant vis-à-vis the racialized category of proletarian "worker." This is expressed in stark terms in the section of the form (numbers 8 and 9) noting Sweet's occupation. Next to the section indicating the dead person's "trade, profession, or particular kind of work done, as spinner, sawyer, bookkeeper, etc.," the only word that appears is "laborer"—while the section pertaining to his particular "industry or business in which work was done" is again followed by the scribbled notation of "unknown." Sweet's anomalous status as *just laborer* stands in stark contrast to the occupational positions of the white victims of the fire whose death certificates I have been able to recover—victims with Depression-era occupations indicative of their status as members of the industrial white proletariat such as "mechanic" and "truck driver." Sweet's social, economic, and industrial (non)status underlines the infamous "last hired first fired" modality of racial capitalism—how the black migrant laboring body was branded as the very antithesis to industrial productivity even after arriving in the industrialized North—and how, as in the white supremacist South, the racist ideological framework of the white supremacist North argued that the migrant Negro could only be "productive" with the spur of repression. The banality of state terror indicated with this document culminates in the section that attributes the cause of Sweet's death to "conflagration: Ohio Penitentiary." What is obscured in this attempted seizure of the semantics of mass civil and untimely death at the Ohio Penitentiary is the fact that culpability in the case of Joe Sweet and the other 321 deaths that occurred in the fire begins and ends with the racial capitalist carceral state. In other words, and at the risk of stating the obvious: if Sweet and the other victims of the fire were never entombed within their prison cells in the first place, then they would never have burned alive in them. Moreover, as I state throughout the book, an unhistorical accounting of state terror within necropolitical sites such as the Ohio Penitentiary cannot be reduced to biological death counts alone—that is, the terror of "life" that Himes and almost five thousand other prisoners endured after the fire represented an inhumanly banal double for the spectacular horror of the prison holocaust. Himes summed up the unspeakable death-in-life predicament of the fire "survivor" shortly after his release: "The only difference between a convict and a dead man is that the dead man don't have to get up."[36]

Joe Sweet's moaning resurfacing from within the bureaucratic remains of the Ohio Penitentiary fire charges us with hearing how the black laboring body continued to be branded as fungible, enslavable, and disposable after drifting northward during the Great Migration in search of substantive freedom. His de facto murder at the hands of the state represents nothing if not a morbid indicator or a systematic structure of violence, dispossession, and criminalization that decimated a large number of those black migrants who came to northern cities from 1910 to 1930. It is important to note, however, that the white panic that attended the mass movement of southern black people across the Ohio River was far from unprecedented by the eve of World War I. As discussed in chapter 2, Ohio was among the

northern Jim Crow apartheid states that incorporated racially restrictionist laws aimed at curtailing escaped slaves and "free" black migrants from
crossing their borders.

The white supremacist antipathy that informed Ohio's "Black Laws"
(1807–49), and that generated the forms of state and vigilante terrorism
against those black people who did find themselves in the state in spite of
their legally barred existence, is expressed in starkest terms by the words of
a member of the Ohio legislature and chairperson of the "Special Committee to Investigate the Negro Problem" in 1827, a time when the state began
to see its first significant rise in a migrant, fugitive black population:

> The negroes [sic] are in many parts of the state a serious political
> and moral evil. Although they are nominally free, that *freedom
> confers only the privilege of being more idle and vicious than slaves.*
> This is obvious to every man who witnesses the effect in our towns
> and villages and turns his attention to the relative proportion of
> crime between the colored and white population of the State.
> *The convicts in our penitentiary with reference to the whole colored
> and white population of the State are as eight of the former to one of
> the latter.*
>
>   Besides, the colored population has a tendency to depress and
> discourage the white laboring classes of the State, who are her
> source of wealth and peace. Destitute of the blessings of education
> and of moral and religious instruction, with no incentive to
> industry or the acquisition of an honorable reputation, and devoid
> of the intelligence and moral restraint necessary to qualify them for
> the privileges and immunities of citizens, *they form an excrescence
> on the body politic,* which, if it cannot be removed, should not be
> permitted to increase by emigration.[37]

In 1832, a member of another "Negro Problem" committee in the legislature focused more specifically on the degenerating effect that an increase
of black migrants would have on the state's white citizenry: "White men
will not degrade themselves in society by adopting the employment of,
and coming into competition with the blacks, a people of a degraded and
dependent condition and of dissolute conduct, a people upon whom society has affixed the brand of infamy from their birth; with whom it is considered disgraceful for the meanest white man to associate."[38]

Such testimony signifies how Joe Sweet and other black migrants who entered the state of Ohio in the context of Himes's imprisonment encountered an already well-embedded white supremacist ideological terrain that had long approached "free" migrant blackness as a contaminating threat. In the remarkable words of the legislator, the nominally emancipated black body was cast as a biometaphysical *excrescence* on the (white) social body— or what the *Oxford English Dictionary* defines as an *abnormal, morbid, or disfiguring growth*. Notwithstanding the impracticality of collectively removing or barring this dangerous abnormality through deportation or colonization, the nineteenth-century Black Laws worked in a manner akin to the more often discussed state-level white supremacist laws of southern states known as the Black Codes, which signified the state's repressive bearing toward those migrants who did settle in Ohio. As Leon Litwack observes, they "reminded Negroes of their inferior position in society and provided whites with a convenient excuse for mob violence and frequent harassment of the Negro population."[39] Early black migrants to Ohio and other northern states consequently dealt with formations of state and vigilante terror and structural dispossession that continued right up to the eve of the Great Migration, such as lynchings and organized white mob violence; segregated public accommodations, education, and employment; and police brutality, racial profiling, and disproportionate imprisonment—conditions of northern racial apartheid and domestic warfare that led to the mass exodus of over half the black population of Cincinnati to Canada in 1829.[40] Here, by jettisoning the fictive border that liberal bourgeois historiography has successfully erected between pre- and post-1865 social relations—and between northern and southern racial relations—we can begin to understand how the predicament of early "free" and fugitive black people represented a haunting prologue of the menaced social experience of black people after the arrival of collective de jure freedom. In so doing, we come to realize that the dubious experiential synchronicity of slavery and freedom is grounded not only in the terrorized experience of antebellum slaves but also in the systematic targeting of early "free" and fugitive northern black bodies with police brutality, arrest, and chattelized incarceration. Indeed, the legislator's reference to an imprisonment rate of eight black people to one white person in 1827 signals the degree to which, in lieu of actual large-scale banishment, the northern white supremacist state had already seized upon racialized imprisonment as one of its most actionable means of *free Negro removal*.

Insofar as the mid-nineteenth-century black migrant population was viewed as a degrading excrescence on the social body—a contaminating element in need of social and legal excision—its highly disproportionate imprisonment represented a dress rehearsal for the state's handling of the putatively "immoral," "idle," and "dependent" individuals who would stream across Ohio's borders in large numbers during the Great Migration. On a regional scale, the interested white supremacist cultural fable of black migrant criminality and social degeneracy would produce devastating consequences for those seeking to rid themselves of the violence, dispossession, and terror of southern Jim Crow apartheid. That is, upon the northward movement of black southern migrants in large numbers in the early to mid-twentieth century, the mythos of atavism, unproductivity, and metaphysical incorrigibility that had attached to their bodies with the advent of de jure emancipation in the South translated into ghettoization, structural poverty, police and vigilante brutality, and grossly disproportionate imprisonment in the white supremacist North. Indeed, as Scott Christianson notes, by 1926 "a Detroit study reported that twice as many blacks as whites were being sentenced to prison for roughly comparable offenses. About the same time a survey of Pennsylvania's Western Penitentiary found that blacks were being held at a rate nearly fourteen times greater than whites."[41] When looking at Ohio specifically, we find that the socially instrumentalist white racial panic that surrounded the arrival of the so-called shiftless, loafing, and criminal southern migrant figure led to a black incarceration rate that far surpassed the national average. Specifically, in 1923, the state had a total of 4,021 prisoners, with black captives making up 1,030 of the total, or 25 percent. In the same period, however, black people constituted only 3 percent of the total population of Ohio (approximately 220,000), equating to an imprisonment rate of 470 per 100,000, or almost double the rate at which black people were being imprisoned at that time in Alabama.[42] Moreover, just as in the case of the terroristic regimes of racial capitalist misogynist imprisonment that befell black people in the South after 1865, the neo-enslavement of southern migrants such as Joe Sweet, and other impoverished black people within "modern" northern prison carceral spaces such as Sing Sing (New York), Jackson (Michigan), and the Ohio Penitentiary, was conjured into sociological proof that the "Negro Problem" was the inevitable result of innate black social pathology, unproductivity, and criminality rather than a fatally banal outcome of America's transgeographical, transnational, and transepochal *problem of structural white supremacy*.

Yesterday Resurrected: A Black "Queer, Ghostly Voice"

Notwithstanding what became a national obsessive focus on and racist ideological construction of the "criminal" black migrant figure in U.S. mass media and sociological discourse in the early to mid-twentieth century, the voices of those who experienced northern penal neoslavery after their arrival to police-occupied black urban neighborhoods such as Harlem, Chicago's South Side, the Hill District in Pittsburgh, Detroit's "Black Bottom," and the Scovill/Central District in Cleveland remain virtually inaudible within U.S. cultural history and penal historiography. One explanation for this absent-presence is that, unlike those black subjects who faced penal neoslavery on the chain gang and prison plantation, the tens of thousands of black southern migrants who ended up being detained in northern jails, penitentiaries, and reformatories never became objects of the sort of primitivist white folkloric desire that brought the recorded voices of Lead Belly, Robert Pete Williams, Son House, Bukka White, and other incarcerated southern blues and folk virtuosos into public notice beginning in the early 1930s. In fact, from the romantically racist standpoint of white folklorists such as John and Alan Lomax, Dorothy Scarborough, and Harry Odum, the only place to find an "authentic" black folk/blues sound was a properly "premodern," that is, southern rural, "Negro" space—none of which was considered more *authentically Negro* than chain gangs, prison plantations, and cane fields.[43]

The virtual absence of the northern black neoslave voice in white folkloric scholarship—and *recorded* blues/folk music—is matched in the area of U.S. penal historiography. As the critically important work of Khalil Gibran Muhammad indicates, histories of black criminalization and imprisonment before the civil rights movement focus nearly exclusively on southern localities of neoslavery, while

> the prevailing history of the northern criminal justice system, starting with the nineteenth-century, has been a modernizing narrative, one in which the development of everything from prisons to policing to juvenile justice to probation and parole has turned almost exclusively on the experiences of native-born whites and European immigrants . . . giving the impression that the history of racial criminalization began and ended in the Jim Crow South.[44]

If, as I have stressed throughout this book, the historically submerged voices of black southern neoslaves such as Odea Mathews, John McElroy, and James Bruce represent spectral soundings of neoslavery that still echo from the southern zones of state terror such as Angola prison plantation, then *Yesterday Will Make You Cry* provides us with a vital, if ideologically problematic, point of entry into how the ghostly sounds and unendurable experiences of southern neoslavery reverberated into spaces of northern penal modernity right along with the historically anonymous black southern migrants who became entombed within them. My mentioning of the historically submerged name of James Bruce—the black drag artist whose performative enslavement, militant prison escape, and legally justified murder were the subject of the last section of chapter 3—bears particular significance here in that one of the main sources of black neoslave sound in Himes's prison autobiography is supplied by an imprisoned black queer musician by the name of Aubert LaCarlton Collins, or "Prince Rico." Arriving late into the action of *Yesterday,* Rico is a self-described "hobo," carnival performer, and cabaret drag queen, who gets arrested in Ohio after surviving a year-long sentence on a Florida chain gang.[45] As a former southern prison slave who comes north only to be reenslaved, Rico not only ends up supplying a haunting northern reversioning of southern chain-gang songs with the prison's Black Bottom, but he also represents the third and most intense of Jimmy's intimate liaisons in the novel. In fact, Jimmy's love affair with Rico—an affair whose eroticism is produced as much through artistic and intellectual communion as through sexual union[46]— is the primary catalyst for Jimmy's first successful attempts at redressing his experience of surviving the prison fire through writing.

However, as Himes discusses in his correspondence with Carl Van Vechten, it was Jimmy's openly avowed love for Rico that was the main target of the wholesale editorial expurgation of *Cast the First Stone* before its publication in 1952. In a letter dated March 11, 1953, Himes attempts to explain what Van Vechten immediately recognized as a severe excision in the original manuscript: "About CAST THE FIRST STONE.... In my contract I had to give Cecil Goldbeck at Coward-McCann the complete right to cut it as he saw fit. He cut 250 pages from the original script of 650 pages, and the part he cut was mostly the heart, the pulsebeat and emotion of the story."[47] This editorial closeting of the "pulsebeat and emotion" of *Yesterday Will Make You Cry* did not have to do with its portrayal of prison "homosexuality" per se, but with the fact that the love affair between

Jimmy and Rico (or Dido, as he is named in *Cast the First Stone*) manages to exceed the bounds of what has been described as the "situational" sexual culture of the penitentiary. That is, their bond is not reducible to the homo/transphobic framework that defines sex in prisons as a matter of environmentally determined moral *degeneracy* grounded in the sexually "normal" prisoner's forced removal from heteronormative sexual relations.[48] That Himes's prison autobiography situates its protagonist in a romantic love affair with another prisoner may come as somewhat of a surprise given his well-known penchant for producing hard-boiled, hypermasculinist, and openly misogynist stories. Indeed in his introduction to *Black on Black* (1973), a collection of his fictional works, he informs the reader that "these writings are admittedly chauvinistic. You will conclude if you read them that black protest and black heterosexuality are my two chief obsessions."[49] However, in another section of the letter to Van Vechten, Himes unveils that he was not always so categorical in his sexual obsessions within his fiction or within his own life: "About Rico: he was the boy in the story, entire and absolute, and *I was in love with him more, perhaps, than I have ever been in love with anyone before or since.* We had a full and complete and very touching love affair, and fulfilled each other emotionally, spiritually and physically; and then it was over. When I left the prison and went to the [penal] farm it wasn't over; I don't know when it got over, but when it got over, it was completely over."[50]

Himes's incredibly candid revelation of his romantic attachment with Rico as having been possibly the greatest love of his life, "before or since" his imprisonment, short-circuits any claim that their relationship was merely an expression of a necessary adaptation on Himes's part to the circumstance of incarceration. Moreover, Himes's portrait of the mental, spiritual, and physical fulfillment he found with Rico expresses the degree to which the relationship played an integral role in allowing the writer to survive the last three years of confinement in the Ohio Penitentiary. Indeed, by the time Rico enters the action of *Yesterday* "wearing a banjo ukulele strung from his neck by a woven chain of shoe strings," the death simulating routine of imprisonment, along with the ever-recurring rememory of the prison holocaust, has driven Himes's fictive persona perilously close to insanity.[51] Prior to Rico's arrival, Jimmy had attempted to stave off the prison's "ever-lasting pattern" of living death by shutting down his emotive self and repressing his memories of the "free-world"—a numbed "stage of senselessness" that recalls what Morrison describes as the "tin-can" that

Paul D erected around his heart in order to protect himself from the rememory of the chain gang in *Beloved*. However, soon after meeting Rico, Jimmy allows himself to open up again, emotionally, artistically, and sexually: "Everything touched Jimmy that spring. He was too emotional; he had never been so emotional. Everything was soft inside of him and at the slightest touch he'd bubble over, like foam. A single note from Rico's ukulele touched him. A bar of melody. A visit from his mother." Not only does Rico's entrance lead to Jimmy's consummating a relationship sexually for the first time in four years of imprisonment, but it also enables him to overcome what had been a series of unsuccessful attempts at writing his first short story. As Jimmy explains to his mother during a visit: "He's the most intelligent convict I've met since I've been in prison. . . . He writes a little too. And he's helping me to no end with my own writing. I think I'm going to get somewhere now."[52]

However, as much as Rico functions as both sexual and artistic partner— as lover and muse—he also represents a source of abjection and repulsion. Indeed it is Rico's willing and seemingly all-too-natural adoption of the role of "woman" in their relationship that quickly identifies him to Himes, the entire prison population, and administration as "girl-boy"—one whom in prison sex culture is interpellated as a pathologically feminine (and anatomically male) queer body.[53] While Himes describes himself as having been immediately captivated by Rico, who for him had a "picturesqueness [that] immediately set him apart from other convicts," he is also repelled by what he considers to be a "disturbing girlishness to his face" and the unmanly character of his "swirling" gait: "Watching him walk off, Jimmy was repulsed by the grotesqueness of his carriage. He'd look so much better if he carried his shoulders erect." But it is not until Jimmy/Himes hears Rico's stories of his sexual life as a carnival performer, drag queen, and "roustabout" that Jimmy's feelings of antipathy reach their peak. "Hearing Rico talk thus, he filled with a squashy mixture of jealousy and chagrin and a sort of impotent fury. How could [Rico] have ever been anything else? he asked himself, looking at his wet red lips and smoky smoldering eyes. How could I have possibly been the first? But he prayed that he was; he fought to make himself believe it in the face of all contradictory evidence."[54] Here Himes intimates that he was desperately invested in Rico being a "virgin woman"; that is, he was not so much repulsed by Rico's femininity as by the unbearable prospect that he may have allowed another man to perform the penetrative role in sex before arriving at the prison. Whereas before

hearing the stories of Rico's exploits the narrator expresses the romantic homophobic idea that "there was something about their relationship
which transcended the sordid aspects of homosexuality and even attained
a touch of sacredness," these stories ultimately lead to Himes's emotional
rejection of Rico. This rejection is clearly expressed near the end of the narrative, when Jimmy physically strikes his "woman" in the face—a moment
of misogynist homo/transphobic violence that we learn is a direct reflec-
tion of Himes's deep-seated anxieties vis-à-vis his own pre-imprisonment
masculinity and sexuality.[55]

As pointed out above in the brilliant essay by Marlon Ross, critics who
actually did address the queer plot in Himes's prison autobiography after
its first release as *Cast the First Stone* read it in a similar vein as they read his
choice of a white protagonist. They saw it as a detraction and distraction
from the "real" work of racial protest with which a black man was supposed
to be consumed after the white publishing industry's crowning of Richard
Wright as the quintessential model of authentic "Negro" writing.[56] Indeed,
the editor's choice of expurgating the essence of Jimmy's love affair with
Rico/Dido is suggestive of the degree to which the white publishing industry attempted to conform this complicated and largely unprecedented narrative to its own grossly simplistic, heteronormative, and reductive white
liberal sociological notion of what counted as bona fide "black" literature.
But here I am less interested in the troubling history of what led to the
submergence of the novel's (black) queer plot by its editors than in what
critical, epistemic, and neo-abolitionist possibilities are generated by Rico's
spectral resurfacing in *Yesterday Will Make You Cry* and in our current
moment of prison–industrial genocide.[57] In other words, I am concerned
with how, far from detracting from *Yesterday's* exposition of penal law's
fatal reapplication of punitive difference to racialized subjects, the reemergence of Rico and other socially and criminally "blackened" queer bodies
in the text represents an epistemically generative representation of the
intersectional and interdependent vectors of racialized, classed, and sexualized alterity in zones of chattelized carcerality—a dialectic of punitive
difference that is shown to be especially dehumanizing when, as in Rico's
case, it is focalized onto a single incarcerated body.

Similar to the case of James Bruce, we have no way of ascertaining
exactly how Aubert LaCarlton Collins identified himself in terms of gender or sexuality upon his imprisonment or any other time of his life. However, what I am interested in here is the degree to which the recovery of the

story of another black prisoner who was branded as "girl-boy"—or *nigger punk*, as other black queer bodies are branded in *Cast the First Stone*—underlines the sexualized and gendered aspects of what I referred to above as the prison's tendency to reascribe deadly punitive difference onto bodies branded as ontologically inassimilable, and metaphysically incorrigible, in the "free-world." In this way, the haunting presence of Rico and other queer black bodies in *Yesterday Will Make You Cry* registers the epistemically productive and politically necessary nature of incorporating the critical interventions of queer of color critique, black feminist theory, and radical queer/transgender studies into the study of white supremacist criminalization and neoslavery—methodologies that take for granted the degree to which racialized, classed, gendered, and sexualized violence function in dynamic articulation with one another under racial capitalist heteropatriarchy.[58] Indeed, what Rico's arrest, imprisonment, and sexualized/gendered punishment in the Ohio Penitentiary represents is the fact that many of the black migrant men, women, and gender-nonconforming people who were rounded up in so-called vice districts in northern cities such as the Scovill/Central area in Cleveland were in fact *queer* black migrant bodies—persons whose profiling as both racially and sexually "degenerate" analogizes the ways in which the northern white supremacist image of migrant subjectivity being an "excrescence" on the national body was often predicated on the attachment of sexual and/or gender difference onto the discursive grid of black abnormality and social enmity.[59] As Roderick Ferguson asserts, the white supremacist apartheid state's geographical cordoning of public nonheteronormative being to poor black neighborhoods in the age of the Great Migration expressed the structural entanglements of racial and sexual/gender alterity: "African American neighborhoods, popularized as the terrain of prostitutes, homosexuals, rent parties, black and tans, interracial liaisons, speakeasies, and juvenile delinquency, epitomized moral degeneracy and the perverse results of industrialization. . . . Vice worked in tandem with residential segregation and thereby established a formal relationship between racial exclusion and sexual regulation."[60]

If the terrorizing structure of U.S. penal law rests on a dynamic interchange between punitive homogenization (a relative suspension of socially constructed difference under the collectively stigmatizing sign of "convict") and punitive redifferentiation (the carceral state's reestablishment of repressively productive social taxonomies in respect to bodies marked as criminally deviant and metaphysically incorrigible), then the practice of racialized sexual surveillance in *Yesterday* signifies how what Ferguson describes as a formal relationship between racial and sexual exclusion in zones of social incarceration is taken to its dominative extreme under regimes of official incarceration.[61] Indeed, as in the case of those prisoners whom penal law hails as "nigger," bodies in Himes's text that end up being branded as "girl-boy," "whore," and "nigger punk" also experience the prison's spatial solution to the managerial problem of dangerous heterogeneity behind the walls.[62] That is, like those black prisoners who are relegated to the de facto punishment unit of 1-I, the "Black Bottom," those bodies identified as sexually degenerate are segregated to the Ohio Penitentiary's other ontologically determined prison-within-a-prison, known as "5-D"—the "company of degenerates."[63]

While Himes's misogynist and homo/transphobic conception of Rico's personhood is what ultimately determines his estrangement from his greatest life love after his release from the penitentiary, the most powerful impediment to the couple's attempts at rescuing something of a sexual, artistic, and romantic life out of conditions of living death at the peak of their bond is the prison's organized systems of sexual panopticism and sexual caste, formations of terroristic surveillance that in their proscription of authentic intimacy attest to the reality of Assata Shakur's radical poetic contention: "Love is contraband in Hell."[64] Once Rico and Himes's public displays of nonrepressive erotic attachment signal to their fellow prisoners and administrators that theirs is a relationship based upon intimacy and love rather than institutionally sanctioned rape and domination, the prison administrators immediately separate Jimmy and Rico and transfer them both to the "degenerate company"—a sentence of punitive segregation by which they are subjected to a solitary confinement and allowed out of their cells only three times a day for meals.[65] That the state's ascription of sexual abnormality onto the prisoner operates in dialectical, mutually constitutive, and cross-fertilizing relation with the brand of racial alterity is expressed in stark terms in the thoughts of Jimmy/Himes after being transferred into solitary: "And now they had the name, Jimmy thought. He was going out, sooner or later. . . . But Rico had to stay there for years to come. And when they put the name on you, it stuck. You were a 'lousy whore' forevermore. No matter how you played it."[66] Whereas the brand of "lousy whore" meant punitive isolation for Himes and Rico, it leads to additional formations of terror for other queer and "turn-out" bodies in the text, ranging from serialized rape to punitively motivated suicide.

As D. Morgan Bassichis, Dean Spade, and others have pointed out, the repressive isolation of and de facto social and penal warfare against sexualized and gendered difference continues to leave incarcerated queer and trans women, men, gender-nonconforming, and intersex people (most of whom are black and brown) vulnerable to particularly brutal regimes of civil death under today's prison–industrial complex.[67] These gendered and sexualized formations of terror and neo-enslavement range from physical brutality, to serialized rape by fellow prisoners and prison staff, to being turned into a fungible object of sexual exchange through sex trafficking—de facto elements of chattelized carcerality that respect no boundaries as to race, gender, or sexual identification even as women and queer bodies are their most common targets.[68] Indeed, while queer-identified and women prisoners in today's prison–industrial complex are often the most vulnerable to gendered and sexualized abuse, the indiscriminate nature of rape and sexual violence as a weapon of prison warfare is also expressed in the abject positionality of the "turn-out" or "punk"—a hetero/male-identified body who, in the heteronormative discourse of male prison sex culture, has had his "manhood" forcibly deconstructed through serialized rape and sexual slavery.[69]

One unspeakable modern example of this situation is offered in the second epigraph to this chapter by an anonymous, hetero-identified black male who faced ritualized imprisonment at a moment, in the early 1980s, when the Reagan administration's version of the tough-on-crime domestic warfare modality of the Nixon/Goldwater era inaugurated the largest increase in officially incarcerated people in post-1865 U.S. history.[70] The unidentified subject describes himself as a "35 year-old Black man, married, and an ex-offender—and an ex-punk," who was first imprisoned as a young teenager. He recalls how ritualized sexual rupture greeted him immediately upon his first experience of imprisonment in a boy's reformatory—a form of subjection that he would face in each of the seventeen years of his confinement in youth and adult facilities:

When I was 14 I got busted for "joy-riding" . . . and sentenced to a year at [a reform school]. The first day there I was put into a dorm and one of the dudes . . . beat me badly in front of the other guys. He topped his beating off by raping me and established *my identity as a "nigger punk."* I spent that year servicing the boys in the dorm and any of their friends that wanted sex. . . . That was when I realized that my position wasn't too different from my ancestors and that for the rest of the year *I wasn't any different from a plantation slave.*[71]

Himes repeatedly, and uncritically, alludes to the repressively constructed racial/sexual positionality elaborated here—that of *nigger punk*—in the 1952 version of his prison autobiography. And, while prison rape moves at the margins of a story based on the redressive capacities of his love affair with Rico, the unspeakably banal practice of sexualized and gendered carceral terror completely encircles the romance plot in *Yesterday*, a fact revealed both in the punitive annulment of Himes and Rico's relatively noncoercive relationship, and in moments such as the fire scene, when the narrator describes seeing an array of "wolves" turning the confusion of the holocaust into an opportunity to rape "that punk they'd always wanted to have." Even as the loving sexual and artistic relationship between Himes and Rico expresses the problematic aspects of the ascription of "situational homosexuality," or coerced same-sex relations, onto *all* sexual encounters in prison, the pervasiveness of sexual violence in the novel—and that which is expressed in the testimony offered by a "nigger punk" some five decades after Himes's imprisonment—suggests the degree to which the thought categories we bring to bear onto sexual relations in the "free-world" cannot be grafted unproblematically onto the death-simulating predicaments of the prison world.[72] Again, as in the case of chattel slavery, critical categories such as sexual/gender "self-identification," "sexual object choice," and homo/hetero-erotic "desire" are rendered vexing, if not completely inapplicable, in respect to unsocial spaces wherein human beings are transmuted into objects of natal alienation, sexual exchange, sexual deprivation, legalized terror, and socially acceptable/pleasurable entombment. Furthermore, the anonymous black man's assertion of the time-bending capacities of his incarceration in a putatively "modern" northern carceral system in the 1980s resonates directly with the other black neoslaves' voices who have guided this book insofar as it functions at the level of unhistorical counter-knowledge production. That is, his pained elaboration of how the de facto state punishment regime of serialized rape shuttled his body into a chattelized predicament dubiously akin to what his ancestors endured on the pre-1865 slave plantation amounts to a late twentieth-century re-sounding of the timelessness of chattelized imprisonment. And, as such, it also represents a ghostly reminder of how the Middle Passage carceral model continues to reactivate from the very foundations of U.S. penal modernity, whether practiced on a modern slave plantation such as Angola or a land-based slave ship such as the Ohio Penitentiary.

In a moment just before Jimmy/Himes walks out of the Ohio Penitentiary on his way to a prison farm that will take him a step away from freedom and a step closer to literary stardom, the narrator of *Yesterday* describes how Rico offers one final expression of his love for Jimmy in "a queer, and ghostly voice."[73] The moment unconsciously captures the fact that, like the other neoslave voices I have introduced in this book, the haunting refrains of Aubert LaCarlton Collins continue to resonate in the pages of Himes's buried prison autobiography, notwithstanding the apparent closure that occurs at the end of the narrative announcing that both Himes's imprisonment and the story of his love affair with Rico are "completely over." Like Robert Pete Williams, Odea Mathews, John McElroy, Jackson and Mentha Morrison, and James Bruce, Prince Rico presents us with a historically muted but irrepressibly undead sounding of the degree to which the formations of chattelized carcerality that were endured by African subjects in the barracoons, slave holds, slave pens, and plantations of the Middle Passage and plantation slavery have never come anywhere close to being over. And just as important, Rico, the survivor of a southern chain gang whose northern migration landed him in a zone of progressive carceral dehumanization, continues to beckon to us from the sepulcher-like enclosures of official history, demanding that we recognize the degree to which prison slavery has always been (and remains) a national rather than sectional modality of U.S. empire.

Indeed, like other black neoslaves who have guided the production of this book, Prince Rico, the survivor of neoslavery on a southern chain gang and a northern penitentiary, continues to haunt the current moment of prison–industrial genocide from outside the margins of U.S. dominant historiography, ukulele banjo in hand, offering a sonic reminder of the unhistorical truth contained in Malcolm X's "Ballot or the Bullet" (1964) speech: "If you're black, you were born in jail, in the North as well as the South. Stop talking about the South! Long as you're south of the Canadian border, you're south." Rico's submerged black queer ghostly voice also beckons us from another of America's many buried temporal boxes—a news item from 1935 that was intended as a bit of comical and pastoral relief in respect to an Ohio Penitentiary system still reeling from the public relations disaster of the prison fire. The article begins with an introduction of its picturesque subject: "Prince Rico, a Georgia Negro doing a robbery 'stretch' at Ohio Penitentiary, would like to weave into an opera the threads of Negro working chanteys he has collected [in] 23 years of custody in the north and south." The first song that Rico sings for the reporter is transcribed in the piece as such:

> Every mail day,
> Mail day I get a letter;
> Cryin' son come home,
> Lord, Lord, my son come home.
>
> I never had no—
> Never had no ready money;
> I couldn't get home,
> Lord, Lord, I couldn't go home.
>
> I'm gonna roll here,
> Roll here a few days longer;
> And then go home,
> Lord, Lord, and then go home.
>
> If I can make it,
> June, July and August;
> I'll be a man,
> Lord, Lord, I'll be a man.
>
> But look up yonder,
> Hot boilin' sun is turnin' over;
> It won't go down,
> Lord, Lord, it won't go down.[74]

Whereas the reporter receives this song as a quaint, premodern, anachronistic expression of a peculiarly southern experience, Rico's performative importation of the chain-gang dirge of living death, (un)productive neoslave labor, and natal alienation into the space of modern northern carcerality suggests the degree to which songs of southern neoslavery continued to hold unspeakable prescience for those who migrated across the Mason-Dixon line in search of a substantive reprieve from social apartheid, penal reenslavement, and domestic warfare only to find "modernized" versions of these formations of unfreedom awaiting them in the mythic North. Again, the "poignant and stirring" wails that Himes's fictive persona hears echoing nightly throughout the Ohio Penitentiary's Black Bottom amount to a collectively authored black chorus that was as instrumental in the outpouring of Himes's writerly voice as his artistically and physically intimate exchanges with Rico. As I have stated earlier in reference to the incarcerated wailings of other black neoslaves such as Odea Mathews, John McElroy, Robert Pete Williams, and James Bruce, the northern reversioning of the chain-gang song by Prince Rico and other anonymous black migrant neoslaves in *Yesterday Will Make You Cry*, represent a collectively authored spectral demand on the perilous now as much as they serve as revelations of America's neoslavery past—a living, open wound, history that finds one out of every nine black men between the ages of twenty and thirty-four currently entombed within today's carceral Black Bottoms, while black, brown, and poor women prisoners endure modern versions of the Middle Passage carceral model and colonial genocide ranging from ritualized rape and sexual assault, to shackled childbirths, to mass forced sterilization.[75]

When received in this light, the ghostly neo-abolitionist voices that have coauthored this work demand that we read today's legally perpetrated and socially accepted terror system of penal neoslavery as a continuance rather than a break from America's centuries-long history of chattelized imprisonment and white supremacist genocide—that we acknowledge that slavery's unspeakable yesterday is indeed *always now*, even as liberal bourgeois history and white supremacist "postracial" cultural mythology continue to pronounce its prehistorical death. As such, the songs of neoslavery that were performed through the historically anonymous and ostensibly nonpolitical ghostly voices of black neoslaves from the southern chain gang to the Depression-era penitentiary can still be heard emanating from today's temporal boxes of U.S. neoslavery such as Angola, Chowchilla, Attica, Guantánamo Bay, and the SHU boxes of Pelican Bay and Corcoran—the last three of which have recently witnessed hunger strikes by thousands of black, Latino, Asian, Indigenous, poor white, and Muslim prisoners, whose soundings against indefinite solitary confinement, state-of-the-art (in)human entombment, and U.S. state terrorism make a renewed neo-abolitionist demand on everyone within striking distance of these words:

If you are reading these words, you can no longer claim ignorance; to stand idly by now would be complicity. A wise man once said, "All that is necessary for evil men to prevail is for good men to do nothing." We are under no illusions. The ultimate arbiter of our fate—and this society's fate—is the people. YOU. YOU must rise up against this injustice and inhumanity. YOU must let the state know that substantive change at every level of society is something the people demand.[76]

Acknowledgments

W HEN SITTING DOWN TO WRITE THESE WORDS after so many
years of working on this project, the first thing that came to mind
was something my grandfather once said to me, when I was twelve years
old, as we sat near a pool table that still occupies the basement of his home
in Denver, Colorado. He said: "Grandson, you gotta know how to dig a
ditch." For years these words represented something of a black vernacular
riddle for me. As time passed, however, I began to understand something
of the multilevel meaning of this saying that my grandfather picked up as
he worked, from the age of nine, in the cotton fields that surrounded the
black section of DeWitt, Arkansas—an area that many of the town's white
residents referred to as "Nigger Hill." The first level of meaning that I
picked up from that phrase had to do with the fact that no amount of book
learning could ever take the place of the sort of common survival sense
that was required for him and his community of hard-laboring agricultural
and domestic workers to literally "make a day" in places like DeWitt.

Through facing what at times seemed an impossible task of completing
an academic book, however, I became aware of a second level of meaning
within my grandfather's phrase. That is, I came to realize that no matter
what kind of "work" one faces, the pain of the task at hand can indeed be
outstripped by the reward of never giving up the struggle, no matter what
form the struggle takes. And while the process of writing a book, or slog-
ging through academia as a black male, can in no way be mistaken for the
infinite hardships that my grandfather and other black men, women, and
children in southern plantation fields endured, the struggle of surviving
academia as a person of color is, in a very real sense, akin to digging a very
long ditch. So, as I look back on the production of this book, and the many
stories of neoslavery that I have unburied in the course of "diggin' in the
crates" of U.S. white supremacist history, I want to dispatch a normative
formal element of the acknowledgments genre by first thanking my grandfather, R. E. "Tunie" Childs, for being the only father I ever had, and for the

many life lessons he imparted to me—whether we were sitting around his pool table listening to Al Green, relaxing on a fishing boat, or cleaning an office building as I worked my first "real job" as a janitor in his and my grandmother's cleaning service. Here I also wish to express my deep gratitude to my beautiful grandmother, Sonja Childs, who also added a hefty share of lessons and love in these same ritualized spaces of my early life.

As to the academic community that I have been privileged enough to be a part of over the years, I must begin by recognizing the mentorship of Saidiya Hartman, my dissertation director at UC Berkeley. Anyone who takes the time to read what is contained in the pages of this book will recognize the profound influence that her groundbreaking scholarship has had on my intellectual path. I would also like to thank Ruth Wilson Gilmore, Marcial Gonzalez, and Hertha D. Sweet Wong, who offered generous support during my time at Berkeley. I would never have made it into a PhD program in the first place were it not for the mentors I had while in the Master's Program in Afro-American Studies at UCLA. In particular, the intellectual and pedagogical guidance of Valerie Smith and Richard Yarborough have stayed with me until this day. I will never forget everything they have done for me (and continue to do).

Since my arrival at UCSD, I have had the privilege of working with an incredible group of friends and colleagues who supplied the sort of vibrant intellectual community that I needed in order to bring this project to fruition. Lisa Lowe offered a tremendous example of how to be a politically engaged scholar, teacher, and mentor. I have also received invaluable inspiration, feedback, and support from Page duBois, Jaime Concha, Yen Le Espiritu, Ross Frank, Daniel Widener, Curtis Marez, Natalia Molina, David Pellow, and Shelley Streeby.

Very special thanks go to John Blanco, Fatima El-Tayeb, Sara Johnson, and Luis Martín-Cabrera for their friendship, intellectual power, political commitment, and unwavering dedication to our students.

I also want to express my sincere appreciation to colleagues at other universities throughout the United States. Dylan Rodríguez and Randall Williams offered generous and insightful comments, many of which are reflected directly in the final version of the book. My deepest gratitude extends to Sarika Chandra, Jennifer Scappettone, Lisa Ze Winters, and Carter Mathes—de facto relatives who also happen to be incredible scholars. Indeed I must thank the entire Mathes family for providing me with a radiant (Ital) example of what a truly loving home can be from Oakland to East Orange.

I would also like to express my appreciation to the incredible students I have worked with over the years at both the undergraduate and graduate level. Your intellectual imagination and political fervor have inspired the writing of this book and my conception of what it means to be a scholar-activist. Great thanks also go to a number of prison abolitionist and grassroots community organizations that have helped to shape my vision of radical social analysis and action over the years. In this regard, I would like to mention the Malcolm X Grassroots Movement, All of Us or None, Critical Resistance, CURB, and the Chicano-Mexicano Prison Project. I also want to offer my thanks and deepest respect to Robert Hillary King (aka Robert King Wilkerson) of the Angola 3 for his wisdom, courage, and black radical leadership—and for honoring me with many long conversations about the international neoplantation that is the prison–industrial complex. The word "inspiration" does not capture what you, Albert Woodfox, and the late Herman Wallace have meant to me since I first heard of your living burial at Angola prison plantation. I would also like to express comradely gratitude to Henry "Hank" Jones and Ray Boudreaux of the San Francisco 8 for your time, guidance, and interminable antiprison work.

As anyone who conducts archive-based scholarship knows, such projects would be impossible without the technical acumen and generosity of a number of librarians and archivists. In this regard, I would like to thank Jennifer Hafner and Owen Lourie from the Maryland State Archives and Vincent Golden from the American Antiquarian Society. Special appreciation goes to Marc Wellman from the State Library of Louisiana, who offered me expert archival assistance for my research on Angola.

Essential financial support for this project was provided by the Scholars-in-Residence Program at the Schomburg Center for Research in Black Culture in Harlem. My residency at the Schomburg was also made possible through a grant from the National Endowment for the Humanities. While at the Schomburg, I had the distinct pleasure of working with an amazing group of scholars, archivists, and mentors: I especially want to thank Colin Palmer and Diana Lachatanere. My research was also supported by a postdoctoral fellowship in African American Literature at Rutgers University. It was during my time at Rutgers that I came to realize that Cheryl Wall's incredible scholarship is matched by a tremendous commitment to the mentorship of junior black scholars. I also received integral support through the UC President's Postdoctoral Program, during which time I had the distinct privilege of working with Cheryl Harris at the UCLA School of Law. My research was also supported by the Hellman Fund.

Much appreciation goes to my editor, Richard Morrison, at the University of Minnesota Press for believing in this project from the outset.

Tracy Curry, Stevie Harris, Bryan Massengale, Jason Pipes, and Isadora Romero have been sisters and brothers to me for most of my life. Thanks for everything you have done to help guide me on this journey.

As to my immediate family, I love you all beyond measure. To my brother, Derick London: we are living our father's redemption. For my younger brother and sister, Sean and Rachelle: you are more important to me than I have the power to describe. I am so very proud of you both. To my mother, JoAnna: we have come so far since that sunrise ride out of Tulsa. No one would ever have believed that we would have made it this far. Thank you so much for your sacrifice and strength. For Saranella, my partner and love: you have anguished with me over every word (and thousands of miles of moves). I can never tell you enough of my deep gratitude, love, and respect for who you are, and how happy I am with the home we have made together with our son. Kahlil Patrice, my joy, my heart, I hope to be able to say one day that I have offered you something approaching what you have already given to my life.

Notes

Introduction

1. Angela Y. Davis, "Racialized Punishment and Prison Abolition," in *The Angela Davis Reader*, ed. Joy James (Malden, Mass.: Blackwell, 1998), 99. As Davis points out, however, Foucault became personally aware that the "disciplinary" rubric with which he approached the birth of the modern prison was inapplicable to white supremacist carcerality upon his visit to Attica (New York) in 1972 (a year after the prisoner uprising and massacre that led to the deaths of thirty-nine prisoners and guard hostages): "At the time of the creation of Auburn and the Philadelphia prison [in the nineteenth century], which served as models (with very little change until now) for the great machines of incarceration, it was believed that something indeed was produced: 'virtuous men.' Now we know . . . that nothing at all is produced. That it is a question simply of a great sleight of hand, a curious mechanism of circular elimination: society eliminates by sending to prison people whom prison breaks up, crushes, physically eliminates; the prison eliminates them by 'freeing' them and sending them back to society; . . . the state in which they come out insures that society will eliminate them once again, sending them to prison. . . . Attica is a machine for elimination, a form of prodigious stomach, a kidney that consumes, destroys, breaks up and the rejects, and that consumes in order to eliminate what is has already eliminated" (ibid., 98). Note how Foucault's newfound recognition of the propensity of the "modern," "disciplinary," prison to produce and consume dead and living dead bodies through structurally recidivist ingestion, ejection, and elimination bears stark resemblance to descriptions by slaves of their fear that they would be eaten by white men in the early modern chattelized carceral formations of the coffle, slave dungeon, and slave ship. See Ottobah Cugoano, *Narrative of the Enslavement of Ottobah Cugoano, a Native of Africa, Published by Himself in the Year 1787*, in *The Negro's Memorial 1825, or, Abolitionist's Catechism by an Abolitionist* (London: Hatchard and Co., 1825), 123; and Olaudah Equiano, *The Interesting Narrative of the Life of Olaudah Equiano, or Gustavus Vassa, the African. Written by Himself* (London: O. Equiano, 1789), 97. For a brilliant theoretical reading of chattel slavery as a process of cannibalistic/capitalistic ingestion, see Saidiya Hartman, *Lose Your Mother: A Journey Along the Atlantic Slave Route* (New York: Farrar, Straus and Giroux, 2007), 110–21.

My use of the term "neo-abolitionist" in reference to the antiprison scholar-ship and activism of Angela Y. Davis derives from the pathbreaking critical prison studies and neo-abolitionist work of Joy James. See, for example, Joy James, Intro-duction to *The New Abolitionists: (Neo)Slave Narratives and Contemporary Prison Writings,* ed. Joy James (New York: State University of New York Press, 2005).

2. The term "racial capitalism" derives from Cedric Robinson's seminal work on the relationship between the pan-African black radical tradition and European Marxist theory, *Black Marxism: The Making of the Black Radical Tradition* (Chapel Hill: University of North Carolina Press, 2000). The term highlights the material-ity of white supremacy within occidental modernity—a structural formation that for Robinson is untheorized within the European Marxist tradition, a mode of thought that, in its reductive economistic form, defines racism as merely a super-structural mode of idealist sociality, or a machination of "false consciousness," rather than as a material (and fatally corporealized) modality of Euro-American imperial history. Throughout this work, I rephrase Robinson's original term, using "racial capitalist misogyny," in order to highlight the degree to which gender dom-ination also functions as a material ideological formation of global capitalism. This should in no way be read as an argument for a shuttling of all Marxisms in respect to the interlocking repressive systems of class, race, and gender repression, however, since many Marxist theorists have indeed treated social structures in a truly dialectical fashion, taking for granted the poly-determinant nature of social relations. See, for example, Stuart Hall, "Articulation and Societies Structured in Dominance," in *Sociological Theories: Race and Colonialism* (Paris: UNESCO, 1980); and Ruth Wilson Gilmore, *Golden Gulag: Prisons, Surplus, Crisis, and Opposition in Globalizing California* (Berkeley: University of California Press, 2007).

3. Orlando Patterson defines social death as the death-in-life situation of the slave whereby biological death is at once threatened via physical terror and simu-lated through her forced removal from lines of kinship and communal/cultural sociality—what he describes as "natal alienation." Patterson, *Slavery and Social Death* (Cambridge: Harvard University Press, 1982). See also Claude Meillassoux, *The Anthropology of Slavery* (Chicago: University of Chicago Press, 1991). For an illuminating treatment of the legal concept of "civil death"—a term derived from early modern English common law signaling the felon's forfeiture of all rights, properties, etc., relative to the status of *living* "citizen," see Colin Dayan, "Legal Slaves and Civil Bodies," in *Materializing Democracy,* ed. Russ Castronovo and Dana Nelson (Durham: Duke University Press, 2002).

Throughout this book I use the terms "racial genocide" and "prison–industrial genocide" in keeping with William Patterson's theorization of racial genocide in his historic petition to the United Nations in 1951, charging the U.S. government with genocide against black people within its borders. Citing the UN Genocide Convention of 1948, the black Communist and his fellow petitioners argued that the situation of black people in the United States undoubtedly raised to the level of a systematic "killing members of [a] group" with the intent to destroy it *in whole or in part.* Significantly it was Patterson's work on behalf of black people who had been victimized by state violence in the form of mass imprisonment and legal lynching (both by police and in prisons via the electric chair) that informed his theorization of racial genocide in the United States. While focusing on extralegal formations such as the KKK, the petition also cites the structural pattern of police and carceral terror versus black people: "Our evidence concerns the thousands of Negroes who over the years have been beaten to death on chain gangs and in the back rooms of sheriff's offices, in the cells of county jails, in precinct police stations and on city streets." William Patterson, *We Charge Genocide: The Crime of Government Against the Negro People* (New York: International Publishers, 1970), xiv, 4. Of course, this element of the genocide charge rings all-too-relevant in our current context of legal and extralegal terror against black and Latina/o people such as Trayvon Martin, Ramarley Graham, and Valeria Alvarado. Indeed, as of the month of July in 2012, the United States (over)saw the killing of 120 black men, women, and minors by police, security guards, and vigilantes—that is, one black person murdered every thirty-six hours. Malcolm X Grassroots Movement, "Report on the Extrajudicial Killing of 120 Black People by Police, Security Guards, or Self-Appointed Law Enforcers" (updated edition, July 16, 2012), http://mxgm.org/report-on-the-extrajudicial-killings-of-110-black-people/. Although we are right to focus on the spectacular murder of black people, Latina/os, and other socially stigmatized bodies in zones of social incarceration, the greatest emblem of U.S. racial capitalist genocide comes in the more (apparently) banal form of mass imprisonment, in which one out of nine black men between the ages of twenty and thirty-four are entombed in the United States. For an important study of mass imprisonment as a genocidal formation, see Dylan Rodríguez, *Forced Passages: Imprisoned Radical Intellectuals and the U.S. Prison Regime* (Minneapolis: University of Minnesota Press, 2006). See also Michelle Alexander, *The New Jim Crow: Mass Incarceration in the Age of Colorblindness* (New York: The New Press, 2010). And for an equally important study of U.S. genocidal practice versus the Indigenous peoples of the Americas, see Ward Churchill, *A Little Matter of Genocide: Holocaust Denial in the Americas, 1492 to the Present* (San Francisco: City Lights, 2001).

4. *Ruffin v. Commonwealth,* 62 VA 790 (1871): 795–96. I should point out here that Paul Wright, an imprisoned writer and coeditor of *Prison Legal News,* also uses *Ruffin's* language as a title for his important article on the practice of neoslave labor in U.S. prisons. Wright, "Slaves of the State: Prison Laborers Do Time in Factories with Fences," *Washington Free Press,* Seattle, WFP Collective, October–November 1995.

5. In discussing the criminalization of black life in particular, Angela Y. Davis cites how the remarkably high number of black people, and black men in particular,

in U.S. prisons, jails, and under some form of "correctional" supervision under-lines the fact that blackness is the most penalized crime under U.S. racial capitalist misogynist law: "One has a greater chance of going to jail or prison if one is a black man than if one is actually a law-breaker. While most imprisoned young black men may have broken a law, it is the fact that they are young black men rather than the fact that they are law-breakers which brings them into contact with the crimi-nal justice system." Davis, "Racialized Punishment and Prison Abolition," 104. What the work of Davis and other prison abolitionists has shown us, however, is that the retail "crimes" of individual black, brown, Indigenous, and poor people are direct results of the wholesale crimes of structural poverty, joblessness, and racist legality as practiced by the racial capitalist heteropatriarchal colonial state. My description of the relationship between the "retail," or individual criminality, and "wholesale" criminality, or structural terror performed by the U.S. imperial state, derives from Noam Chomsky and Edward Herman, *The Washington Con-nection and Third World Fascism, Volume 1* (Boston: South End Press, 1979), 85–94. See also Gregg Barak, *Crimes by the Capitalist State: An Introduction to State Crim-inality* (New York: State University of New York Press, 1991).

For a brilliant analysis of the degree to which the hyperisolating structure of residential segregation in the United States has amounted to a long-standing national (as opposed to sectional/southern) system of social apartheid, see Doug-las Massey and Nancy Denton, *American Apartheid* (Cambridge: Harvard Uni-versity Press, 1993). I have placed the term "America" in quotation marks here to demonstrate that the common attribution of this term to the empire of *the Amer-icas* is a galling indicator of U.S. hemispherical chauvinism and racism. I am indebted to the South African poet and liberation activist Keorapetse "Willie" Kgositsile for first drawing my attention to this example of U.S. cultural imperial-ism. For the remainder of the book, for the sake of readability, I will not employ quotation marks when using this term; however, I will use "U.S." when syntacti-cally possible.

6. Saidiya Hartman, *Scenes of Subjection: Terror, Slavery, and Self-Making in Nineteenth-Century America* (Oxford: Oxford University Press, 1997), 14.

7. Avery Gordon, *Ghostly Matters: Haunting and the Sociological Imagination* (Minneapolis: University of Minnesota Press, 1996), 64. On the imperative polit-ical practice of spectral listening, Gordon states that "we will have to learn to lis-ten to ghosts, rather than banish them, as the precondition for establishing our . . . knowledge" (ibid., 23). I would like to thank Ryan Heryford for bringing my attention to this particular aspect of Gordon's work in his riveting discussion of neoslave song, unpublished manuscript. My *hearing* of the spectrally produced testimonies, soundings, and subterranean histories of black neoslaves is greatly indebted to Gordon's intellectually stimulating and politically courageous treatment of haunting as a material and social practice. I should add here that my attention

to the countless unquiet revenants of U.S. genocidal history has also drawn heavily from Toni Morrison and her narrative-epistemic charting of the ways in which slavery haunts U.S. postbellum life—a point that is articulated most clearly in the masterpiece that is *Beloved,* a work that I discuss at length in chapter 1.

8. My use of the term "unhistory" derives from Bob Kaufman's poem "Unhistorical Events," in which the surrealist poet addresses Guillaume Apollinaire, the French poet and playwright who is credited with coining the term "surrealism," and with writing one of the first works to be described under that aesthetic heading, a play entitled *The Breasts of Tiresias* (1917). Kaufman's poem issues a refrain, "Apollinaire never . . . ," followed by a series of people and events that even the ostensible father of surrealism "never" would have known or experienced—a man named "Rock Gut Charlie / who gave fifty cents to a policeman / driving around in a 1927 Nash," and a woman named "Lady Choppy Wine / peerless female drunk, who talked to shrubs / and made children sing in the streets." "Unhistorical Events," *Cranial Guitar: Selected Poems by Bob Kaufman,* intro. Gerald Nicosia, ed. David Henderson (Minneapolis: Coffee House Press, 1996), 53. The poem (like the invisibilized life and work of Bob Kaufman himself) highlights the degree to which racialized and criminalized subjects are historically disappeared even within Western aesthetic and social arenas, such as surrealism, that attempt to cut against the grain of normative historical, cultural, and experiential perception. Kaufman definitely knew of what he spoke in terms of the unhistorical experiences of one such as Rock Gut Charlie, who was forced to be on all-too-intimate terms with police. The poet and activist was arrested thirty-six times in one calendar year (c. 1959) for his openly interracial romantic liaisons and his politicized poetic performances. He was incarcerated in a number of local and state jails, prisons, and mental institutions on both coasts, including San Francisco City Prison, The Tombs, Rikers Island, and Bellevue Hospital, in which he was known to have received involuntary shock "therapy." David Henderson, Introduction to *Cranial Guitar,* 13, 16.

9. Mumia Abu-Jamal, *Live from Death Row* (New York: Harper Perennial, 1996), 46, 10. Unless otherwise indicated, italicized portions hereafter will represent the author's emphasis.

10. Abu-Jamal is joined by a large number of other imprisoned black radical theorists in articulating the time-bending experience of neoslavery. See, for example, Angelo Herndon, *Let Me Live* (Ann Arbor: University of Michigan Press, 2007), 279; Assata Shakur, *Assata* (New York: Lawrence Hill Books, 1987), 64; and George Jackson, *Soledad Brother: The Prison Letters of George Jackson* (Chicago: Lawrence Hill Books, 1994), 234. This assertion of the time-bending capacity of imprisonment is not limited to publically recognized political prisoners, however. For similar articulations along these lines by black social prisoners—i.e., those who have been incarcerated for the *politically motivated crime* of being born

black in the United States—see Gloria House, *Tower and Dungeon: A Study of Place and Power in American Culture* (Detroit: Casa de Unidad Press, 1991), 71. For my conception of the nonlinear temporality of black chattelized imprisonment, I am also indebted to Hortense Spillers, namely, as reflected in her exposition of the cyclical nature of white supremacist misogynist discourse under U.S. empire: "Even though the captive flesh/body has been 'liberated' . . . the ruling episteme that releases the dynamics of naming and valuation, remains grounded in the originating metaphors of captivity and mutilation so that it is as if neither time nor history, nor historiography and its topics, shows movement, as the human subject is 'murdered' over and over again. "Mama's Baby, Papa's Maybe: An American Grammar Book," *Diacritics* 17, no. 2 (1987): 68. As we shall see, however, what Spillers describes as an undying pattern of white supremacist epistemological/ rhetorical racial murder of the putatively "liberated" black subject has also been actuated at the level of actual black flesh/corporeality through unceasing formations of liberal white supremacist legal and extralegal terror.

11. James, "American 'Prison Notebooks,'" *Race & Class* 45, no. 3 (January 2004): 37. See also Rodríguez, *Forced Passages*.

12. In speaking of the precarious social position of the dead vis-à-vis the racial capitalist misogynist state's continued manufacture of civilly and biologically dead bodies, I am gesturing toward Walter Benjamin's hauntingly prescient phrase from his "Theses on the Philosophy of History": "Only that historian will have the gift of fanning the spark of hope in the past who is firmly convinced that *even the dead* will not be safe from the enemy if he wins. And this enemy has not ceased to be victorious." Benjamin, *Illuminations* (New York: Schocken Books, 1969), 255.

13. Mentha Morrison to Theodore Roosevelt, *The Peonage Files of the U.S. Department of Justice, 1901–1945* (microform), ed. Pete Daniel, DOJ Case No. 3098-1902. One of the main reasons for the Justice Department's inability to achieve convictions in the majority of peonage cases such as the Morrisons was because it relied on gaining testimony from terrorized peons against their masters at the very sites in which neoslavery occurred, a process that rarely offered neoslaves an opportunity to freely express their grievances due to the immanent threat of torture and death by the peon master. In the case of Jackson Morrison, he denied ever having been tortured on Smith's plantation, notwithstanding his wife's entreaty to President Roosevelt. The federal investigator for the Morrisons' case noted discrepancies in Smith's testimony and those of other peon slaves, and also recognized visible signs of fear when interviewing black peons, a fact that made him believe that they had been terrorized into denying their own enslavement. John Dittmer, *Black Georgia in the Progressive Era, 1900–1920* (Champaign: University of Illinois Press, 1980), 78–79. For the most thoroughgoing analysis of peonage as practiced well into the twentieth century versus black people in the South

and Latina/os in the Southwest, see Pete Daniel, *The Shadow of Slavery: Peonage in the South, 1901–1969* (London: Oxford University Press, 1972).

14. On the conjuring/occult vectors of U.S. legal practice, particularly in respect to racialized imprisonment, solitary confinement, and civil death, see Colin Dayan, "Legal Slaves and Civil Bodies," and *The Law Is a White Dog: How Legal Rituals Make and Unmake Persons* (Princeton: Princeton University Press, 2011).

15. The term "rememory" is borrowed from Toni Morrison's novel *Beloved* (New York: Plume, 1987). It suggests the undead nature of chattel slavery for Africans in the United States after the arrival of de jure freedom. See chapter 1 for my reading of *Beloved*'s chain-gang scene in relation to today's PIC.

16. See, for example, Edward Ayers, *Vengeance and Justice* (New York: Oxford University Press, 1984), and Matthew J. Mancini, *One Dies, Get Another: Convict Leasing in the American South, 1866–1928* (Columbia: University of South Carolina Press, 1996). For an example of a work that does take seriously the central role of racial ideology in the system of southern postbellum imprisonment, but that unfortunately ends up abjecting neoslavery as a distinctly southern and past phenomenon, see Douglas Blackmon, *Slavery by Another Name: The Re-enslavement of Black Americans from the Civil War to World War II* (New York: Doubleday, 2008). While these works do discuss racist ideology in the South, they do so in keeping with the idea that racialized neoslavery was a peculiarly "southern" or "past" problem. They also tend to disengage "convict labor" from chattel slavery by either not discussing the relation between the two systems at all, or by claiming that post-1865 black imprisonment was somehow "worse" than its antebellum counterpart because of the relatively high death counts that occurred with the advent of convict leasing in the late nineteenth century, a claim that unconsciously upholds the notion that the southern antebellum slave plantation amounted to a paternalistic/disciplinary rather than genocidal/dominative system of racial control. As I will discuss below, chattelized incarceration represents a necropolitical system in which "life" itself is transmuted into an approximation of death, and in which biological death is often described by the (neo)slave as preferable to a "life" of legal torture, natal alienation, and chattelized internment. On "necropolitics" and the life-in-death practice of colonial-slave-state sovereignty, see Achille Mbembe, trans. Libby Meintjes, *Public Culture* 15, no. 1 (2003): 11–40.

17. Sylvia Wynter, keynote address at "The State and Soul of Jamaica" conference, University of California, Berkeley, March 31, 1993.

18. Sylvia Wynter, "On Disenchanting Discourse: 'Minority' Literary Criticism and Beyond," in *The Nature and Context of Minority Discourse,* ed. Abdul Jan-Mohamed and David Lloyd (Oxford: Oxford University Press, 1990), 439–48. On the fabulation of the African subject into the fungible "Negro," see also Cedric Robinson, *Black Marxism: The Making of the Black Radical Tradition.* "The 'Negro,' that is the color black, was both a negation of African and a unity of opposition to

white. The construct of Negro, unlike the terms 'African,' 'Moor,' or 'Ethiope,' suggested no situatedness in time, that is history, or space, that is ethno- or politico-geography. The Negro had no civilization, no cultures, no religions, no history, no place, and finally no humanity that might command consideration" (81). Here the racist conjurations of no less lofty a figure than Hegel on the subject of "the Negro" suffice as an example of this branch of white supremacist cultural violence: "The peculiarly African character is difficult to comprehend, for the very reason that in reference to it, we must quite give up the principle which naturally accompanies all *our* ideas—as for example, God, or law—in which the interest of man's volition is involved and in which he realizes his own being." He continues: "The Negro, as already observed, exhibits the natural man in his completely wild and untamed state. We must lay aside all thought of reverence and morality—all that we call feeling—if we would right comprehend him; there is nothing harmonious with humanity to be found in this type of character." The "peculiarly" atavistic, immoral, and not quite human, ontological character of the African is then deployed as a rationale for her continued enslavement (or what Hegel euphemistically describes as a necessarily "gradual" emancipation), and for a conceptualization of the history-less quality of an entire continent: "Slavery is in and for itself injustice, for the essence of humanity is Freedom; but for this man must be matured. At this point we leave Africa, not to mention it again. For it is no historical part of the World; it has no movement or development to exhibit. Historical movements in it—that is in its northern part—belong to the Asiatic or European world. . . . What we properly understand by Africa, is the Unhistorical, Undeveloped Spirit, still involved in the conditions of mere nature, and which had to be presented here only as on the threshold of the World's History." Georg Wilhelm Friedrich Hegel, *Lectures on the Philosophy of History* (London: Bell, 1914), 97, 103. Again, our study, in keeping with Bob Kaufman's poetic deployment of the term "unhistory" (and in strident opposition to Hegel's racist fictional episteme), sites an infinite semantic opacity, counter-historical urgency, and epistemic complexity within the testimonies, soundings, writings, and political practices of "Unhistorical" slaves and neoslaves.

19. For the incarceration rate of young black males, see "One in 100: Behind Bars in America 2008," The Pew Center on the States, 6. As of this writing, one out of every three black men born in the United States can expect to be incarcerated at some point in their lives. "Report to the United National Human Rights Committee Regarding Racial Disparities in the United States Criminal Justice System," The Sentencing Project, August 2013, 1. This startling situation registers the degree to which the PIC operates as a regime of genocidal gendering for black men in the United States.

20. The term "chattel principle" derives from Walter Johnson, ed., *The Chattel Principle: Internal Slaves Trades in the Americas* (New Haven: Yale University Press, 2004).

21. Hartman, *Scenes of Subjection*. For my reading of the epistemic aspects of black neoslave sound, testimony, and political practice, I am indebted to Clyde Woods and his hugely important reading of the epistemological and political currents of black southern vernacular cultural praxis, or what he describes as an unaccounted-for "blues epistemology." Clyde Woods, *Development Arrested: The Blues and Plantation Power in the Mississippi Delta* (London: Verso, 2006).

22. Robert Pete Williams, "Prisoner's Talking Blues," Arhoolie CD 419 (arhoolie.com), Tradition Music Co. (BMI), administered by Bug Music c/o BMG Rights Management.

23. As the greatest modern interpreter of black prisoner folk/blues songs, Odetta Holmes once attempted to explain this often-ignored semantic complexity of neoslave sound after offering a version of "Prettiest Train," a slave work song that appears to be simply about a train going from Jackson, Mississippi, to New Orleans. With her eyes closed to the camera and shaking her head, the black folk/blues maestro states: "What does that song say . . . you say, 'What about that song that means so much to you?' And I, I don't know. There's simplicity of the words, it certainly wouldn't win a poet's prize or anything, but *there is something that is more than what the words are saying.* The words: It's almost like [the words are] an introduction to feelings that the words came out of." "The Last Word: Odetta," December 2, 2008, online video interview, *New York Times,* http://nytimes.com. For a discussion of the semantic opacity of black sound as expressed within Caribbean zones of enslavement, see Edouard Glissant, *Caribbean Discourse: Selected Essays* (Charlottesville, Va.: Caraf Books, 1999), 2, 120–33. For a further discussion of the opacity and counter-historical gravity of slave performative practice, see Hartman, *Scenes of Subjection,* 17–48. See also Nathaniel Mackey, "Cante Moro," in *Disembodied Poetics: Annals of the Jack Kerouac School* (Albuquerque : University of New Mexico Press, 1994), 71–94.

24. Hartman, *Scenes of Subjection,* 36.

25. I am indebted to Randall Williams for the term "counter-conjuration."

26. See John Lomax and Alan Lomax, *Negro Folk Songs as Sung by Lead Belly, "King of the Twelve-String Guitar Players of the World," Long-time Convict in the Penitentiaries of Texas and Louisiana* (New York: Macmillan, 1936), and Charles Wolfe and Kip Lornell, *The Life and Legend of Leadbelly* (New York: HarperCollins, 1992). For a visual example of the Lomaxes' racist exhibition of Lead Belly to northern white audiences, and the degree to which the white folkloric narrative of black vernacular "discovery" pastoralized the scene of neoslavery, see the *March of Time* newsreel, "Leadbelly," vol. 1, episode 2, March 8, 1935, http://www.time.com. As indicated in the newsreel, Lead Belly would end up working not only as an exotic musical showpiece for the Lomaxes but also as driver, cook, shoe-shine "boy," laundryman, and butler for a $1 per week "allowance," an exploitative and

dehumanizing servant positionality that limns the coercive dimensions of the Lomaxian folkloric method.

27. Hartman, *Scenes of Subjection,* 45.

28. William Goodell, *The American Slave Code* (New York: American and Foreign Anti-Slavery Society, 1853), 77 (italics in the original).

29. Sara Johnson, "'You Should Give them Blacks to Eat': Cuban Bloodhounds and the Waging of an Inter-American War of Torture and Terror," *American Quarterly* 61, no. 1 (March 2009): 65–92.

30. On the racial gothic ritual that involved the exchange of body parts of lynch victims, along with the overall machinations of extralegal lynching in the late nineteenth-century, see Ida B. Wells-Barnett, *On Lynchings: Southern Horrors, A Red Record, Mob Rule in New Orleans* (1895; reprint, New York: Arno Press, 1969). For a reading of the way in which extralegal lynching was systematically articulated into the practice of legal lynching, see James Clarke, "Without Fear or Shame: Lynching, Capital Punishment, and the Subculture of Violence in the American South," *British Journal of Political Science* 28, no. 2 (April 1998): 285–88.

31. Mike Ward, Cox News Service, *Savannah News-Press,* November 18, 1990.

32. While sexual terror functions as a quotidian and effectively sanctioned reality inside the prison, it also operates as fodder for public consumptive pleasure in the form of interminable comedic references to prison and jail rape in U.S. popular culture. See, for example, *Saturday Night Live,* "Scared Straight," Episode 3716, aired on NBC, March 3, 2012; *The Boondocks,* "A Date with the Health Inspector," Season 1, Episode 5, aired on Adult Swim/BET J, December 4, 2005; and the film *Let's Go to Prison,* Universal Pictures, 2006. One particularly horrifying scene in *Let's Go to Prison* focuses on the implied rape of an accidentally incarcerated upper-class white male by a black man. The film's trafficking in the perverse public enjoyment that has attached to rape in prisons and jails was also represented in its newspaper advertisement campaign whose primary image consisted of a bar of soap imprinted with the movie's galling four-word title. Indeed "don't drop the soap," a line referencing public fantasies in respect to rape in prison and jail shower stalls, represents a widely deployed comedic witticism meant to elicit easy laughs from the unimprisoned during their consensual consumption of television sketches, movies, and standup routines.

33. For a horrifying example of the imbricated nature of terroristic punishment and sadistic pleasure under modern chattelized imprisonment, see "Maximum Security University," California Prison Focus, 1997. This documentary consists of leaked surveillance footage from the Supermax unit at Corcoran, otherwise known as the Corcoran SHU (Security Housing Unit). The footage reveals the practice of prison administration–sponsored "gladiator" fights, whereby rival prisoners (who are kept in solitary confinement cells for twenty-three hours a day) are shown fighting in prison yards, four of whom are ultimately gunned down

with live 9mm rounds. The film points out how the prison's "integrated yard pol-icy" allowed guards to stage many of the fights at the prison by putting known rivals in the yard together, and how they also reaped perverse recreative pleasure from the gladiatorial spectacle by placing wagers on the fights they set up. As in the case of nearly every killing in California and U.S. prisons, and by police on the streets, state and federal courts determined that each of the five killings that occurred at the Corcoran SHU between 1989 and 1993 amounted to "justifiable homicide."

34. In her seminal work on the writings and political praxis of incarcerated intellectuals, Joy James employs the term "(neo)slave narrative" to signify both the writings and testimonies of political prisoners from the Movement Era to the prison–industrial complex, and the modes of neo-enslaving discourse executed by the "master state" via white supremacist legal, political, and social discourse. See Joy James, "Democracy and Captivity," Introduction to *The New Abolitionists: (Neo)Slave Narratives and Contemporary Prison Writings* (New York: State University of New York, 2005). I do want to clarify, however, that my use of the term "narrative of neoslavery" began with my engagement with the narrative poetics and carceral epistemics of George Jackson, who, in *Soledad Brother* (1971), offers a black Marxist theoretical articulation of the term "neoslavery" and a personal/ political expression of his own neo-enslavement as a black radical political pris-oner. As I will discuss in chapter 1, Jackson offers a multidimensional definition of the term that is inflected as much by the experience of chattelized imprisonment (via indefinite solitary confinement) as by his adoption of a Marxist understand-ing of the hyperexploited labor/social positionality of the black proletarian "wage slave." In what follows, I broaden the generic category of "(neo)slave narrative" as expressed by James and the theoretical articulation of the term "neoslavery" by Jackson to include the soundings, testimonies, and invisible epistemic/political practice of black neoslaves who have never been known as "intellectual" or "polit-ical" or "radical."

35. "Only that historian will have the gift of fanning the spark of hope in the past who is firmly convinced that *even the dead* will not be safe from the enemy if he wins. And this enemy has not ceased to be victorious." Benjamin, *Illuminations,* 255.

1. "You Ain't Seen Nothin' Yet"

1. "Prison and Jail Inmates, 1995," U.S. Department of Justice (DOJ) Statis-tics, August 1998, www.ojp.usdoj.gov/bjs/abstract/pji95.htm/.

2. North Carolina Department of Correction, press release, November 1, 1994, www.doc.state.nc.us/ NEWS/1996/96news/oldcages.htm/.

3. Ibid.

4. Alex Lichtenstein, *Twice the Work of Free Labor: The Political Economy of Convict Labor in the New South* (London: Verso, 1996), 185. See also David Oshinsky, *"Worse Than Slavery": Parchman Farm and the Ordeal of Justice* (New York: Simon and Schuster, 1996); Milfred Fierce, *Slavery Revisited: Blacks and the Convict Lease System, 1865–1933* (New York: City University of New York, 1994); Angela Y. Davis, "From the Prison of Slavery to the Slavery of Prison: Frederick Douglass and the Convict Lease System," in *The Angela Davis Reader*, 74–95, and Matthew J. Mancini, *One Dies, Get Another*.

5. Walter Wilson, *Forced Labor in the United States* (New York: International Publishers, 1933), 80.

6. Again, along with the fictional epistemics of Toni Morrison on the materiality of ghosts, my analysis of the political and social practice of haunting within zones of state terror draws inspiration from Avery Gordon's incisive work, *Ghostly Matters*, a work that also offers a provocative reading of spectral practice in *Beloved*.

7. I am indebted to Dylan Rodríguez for helping me to conceive of the degree to which *Beloved* elaborates a black diasporic counter to prevailing modes of U.S. and European penology that elide the centrality of race in the construction of modern carcerality (namely, in treating of the modern prison as a reformatory and progressive institution), and that completely invisibilize the Middle Passage as a primal source of modern carcerality.

8. The Security Housing Unit, or "SHU," refers to prisons or sections of prisons wherein individuals are subjected to twenty-three-plus hours a day of solitary confinement in six-by-eight-foot cells that often have "boxcar"-style windowless steel doors designed for total sensory deprivation. For more on the use of isolation as a technique in modern racialized punishment, see Dylan Rodríguez, *Forced Passages: Imprisoned Radical Intellectuals and the U.S. Prison Regime* (Minneapolis: University of Minnesota Press, 2006), 223–56. See also George Jackson, *Soledad Brother: The Prison Letters of George Jackson* (Chicago: Lawrence Hill Books, 1994), 233; Melvin Farmer, *The New Slave Ship* (Los Angeles: Milligan Books, 1998).

9. This book has been influenced by Ruth Wilson Gilmore's brilliant analysis in *Golden Gulag*. I take issue, however, with Gilmore's attempted refutation of the argument that the prison–industrial complex (PIC) represents an extension and reconfiguration of slavery. For her, that most of those entombed within the modern penitentiary are not actually producing goods for corporations registers the insufficiency of the "new slavery argument" (20–21). In my estimation, the mass human warehousing of today's PIC is a direct analogue of the cargoing of human beings that took place during chattel slavery. That those who are subjected to the civil death of imprisonment are not performing labor for the open market, at least not on a large scale, in no way diminishes the reality that they serve as *human commodities* for a multibillion-dollar punishment industry. The object of human commodification in today's neoslavery is therefore not the neoslaves' *labor* but

their warehoused *bodies* and the nexus of profitability resulting from their natal alienation and civil/living death. As Steven Dozinger explains, companies that "service the criminal justice system need sufficient quantities of raw materials to guarantee long term growth. . . . In the criminal justice field *the raw material is prisoners,* and industry will do what is necessary to guarantee a steady supply." Angela Y. Davis, *Are Prisons Obsolete?* (New York: Seven Stories Press, 2003), 94. For incarceration rates of young black males, see "One in 100: Behind Bars in America 2008," The Pew Center on the States, 6.

10. For critical assessments of pre-1865 oriented neoslave narratives, see Bernard Bell, *The Afro-American Novel and Its Tradition* (Amherst: University of Massachusetts Press, 1987); Ashraf Rushdy, *Neo-slave Narratives: Studies in the Social Logic of a Literary Form* (Oxford: Oxford University Press, 1999); Caroline Rody, *The Daughter's Return: African-American and Caribbean Women's Fictions of History* (Oxford: Oxford University Press, 2001); Angelyn Mitchell, *The Freedom to Remember: Narrative, Slavery, and Gender in Contemporary Black Women's Fiction* (New Brunswick: Rutgers University Press, 2002); and Arlene Keizer, *Black Subjects: Identity Formation in the Contemporary Narrative of Slavery* (Ithaca: Cornell University Press, 2004).

11. Joy James offers a similar resignification of the generic category of the "neo-slave narrative" in her work on U.S. imprisoned intellectualism and neo-abolitionism. See Joy James, "Democracy and Captivity," Introduction to *The New Abolitionists: (Neo)Slave Narratives and Contemporary Prison Writings* (New York: State University of New York Press, 2005). For James, the (neo)slave narrative represents a category inclusive of works produced by prison slaves and the modes of repressive storytelling produced by the "master state" via white supremacist misogynist law. In what follows, I expand upon James's critically important intervention by including the neoslavery writings, testimonies, soundings, and political practices of neo-slaves ranging back to 1865—that is, those black neo-slaves whose formations of cultural, political, and performative redress have been largely disqualified from historiographic view but that represented the foundation for later neo-abolitionism.

12. Rodríguez, *Forced Passages,* 239.

13. Robert Broad, "Giving Blood to the Scraps, Haints, History, and Hosea in *Beloved,*" *African American Review* 28, no. 2 (Summer 1994): 189–97.

14. Toni Morrison, *Beloved* (New York: Plume, 1987), 210–11.

15. Daniel Mannix, *Black Cargoes: A History of the Atlantic Slave Trade* (New York: Viking, 1962), 106.

16. Ibid., 106–7.

17. Joseph Inikori and Stanley Engerman, eds., *The Atlantic Slave Trade: Effects on Economies, Societies, and Peoples in Africa, the Americas, and Europe* (Durham: Duke University Press, 1992); Walter Rodney, *How Europe Underdeveloped Africa*

(Washington, D.C.: Howard University, 1982); Saidiya Hartman, *Scenes of Subjection: Terror, Slavery, and Self-Making in Nineteenth-Century America* (Oxford: Oxford University Press, 1997), 225; Stephanie Smallwood, *Saltwater Slavery: A Middle Passage from Africa to American Diaspora* (Cambridge: Harvard University Press, 2007), 150–51; Rodríguez, *Forced Passages*, 233.

18. See also Rodríguez, *Forced Passages*, 234–37.

19. Morrison, *Beloved*, 200.

20. Colin Dayan, "Legal Slaves and Civil Bodies," in *Materializing Democracy*, ed. Russ Castronovo and Dana Nelson (Durham: Duke University Press, 2002), 69.

21. Rodríguez, *Forced Passages*, 233–37. See Sylvia Wynter, "On Disenchanting Discourse: 'Minority' Literary Criticism and Beyond," in *The Nature and Context of Minority Discourse*, ed. Abdul JanMohamed and David Lloyd (Oxford: Oxford University Press, 1990), 439–48.

22. Hartman, *Scenes of Subjection*, 17–48. I am indebted to Saidiya Hartman for first drawing my attention to the way in which black existence vis-à-vis the racist productions of history, knowledge, and law most often amount to a process of collectivized *disqualification*. See also Michel Foucault, *"Society Must be Defended": Lectures at the Collège de France, 1975–1976* (New York: Picador, 2003), 77.

23. Wynter, "On Disenchanting Discourse," 446–47; see Cedric Robinson, *Black Marxism: The Making of the Black Radical Tradition* (Chapel Hill: University of North Carolina Press, 2000).

24. Sylvia Wynter, keynote address at "The State and Soul of Jamaica" conference, University of California, Berkeley, March 31, 1993.

25. Hartman, *Scenes of Subjection*, 17–48, 140–45.

26. George Frances Dow, *Slave Ships and Slaving* (Cambridge, Md.: Cornell Maritime Press, 1968), xix.

27. Hartman, *Scenes of Subjection*, 36.

28. Mbembe, "Necropolitics."

29. Louis Althusser, "Ideology and Ideological State Apparatus (Notes Towards an Investigation)," in *Lenin and Philosophy* (New York: Monthly Review Press, 1971).

30. Morrison, *Beloved*, 29.

31. Smallwood, *Saltwater Slavery*, 125, 135.

32. Morrison, *Beloved*, 106.

33. Ibid., 107.

34. Ibid., 105.

35. See, for example, David Lawrence, "Fleshy Ghosts and Ghostly Flesh: The Word and the Body in *Beloved*," in *Toni Morrison's Fiction: Contemporary Criticism*, ed. David Middleton (New York: Garland, 1996), 231–46.

36. Morrison, *Beloved*, 211–12.

37. Ibid., 39.

38. The interconnected spatial and racial frameworks of the slave ship, the plantation, and the chain gang are also registered by Paul D and his fellow chain-gang captives' experience of sexual violence and rape—central techniques of (neo)slavery, sadism, and punishment that are also central to today's prison–industrial complex.

39. See also Avery Gordon, *Ghostly Matters: Haunting and the Sociological Imagination* (Minneapolis: University of Minnesota Press, 1996).

40. As stated above, Justice J. Christian asserted the idea that as a "slave of the state" the prison laborer had no constitutionally protected rights and was consequently *"civiliter mortuus,"* that is, civilly dead. *Ruffin v. Commonwealth* 62 VA 790 (1871): 795–96.

41. Morrison, *Beloved*, 41.

42. Walter Wilson, "Chain Gangs and Profit," *Harper's*, April 1933, 539–40.

43. For a photo documentation of the chain-gang cage and other aspects of the prison slavery, see John Spivak's muckraking novel *Georgia Nigger* (1932; reprint, Montclair, N.J.: Patterson Smith, 1969). See also W. E. B. Du Bois, *Black Reconstruction in America, 1860–1880* (1935; New York: Atheneum, 1992), 698.

44. See Du Bois, *Black Reconstruction in America,* 698, and Spivak, *Georgia Nigger.*

45. Giorgio Agamben, *Homo Sacer: Sovereign Power and Bare Life,* trans. Daniel Heller-Roazen (Stanford: Stanford University Press, 1998), 166.

46. Ibid., 159.

47. Ibid.

48. Ibid., 20.

49. Aimé Césaire, *Discourse on Colonialism*, trans. Joan Pinkham (London: Monthly Review Press, 1972); Frantz Fanon, *The Wretched of the Earth* (New York: Grove Press, 1991); Ward Churchill, *A Little Matter of Genocide: Holocaust Denial in the Americas, 1492 to the Present* (San Francisco: City Lights, 1997); Hannah Arendt, *The Origins of Totalitarianism* (New York: Harcourt Brace Jovanovich, 1973); Mbembe, "Necropolitics."

50. Mbembe, "Necropolitics," 17, 23.

51. Joy James, "Erasing the Spectacle of State Violence," in *Resisting State Violence: Radicalism, Gender, and Race in U.S. Culture* (Minneapolis: University of Minnesota Press, 1996), 24–43. See also Angela Y. Davis, "Racialized Punishment and Prison Abolition," in *The Angela Davis Reader,* ed. Joy James (Malden, Mass.: Blackwell, 1998), 99. Michel Foucault, *Discipline and Punish,* trans. Alan Sheridan (New York: Vintage Books, 1979), 263.

52. Foucault, *Discipline and Punish,* 263–64.

53. Robinson, *Black Marxism,* 239.

54. Oshinsky adds that, in 1882, "126 of 735 black state convicts perished, as opposed to 2 of 83 whites. Not a single leased convict ever lived long enough to

serve a sentence of ten years or more." In 1870, Alabama officials "reported that more than 40 percent of their convicts had died, prompting a doctor to warn that if the trend continued, the entire convict population would be wiped out within three years." Oshinsky, "*Worse Than Slavery,*" 46, 79.

55. Morrison, *Beloved,* 110.

56. For analysis of the *arwhoolie,* see Sterling Brown, "Folk Literature" (1941), in *A Son's Return: Selected Essays of Sterling A. Brown,* ed. Mark A. Sanders (Boston: Northeastern University Press, 1996), 221–22; and Amiri Baraka [LeRoi Jones], *Blues People* (New York: Morrow Quill, 1963), 67–68.

57. Morrison, *Beloved,* 109.

58. Amílcar Cabral, "Tell No Lies, Claim No Easy Victories," in *Revolution in Guinea: Selected Texts* (New York: Monthly Review Press, 1972), 86.

59. Hartman, *Scenes of Subjection,* 61–78. See Sylvia Wynter, "On Disenchanting Discourse: 'Minority' Literary Criticism and Beyond," in *The Nature and Context of Minority Discourse,* ed. Abdul JanMohamed and David Lloyd (Oxford: Oxford University Press, 1990), 443–57; and Rodríguez, *Forced Passages,* 75–144.

60. For a discussion of anticolonial renderings of the zombie figure within Caribbean literature, see Lizabeth Paravisini-Gebert, "Colonial and Post-Colonial Gothic: The Caribbean," in *The Cambridge Companion to Gothic Fiction* (Cambridge: Cambridge University Press, 2002), 248–53.

61. Morrison, *Beloved,* 273.

62. Joy James, "American 'Prison Notebooks,'" *Race & Class* 45, no. 3 (2004): 35–44. See also James, *Imprisoned Intellectuals: America's Political Prisoners Write on Life, Liberation, and Rebellion* (Lanham, Md.: Rowman and Littlefield, 2003); and Rodríguez, *Forced Passages.*

63. For a further articulation of the wage- and no-wage "neoslave" predicament of black people, and especially black women, after 1865, see Jacqueline Jones, *Labor of Love, Labor of Sorrow: Black Women and the Family, from Slavery to the Present* (New York: Vintage Books, 1985), 153.

64. Jackson, *Soledad Brother,* 234.

65. The indefinite quarantining of political prisoners such as Jackson functioned as a testing ground for today's supermaximum-security prisons and special housing units. The trend of converting either a section or an entire prison into a "lockdown" zone wherein prisoners spend 23.5 or more hours a day in solitary confinement had its methodological beginning at Marion Prison, Illinois, in 1981.

66. Dayan, "Legal Slaves and Civil Bodies," 69.

67. Césaire, *Discourse on Colonialism.*

68. Benjamin, "Theses on the Philosophy of History," 257.

69. Wynter, "On Disenchanting Discourse."

70. Alex Lichtenstein, "Good Roads and Chain Gangs in the Progressive South: 'The Negro Convict Is a Slave,'" *Journal of Southern History* 59, no. 1 (February 1993): 85–110.

71. Smallwood, *Saltwater Slavery*, 207.

72. *Westbrook v. The State*, 133 GA 578 (1909).

73. Ibid., 578, 579.

74. Ibid., 582.

75. Ibid., 585.

2. "Except as Punishment for a Crime"

1. The transcription of the advertisement for the courthouse auctioning of John Johnson, Gassaway Price, Harriet Purdy, and Dilly Harris is taken from *The Annapolis Gazette*, December 20, 1866, 2. The notice for the sale of Richard Harris is from an unpublished transcript of a hearing of the House Judiciary Committee, "Sale of Negroes in Maryland," January 11, 1867, 6. See also a speech delivered by Charles Sumner, "Sale of Persons Into Slavery," Senate Debates, January 3, 1867, Congressional Globe, 39th Cong., 2nd sess., 238. I am indebted to Ervin Goodson for my initial introduction to the existence of such "post" slavery prison slave advertisements (unpublished manuscript). I am equally indebted to Robyn Spencer for sharing this manuscript with me during our residency at the Schomburg Center for Research in Black Culture, Harlem, New York, in 2011. Colin Dayan also discusses the auctionings of Purdy and Harris in the context of the congressional debates on the exception clause in *The Law Is a White Dog: How Legal Rituals Make and Unmake Persons* (Princeton: Princeton University Press, 2011), 62–63.

Unreported in congressional discussions of the Maryland auctions was the level to which state officials such as sheriffs, county clerk, lawyers, and judges stood to collect a commission from the sale or lease of every black body convicted of petty offenses. As I will discuss in reference to criminal-surety and convict leasing, the large-scale leasing, subleasing, and possession of "free" black bodies through criminal sanction under racial apartheid underlines the degree to which neoslavery is a system of both private and public profit making. Importantly, the postbellum public profiteering on the incarceration and sale of black bodies actually has its roots in antebellum slavery. As Thomas Russell points out, a large percentage of slave auctions in the antebellum South were conducted by the state at courthouses, with public officials collecting major profits from the fees and commissions associated with the auctioning of slaves and free black people convicted of crimes. He observes that "the central role of the courts in the conduct of slave sales" belies the commonly held view of "slavery as taking place within a realm of purely private ordering." "Slave Auctions on the Courthouse Steps: Court Sales of Slaves in Antebellum South Carolina," in *Slavery and the Law*, ed. Paul Finkleman (Lanham, Md.: Rowman and Littlefield, 2002), 330. The practice of auctioning prisoners to private parties in the United States can be traced as far back as the

Colonial period, when the process was applied to both black and white subjects. Rebecca McLennan, *The Crisis of Imprisonment* (New York: Cambridge University, 2008), 30–31. According to McLennan, the original legal ritual of selling prisoners "for a slave" remained on the statute books in states such as Massachusetts and Maryland until as late as 1786. However, as the postbellum advertisements for the sale of criminalized free black people in Maryland nearly a century later make clear, blackness functions as the condition of possibility for the resuscitation *and intensification* of ostensibly obsolete punitive and dominative methodologies.

2. Anne Arundel County, Maryland, Circuit Court Docket, October Term, 1866, "Presentments" and "Criminal Appearances," 280, 282, 318, Maryland State Archives; "Sale of Negroes in Maryland," 9. For further discussion of the auctioning of Purdy and Harris, see Dayan, *The Law Is a White Dog*, 62.

3. "This is how one pictures the angel of history," Walter Benjamin writes, his "face is turned to the past. Where we perceive a chain of events, he sees one single catastrophe which keeps piling wreckage upon wreckage and hurls it in front of his feet. The angel would like to stay, awaken the dead, and make whole what has been smashed. But a storm is blowing from Paradise; it has got caught in his wings with such violence that the angel can no longer lose them. This . . . storm is what we call progress." "Theses on the Philosophy of History," in *Illuminations* (New York: Schocken Books, 1969), 258–59. Saidiya Hartman offers a reverb of this conception of modernity as an accretion of progressive "wreckage" in *Lose Your Mother*, 86, 181.

4. James, "Democracy and Captivity," xxiv. For an illuminating discussion of the violent narrativity of the law vis-à-vis its crafting of the civilly dead, see Dayan, "Legal Slaves and Civil Bodies."

5. While the number of "free Negroes" was 8,043, or 7.2 percent of the total African population in Maryland in 1790, their number increased to 33,927 by 1810, which equated to 23 percent of the total black population. By the eve of the Civil War, the number of free black people had effectively equaled the number of slaves in the state. James Wright, *The Free Negro in Maryland* (New York: Columbia University Press, 1921), 36–37.

6. Alexis de Tocqueville and Gustave de Beaumont took note of the large number of "free Negroes" held captive in Maryland's penitentiary during their tour of U.S. prisons in 1831. For them the large population of free black people explained the apparent demographic contradiction of a state featuring a high rate of imprisonment in spite of its large population of "settled" whites (as opposed to "unenlightened" recent European immigrants). "The states which have many Negroes must . . . produce more crimes. This reason alone would be sufficient to explain the large number of crimes in Maryland: it is, however, not applicable to all the states of the South; but only to those in which manumission is permitted: because we should deceive ourselves greatly were we to believe that the crimes of the

Negroes are avoided by giving them liberty; experience proves, on the contrary, that in the South the number of criminals increase with that of manumitted persons; thus, for the very reason that slavery seems to draw nearer to its ruin, the number of freed persons will increase for a long time in the South, and with it the number of criminals." They go on to argue that, the "freed person commits more crimes than the slave, for a simple reason; because, becoming emancipated, he has to provide for himself, which during his bondage, he was not obliged to do. Brought up in ignorance and brutality, he was accustomed to work like a machine. . . . The day when liberty is granted to him, he receives an instrument, which he does not know how to use, and with which he wounds, if not kills himself." Gustave de Beaumont and Alexis de Tocqueville, *On the Penitentiary System in the United States and Its Application in France* (Carbondale: Southern Illinois University Press, 1964), 93, 210. The liberal penal reformers espoused a prototypical version of the occidental consensus that read the existence of a free black body as a priori evidence of an incorrigible black body, a position that reflected the occult white supremacist social logic that somehow managed to disassociate the "crimes" of the emancipated "Negro" from the wholesale legal criminality and atrocity of hundreds of years of enslavement and their postbellum reconfiguration in de jure and customary forms of economic dispossession, state repression, and social apartheid. Hartman, *Scenes of Subjection,* 125–63.

7. *Laws of Maryland,* 1858, chapter 324.

8. Leon Litwack, *North of Slavery: The Negro in the Free States, 1790–1860* (Chicago: University of Chicago Press, 1961), 64–112. For an example of the northern version of the public auctioning of criminally branded free black subjects according to racially restrictionist statutes, see *Nelson (a mulatto) v. The People of the State of Illinois,* 33 Ill. 390 (1864). This Illinois State Supreme Court case involved an appeal issued by an apparently multiracial subject named "Nelson" (for whom the racist moniker "mulatto" takes the place of a surname) against a lower court decision that had upheld his arrest and scheduled public courthouse auctioning for his violation of a state law banning the immigration of "negroes and mulattos" into the state. According to the Act of 1853, any such black person who entered Illinois after the law's passage was subject to arrest and an assessment of a fine, the nonpayment of which called for the justice of the peace "to commit the negro or mulatto to the custody of the sheriff . . . and the justice of the peace is required forwith to advertise the negro or mulatto, by posting up notices in at least three of the most public places in his district. . . . [T]he justice shall, at public auction, proceed to sell such negro or mulatto to any person who will pay the fine and costs for the shortest period." The lower court's ruling was upheld and "Nelson" was thereby ordered sold as what the court euphemistically termed an "apprentice." As I will discuss, this statute, the Maryland Negro/Slave Code mentioned above, and others of the same sort in both southern and northern states prefigured the

system of "criminal-surety" in the postbellum South, a statutory configuration that led to the courthouse leasing of an untold number of black misdemeanants, and that was one of the main driving forces of the system of publicly administered social incarceration known as "peonage."

9. *Laws of Maryland,* 1858, chapter 324.

10. *Congressional Globe,* 39th Cong., 2nd sess., 239.

11. According to David Oshinsky, Mississippi's implementation of the "Pig Law" was a central component of a nearly 500 percent increase in state prisoners from 1874 to 1877 (from a total of 272 to 1,072). Oshinsky, *"Worse Than Slavery,"* 40–41.

12. Carl Schurz, *Report on the Condition of the South,* 39th Cong., 1st sess., Senate Ex. Doc. No. 2, December 1865.

13. *Report of the Joint Committee on Reconstruction at the First Session, 39th Congress* (Washington, D.C.: Government Printing Office, 1866), 67.

14. Assata Shakur offers one of the first direct articulations of the reenslaving potentiality of the exception clause produced by a black prisoner in narrative form in her black liberationist autobiography, *Assata,* 64–65. For historical and critical accounts that make specific mention of the exception clause, see Angela Y. Davis, "From the Prison of Slavery to the Slavery of Prison," in *The Angela Y. Davis Reader,* 78; Dayan, "Legal Slaves and Civil Bodies," 70; James, "Democracy and Captivity," xxi–xxiv; Lichtenstein, *Twice the Work of Free Labor,* 17, 187; Rodríguez, *Forced Passages,* 17, 36; McLennan, *The Crisis of Imprisonment,* 85; Douglas Blackmon, *Slavery by Another Name,* 53. For one exception to the general cursory treatment of the punishment clause within legal studies, see Scott Howe's brilliant work, "Slavery as Punishment: Original Public Meaning, Cruel and Unusual Punishment, and the Neglected Clause in the Thirteenth Amendment," 51 *Arizona Law Review* 983 (2009). For one of the more substantive legislative histories of the Thirteenth Amendment and exception clause, see Barbara Esposito and Lee Wood, *Prison Slavery* (Silver Spring, Md.: Joel Lithographic, 1982), 92–100.

15. For an excellent discussion of this history of legal hermeneutic expansion and contraction relative to the amendment's prohibition on involuntary servitude, see Risa Goluboff, "The Thirteenth Amendment and the Lost Origins of Civil Rights," 50 *Duke Law Journal* 1609 (2001): 1637–40. See also Benno Schmidt, "Principle and Prejudice: The Supreme Court and Race in the Progressive Era," 82 *Columbia Law Review* 646 (1982), and Daniel, *The Shadow of Slavery.* While Goluboff offers an important account of this history from the late nineteenth century to the New Deal, she makes no mention of the way in which the exception clause normalized involuntary servitude, or prison slavery, even in those decisions that are ostensibly expansive and progressive relative to the Thirteenth Amendment's prohibitive dimensions. The enshrinement of public (or "normal") involuntary servitude in the peonage cases exemplifies the intersections of liberal legality

and white supremacist juridical, legislative, and penal practice. Some legal studies that do mention the punitive exception ultimately end up making the problematic attempt to recuperate the Thirteenth Amendment as a redressive tool for a rights-based approach to the situation of prisoners. See Kamal Ghali, "No Slavery Except as Punishment for a Crime: The Punishment Clause and Sexual Slavery," 55 *UCLA Law Review* 607 (2008), and Raja Raghunath, "A Promise the Nation Cannot Keep: What Prevents the Application of the Thirteenth Amendment in Prison?" *William and Mary Bill of Rights Journal* 18 (2009): 395. For legal studies that read against the grain of this rights-based approach, and that engage with the violence produced by the state's wielding of the exception clause, see Howe, "Slavery as Punishment"; and Dayan, "Legal Slaves and Civil Bodies," 70. See also Kim Shayo Buchanan, "Impunity: Sexual Abuse in Women's Prisons," *Harvard Civil Rights–Civil Liberties Law Review* 42 (2007): 59.

For examples of treatments of the Thirteenth Amendment that posit a relatively uncritical acceptance of the legislation's emancipatory legacy, see Alexander Tsesis, *The Thirteenth Amendment and American Freedom* (New York: New York University Press, 2004); Michael Voreberg, *Final Freedom: The Civil War, the Abolition of Slavery, and the Thirteenth Amendment* (New York: Cambridge University Press, 2001); and George H. Hoemann, *What God Hath Wrought: The Embodiment of Freedom in the Thirteenth Amendment* (New York: Garland, 1987).

16. In the majority opinion for the *Civil Rights Cases,* Bradley asserted that the practice of segregation in public conveyances, places of amusement, and accommodation did not represent a "badge" or "incident" of slavery, thereby finding the two sections of the Civil Rights Act of 1875 that offered redress for such forms of segregation to be unconstitutional. For the court, the argument that social apartheid issued directly from relations of mastery and servitude amounted to "running the slavery argument into the ground." 109 U.S. 3 (1883), 844. This circumscription of the meaning of chattel slavery and the prohibitive power of the Thirteenth Amendment was coupled with an equally damaging restriction of the Fourteenth Amendment. As Hartman argues, the court concerned itself with erecting a cordon between the public and the private (or social), claiming that the Fourteenth Amendment only offered black people avenues of redress against "public" or state-administered violence. She points out the fraudulence of the law's claims to a hands-off relationship with the private sphere, given that the state was fundamentally involved in policing and reproducing social apartheid even on the minutest scale, a fact exemplified most clearly by the public policing of the transits of "Negro" blood via antimiscegenation law. Hartman, *Scenes of Subjection,* 164–206. As I will discuss, however, the juridical and legislative deployment of the exception clause underlines the degree to which the law's protective cloaking of private formations of racial dominance was coupled with its enforcement of the divine right of the state to submit the black body to public formations of terror

and neo-enslavement—a sovereign prerogative reinforced under the cover of prohibitions against specific instances of "private" involuntary servitude.

17. Based on Thomas Jefferson's "Land Ordinance of 1784," the Northwest Ordinance represented the legal establishment of the Northwest Territory. A central aspect of the compact between the states and those white subjects residing north and west of the Ohio River was an ostensible ban against slavery in the region contained in Article Six: "There shall be neither slavery nor involuntary servitude in the said territory, otherwise than in the punishment of crimes whereof the party shall have been duly convicted: Provided, always, That any person escaping into the same, from whom labor or service is lawfully claimed in any one of the original States, such fugitive may be lawfully reclaimed and conveyed to the person claiming his or her labor or service as aforesaid." http://www.early-america.com. Like the Thirteenth Amendment itself, Jefferson's Ordinance supplied a legal mechanism for reenslavement by way of criminal sanction along with the additional chattelizing method of a fugitive slave provision. The backdoor allowance of slavery within the document was not merely a matter of rhetorical violence. For instance, through the "Black Laws" in Illinois, the enslavement of Africans would continue under the euphemistic title of "Negro Indenture" until as late as 1865. The de jure chattel status of nominally liberated blackness was affirmed in *Nance, a colored girl v. John Howard,* in which the Illinois Supreme Court found that "negro and mulatto" servants "are goods and chattels, and can be sold on execution." 1 Ill. 242 (1828): 246. See Elmer Gertz, "The Black Laws of Illinois," *Journal of the Illinois State Historical Society* 56 (Autumn 1963): 454–73.

18. *Congressional Globe,* 38th Cong., 1st sess., 1488.

19. Hartman, *Lose Your Mother,* 145–46.

20. *Congressional Globe,* 39th Cong., 2nd sess., 238.

21. Ibid., 344. The apparent confidence that Sumner and Kasson exhibited regarding the intentions of their fellow members of the Senate and House who were involved in the crafting of the Thirteenth Amendment was grossly misplaced. Comments of Senator Reverdy Johnson (Md.), former U.S. attorney general (and council for John Sanford in *Dred Scott v. Sanford* [1857]), in response to Sumner's above-mentioned speech reveal that there were likely more than a "few" members of the legislative branch who held a dramatically different understanding of the purpose and intention of the Thirteenth Amendment, and whether it placed any sort of proscription on the sale and enslavement of prisoners: "I doubt whether the evil, if it be an evil, can be corrected. Maryland has abolished slavery . . . but the question of whether the abolition of slavery deprives a State of the power of punishing, by a sale of his services, a criminal is quite another inquiry. The constitutional amendment of the United States seems to suppose that there may be slavery or involuntary servitude for crime." *Congressional Globe,* 39th Cong., 2nd sess., 238.

22. Esposito and Wood, *Prison Slavery,* 80.

23. *Congressional Globe,* 39th Cong., 2nd sess., 344–45.

24. Thorsten Sellin, *Slavery and the Penal System* (New York: Elsevier Scientific Publishing Company, 1976); A. Davis, "From the Prison of Slavery to the Slavery of Prison"; Dayan, "Legal Slaves and Civil Bodies"; Esposito and Wood, *Prison Slavery;* David Brion Davis, *The Problem of Slavery in the Age of Revolution* (New York: Oxford University Press, 1999), 453–68; Orlando Patterson, *Slavery and Social Death* (Cambridge: Harvard University Press, 1982), 44–45, 128–29; Howe, "Slavery as Punishment"; Rodríguez, *Forced Passages;* Lichtenstein, *Twice the Work of Free Labor,* 1–36, 8–80, 110–68; Adam Hirsch, *The Rise and Fall of the Penitentiary* (New Haven: Yale University Press, 1992), 71–111. Although Hirsch supplies a great deal of informative details in respect to the teleological connections of the two systems, he quizzically concludes that the noble intentions of penal reformers in respect to "criminals" marked the prison system as substantively distinct from the plantation system (110). The restriction of the social relations of mastery and servitude to a matter of individual intent negates the structural functionalities of both chattel and penal slavery and the material nature of white supremacist state practice.

25. Howe, "Slavery as Punishment," 993.

26. Cesare Beccaria, *On Crimes and Punishments* (Cambridge: Cambridge University Press, 2000), 69.

27. Ibid., 67.

28. W. W. Buckland, *The Roman Law of Slavery* (Cambridge: Cambridge University Press, 1970), 277–78. See also Sellin, *Slavery and the Penal System,* 27–29.

29. David Brion Davis, *The Problem of Slavery in the Age of Revolution,* 453–68; Hartman, *Scenes of Subjection,* 138.

30. David Brion Davis, *The Problem of Slavery in the Age of Revolution,* 456.

31. Jeremy Bentham, *The Rationale of Punishment* (London: Robert Heward, 1830), 165.

32. That the civil stigmatization of imprisonment became imagined as a degrading parody of the racial stigmatization of enslavement within the English public imagination is no surprise given the degree to which this association was rehearsed within the violent metaphorics of the law. Colin Dayan unearths the legal dimensions of the dynamic interface of civil and social death by calling upon Blackstone's description of the metaphysical degradation that attended felony conviction in his *Commentaries on the Laws of England:* "For when it is now clear beyond dispute, that the criminal is no longer fit to live upon the earth, but is to be exterminated as a monster and a bane to society, the law sets a mark of infamy upon him, puts him out of its protection, and takes no further care of him barely to see him executed. He is then called attaint, *attinctus,* stained or blackened" (emphasis in original). She argues that "civil death, the blood 'tainted' by crime, set the stage

for blood 'tainted' by natural inferiority. This discrimination would produce the nonexistence of the person not only in the West Indies but in the United States." Colin Dayan, "Legal Slaves and Civil Bodies," 59.

33. Beaumont and Tocqueville, *On the Penitentiary System in the United States,* 162–63.

34. Bentham, *The Rationale of Punishment,* 82.

35. As Angela Davis observes, "In the philosophical tradition of the penitentiary, labor was a reforming activity. It was supposed to assist the imprisoned individual in his (and on occasion her) putative quest for religious penitence and moral reeducation. Labor was a means to a moral end. In the case of slavery, labor was the only thing that mattered: the individual slaves were constructed essentially as labor units. Thus punishment was designed to maximize labor. And in a larger sense, labor was punishment attached not to crime, but to race." In "Racialized Punishment and Prison Abolition," *The Angela Y. Davis Reader,* 99. Again, this labor-unit philosophy of chattel carcerality was premised on the interested white supremacist fables of black incorrigibility, unproductivity, atavism, and acclimated servility.

36. For histories of the overall profit-centered system of contracted prison labor in the northern and western United States, see Scott Christianson, *With Liberty for Some* (Boston: Northeastern University Press, 1998); Mark Colvin, *Penitentiaries, Reformatories, and Chain Gangs* (New York: St. Martin's Press, 1997), 1–128; Rebecca M. McLennan, *The Crisis of Imprisonment: Protest, Politics, and the Making of the American Penal State, 1776–1941* (Cambridge: Cambridge University Press, 2008). Unfortunately, in her admirable determination to dispel the treatment of profit-centered imprisonment as an exceptionally southern phenomenon, McLennan commits an equally troubling error by eliding the specificity of punishment in the United States against racialized bodies. This occlusion of the centrality of race in U.S. carceral formations allows her to argue that "American penitentiaries . . . constituted a separate and distinct species of involuntary servitude, and not one usefully confounded with chattel slavery" (9). Her conclusion rests on a complete disregard of the specific operation of white supremacy in both southern and northern formations of imprisonment, and a myopic construal of enslavement as strictly a mode of unfree labor rather than a system of racial capitalist domination that continued to be fundamental to black life and death after 1865. See Wynter, "On Disenchanting Discourse"; Robinson, *Black Marxism*; Fanon, *The Wretched of the Earth*; Jackson, *Soledad Brother,* 233. A focus on the chattelized operation of imprisonment across the fictive historical borders proffered by the racial prison state is not dependent on a "confounding" of slavery and imprisonment, but a recognition that the two systems cannot be "usefully" separated in a material or historical sense when viewed from the perspective of bodies marked as both "Negro" and "criminal" under U.S. racial apartheid.

37. Hartman, *Scenes of Subjection*, 164–206. For further discussion of the unviability of categorical distinctions between the public and private, or the state and civil society, see Antonio Gramsci, *Selections from the Prison Notebooks* (New York: International Publishers, 1999), 206–75, and Althusser, "Ideology and Ideological State Apparatuses," 97.

38. The Committee on the Judiciary recommended the "indefinite postponement of the bill (H. R. No. 956) to enforce the thirteenth amendment of the Constitution of the United States." The committee added: "We think the whole subject is covered by the civil rights bill." *Congressional Globe*, 39th Cong., 2nd sess., 1866. Congress would not issue clear-cut statutory enforcement of the Thirteenth Amendment until the early 1950s. See Goluboff, "The Thirteenth Amendment and the Lost Origins of Civil Rights," and Blackmon, *Slavery by Another Name*, 381. While the Department of Justice prosecuted cases that conformed to the narrow definition of peonage offered in *Clyatt* from the early 1900s to World War II—that is, those in which the "basal fact [of] debt was involved—it discarded hundreds of cases presented by black subjects who "only" complained of being enslaved, raped, beaten, and kidnapped without any mention of debt. This federal allowance of neoslavery is given haunting resonance in a letter addressed to Franklin D. Roosevelt by a black woman named Ellen McAllister in 1938, who sought the release of her brother from a Georgia sugarcane camp: "Mr. Roosevelt, Dear Sir.—I have a brother in Aualdia Georgia, he has been there for twelve years and they are working him as a Slave he wants to come home and wants me to help him they don't give him anything but what he eat and what he wear he hasn't done anything. but they are holding him there. . . . The way they gets men in to this place they tells them that they will pay them so much a day or month when they get them in there they don't give them any thing but what they get to eat or wear and don't let them write to their people unless they slip and write." She continues by saying that when her brother tried to escape, the armed plantation guards "liked to beat him to death." Roosevelt's assistant attorney general, Brian McMahon, responded to McAllister's plea for redress by stating: "The statements in your letter have been considered, but it is not clear that your complaint is one falling within the jurisdiction of the Federal Government. The Federal statute deals with holding a person in servitude on account of indebtedness. If you have any additional facts indicating that your brother has been held in involuntary servitude on account of indebtedness, it is suggested that you present the same to the U.S. attorney at Memphis, Tennessee, for his consideration." Letter from Ellen McAllister to Franklin D. Roosevelt (March 7, 1938), and official response (March 26, 1938), in *The Peonage Files of the U.S. Department of Justice, 1901–1945* (microform), ed. Pete Daniel, Reel 9, File 50-0. The federal implementation of definitive statutory protection against "simple" slavery during World War II was largely a propaganda move to counter the unveiling of racial apartheid in democratic

America by the U.S. Left and Japan, the latter of whom hoped to inspire defections of black soldiers looking to escape totalitarianism at "home." See Goluboff, "The Thirteenth Amendment and the Lost Origins of Civil Rights," 1619–28.

39. The Civil Rights Act of 1866, http://www.pbs.org.

40. According to Edward Ayers, Reconstruction-era southern governments turned to convict leasing "as a temporary expedient" based on the infrastructural devastation and economic scarcity left in the wake of the Civil War. From this standpoint, he argues, the "South . . . more or less stumbled into the lease, seeking a way to avoid large expenditures while hoping a truly satisfactory plan would emerge." Ayers, *Vengeance and Justice,* 189. One is left to wonder why virtually no white people were sacrificed by the genocidal operation of this supposedly accidental and "temporary" expedient, which lasted until 1933, and which, in its first few decades, killed anywhere from 10 percent to 60 percent of its black prisoners per annum.

41. Donald Nieman, *To Set the Law in Motion* (New York: KTO Press, 1979), 110. As Nieman also points out, black people were often prevented from removing themselves from debt peonage, physical coercion, and the psychic terror that the Freedmen's Bureau found on the early postbellum plantations, the very federal agency that was created to protect the emancipated from racial violence. Bureau agents regularly enforced an update of the antebellum pass system and forced black people to sign year-long unfree labor contracts (often with their former slave masters), threatening to send those who would refuse with arrest, the chain gang, or lease to private landowners (62). An open letter from the Chairman of the Orangeburg, South Carolina, Commission on Contracts with Freedmen, from just after the war underlines the degree to which the bureau's promotion of "freedom of contract" often equated to peonage or coerced neo-enslavement: "Do not think, because you are free you can choose your own kind of work. . . . Do not think of leaving the plantation where you belong. If you try to go to Charleston, or any other city, you will find no work to do, and nothing to eat. You will starve, or fall sick and die. Stay where you are, in your own homes, even if you are suffering. There is no place better for you anywhere else." Captain Charles Soule, "To the Freed People of Orangeburg District," June 1865. Enclosure contained in a letter from Soule to O. O. Howard (Freedmen's Bureau Commissioner), http://www.history.umd.edu/Freedmen/Soule.htm. I am indebted to Kelley S. Abraham for informing me of this correspondence. Importantly, Soule was no raving southern Redeemer: he was a New Englander and a captain in the 55th Massachusetts Regiment, a unit of black troops in the Civil War. For a masterful exposure of the repressive operation of the liberal discourses of contract and black pseudo-obligation in the aftermath of the war, see Hartman, *Scenes of Subjection,* 164–206.

42. Sellin, *Slavery and the Penal System,* 45.

43. *Black Boy (American Hunger),* in *Richard Wright, the Later Works* (New York: Library of America, 1991), 56.

44. Hartman, *Scenes of Subjection*, 244.

45. A perfect political geographic symbol of what I am describing as public/private carceral hybridity during the era of convict leasing was the industrialized mega-neoslave plantation of James Monroe Smith, otherwise known as "Smithonia." Comprising of twenty thousand acres of land in Oglethorpe County, Georgia, the Confederate colonel's empire included a railroad, a cotton gin, a sawmill, a cottonseed-oil mill, a blacksmith shop, and a guano plant—all of which were operated by a combination of variously unfree black labor, ranging from sharecroppers, to debt peons, to misdemeanants purchased via criminal-surety, to prisoners leased directly from the state. See Dittmer, *Black Georgia in the Progressive Era, 1900–1920*, 78. A portion of Smith's profits came directly from his capacity as a neoslave broker, as he subleased many of his prisoners, including more than sixty black women he originally leased from the state, to other local plantation and business owners. Talitha LeFLouria, "'The Hand That Rocks the Cradle Cuts Cordwood': Exploring Black Women's Lives and Labor in Georgia's Convict Camps, 1865–1917," *Labor: Studies in Working-Class History of the Americas* 8, no. 3 (2011): 58. Department of Justice files reveal that even though black prisoners spoke of being coffled, whipped, beaten, and held captive after their release date, the federal government never attempted to indict the plantation owner. One reason for his legal immunity was the fact that he translated his economic fortune into political power in the form of a stint on the state legislature from 1874 to 1881 and the state senate in 1884. Indeed, this aspect of public profiteering on the entombment of black bodies was endemic to the Georgia lease system from its outset since the first convict lease contracts in the state's history were allotted to two members of the "Bourbon Triumverate": Senator Joseph E. Brown and Governor John B. Brown. Dittmer, *Black Georgia in the Progressive Era*, 83.

46. Walter Wilson gives a detailed description of the "fine/fee" process in "Chain Gangs and Profit," *Harper's Monthly Magazine*, April 1933, 541. See also Oshinsky, *"Worse Than Slavery,"* 41–42.

47. For Wynter, the social and philosophical conjuration of the "Negro" or "nigger" as zero-degree signifier of metaphysical (no)thingness and atavism registers the material and structural nature of white supremacy. She argues that "whilst Marxism's theory of economic subordination provided a dazzling set of explanatory hypotheses" for the Euroamerican Left and members of the black intelligentsia, it does not serve as comprehensive enough of an analytic for full-fledged encounter with the wholesale "ontological subordination" produced under slavery and colonialism. Wynter, "On Disenchanting Discourse," 216. See also Robinson, *Black Marxism*; Frantz Fanon, *Wretched of the Earth*. For my use of the term "afterlife" in respect to the staying power of chattelized law, I am indebted to Saidiya Hartman, *Lose Your Mother* (New York: Farrar, Straus and Giroux, 2007).

48. E. Stagg Whitin, *Penal Servitude* (New York: National Committee on Prison Labor, 1912), 1.

49. A total of 128 miners (including 114 black men and 14 white men) were killed in the explosion at Pratt Consolidated Coal Company's Banner Mine, just outside of Littleton, Alabama, on April 8, 1911, in what still stands as one of the most deadly industrial accidents in U.S. history. *Atlanta Journal Constitution*, April 10, 1911, 1. Of the total dead, 123 were prisoners leased directly to Pratt Consolidated by the state for alleged felonies and misdemeanors. Pratt was the main industrial competitor for Tennessee Coal and Iron Company, or TCI (a subsidiary of U.S. Steel), the largest of a total of four companies that made up Alabama's "penitentiary" system, and that used neoslaves as the engine of the state's booming coal industry. According to Douglas Blackmon, the companies produced a total of nearly fifteen million tons of coal a year by 1910, while entombing more than three thousand black men (and boys) in that year. Blackmon, *Slavery by Another Name*, 331.

50. The hyperfungibility of the black body represents a major connecting link between chattel slavery and the various systems of incarceration to which black people have been subjected since 1865. Studies of convict leasing have nearly unanimously neglected to mention that the legal renting of imprisoned black bodies in the United States actually originated with chattel slavery when, according to Herbert Aptheker, the "leasing of slaves [was often] indulged in by masters who were 'overstocked.'" Aptheker, *American Negro Slave Revolts* (New York: International Publishers, 1969), 123. Such studies have also contended that the high death rates associated with the early years of convict leasing qualify that period as *worse than slavery*. See, for example, Mancini, *One Dies, Get Another*; and Oshinsky, *"Worse Than Slavery."* A centering of black fungibility as a trans-1865 category of white supremacist terror allows us to recognize the ways in which the very processes of being bought, sold, leased, bred, owned, publicly traded, and warehoused have operated as forms of collectivized and legalized racial death. Such a purview also allows for a shuttling of the tendency within histories of neoslavery to exceptionalize it as something that happened "down there" and "back then." See, for example, Blackmon, *Slavery by Another Name*, 381–82. As discussed above, no calculus based on biological death counts alone can account for the interminable catalogue of terror associated with being legally transmuted into an object of public/private property, or the way in which such legal sorcery continues to make mass entombment a socially accepted fact of black, brown, and poor life. As during antebellum plantation imprisonment, the overall system of U.S. neoslavery has been based upon the normalized mass possession of and profiteering on stigmatized black bodies and the protean states of abjection that such hyperfungibility has produced. The "innumerable uses" of civil and state captives from antebellum incarceration through today's prison–industrial complex have involved both express

and unavowed prerogatives of human-as-property ownership, including but not limited to sweat-boxing, shelving, scatological detainment, indefinite solitary confinement, whipping, black-jacking, stretching, natal alienation, justifiable homicide, and rape (and many other sadistic amusements)—a litany of dubious utility that continues to make imprisoned "life" into a dubious simulation of death. On the "innumerable uses" of slave property in the antebellum period, see Goodell, *The American Slave Code,* and Hartman, *Scenes of Subjection.* On the way in which sexual abuse continues to function as a de facto element of the state's punishment of women, see Angela Y. Davis, "Public Imprisonment and Private Violence: Reflections on the Hidden Punishment of Women," 24 *New England Journal on Criminal & Civil Confinement* 339 (1998).

51. For discussion of the system of criminal-surety, see William Cohen, "Negro Involuntary Servitude in the South, 1865–1940: A Preliminary Analysis," *Journal of Southern History,* 42, no. 1 (February 1976): 53–55; and Schmidt, "Principle and Prejudice," 691–701.

52. "Chain Gangs and Profit," 541. Again, this system of public profiteering on the trade in black bodies has roots in the antebellum period, when courts regularly conducted public auctions of both slave and criminally branded "free" black people. Thomas Russell, "Slave Auctions on the Courthouse Steps." For a discussion of the southern prison system as a "trafficking" in "human chattel," see Du Bois, *Black Reconstruction in America,* 697–98. It is important to note here the degree to which this element of public profiteering during the original postbellum prison–industrial complex represents a precursor to the hybridized public/private profit ability of collective human misery under today's PIC. Specifically, one can see this playing out in the huge amount of tax monies that are funneled from national, state, and local coffers to county sheriffs, prison guards, police departments, border-patrol agents, etc.—ostensible "public" entities whose very existence is predicated on the maintenance and expansion of prison slavery and domestic warfare. Along these lines, we might think of the fact that one of the most boisterous sources of opposition to private prisons comes from state prison guards, whose stance against companies such as CCA and Wackenhutt is predicated not on humanitarian grounds but on the fact that they view these companies as direct competition within the overall PIC bonanza.

53. The federal peonage statutes followed the liberal legal logic offered in *Clyatt* (1904), which defined that system of neo-enslavement as "a status or condition of compulsory service, based on the indebtedness of the peon to the master. The basal fact is indebtedness." 197 U.S. 207, 215. As stated above, the Justice Department would repeatedly site this narrow construction of illegal involuntary servitude when refusing to investigate complaints of countless black subjects who spoke of being subjected to "simple" slavery—and its accoutrements, such as corporeal rupture, rape, and kidnapping—without this "basal" element of debt.

The circumscription of black reenslavement to only one specific species of "private" and "contractual" servitude absolved the state's central role in both the overall system of peonage and what it advertised as *purely* "public" formations of penal slavery such as the chain gang, convict leasing, and the prison plantation. What the millions of untold stories emitting from zones of official and social incarceration suggest is that the most "basal" element of black neoslavery was and is white supremacist terror and domination on both a sectional and national scale. On the postbellum system of black indebted servitude, see Hartman, *Scenes of Subjection,* 164–206.

54. *United States v. Reynolds,* 235 U.S. 133 (1914), 145.

55. Rivers would ultimately be released on a habeas corpus petition between the moment of the lower court's upholding of Alabama's criminal-surety statute and the Supreme Court's reversal of that decision; but his release would not happen before his sentencing to the chain gang in consequence of his escape from Broughton. Along with his chain-gang stint, the other major element missing from the court's cataloguing of the circumstances of the case was the fact that *Reynolds* was in fact a "test case." That is, the only reason that the Supreme Court came to decide on the constitutionality of criminal-surety was that both Reynolds and Broughton struck a deal with the Justice Department ahead of the case, which guaranteed that all they would receive in the event that the court struck down the surety law would be a $50 fine. To put this in perspective, after criminal-surety was putatively outlawed in the case, Reynolds and Broughton were made to pay less for subjecting a black person to neo-enslavement than Rivers would ultimately be charged in fines and fees for a petty property offense. That the juridical barring of criminal-surety was largely a performative rather substantive redressive action is underlined by the fact that black subjects would continue to be murdered, raped, and enslaved under this form of public/private mastery until at least the 1960s. The most clear-cut example of this was the "Murder Farm" case (1921), which involved the savage killing of eleven black men who were purchased via surety contracts at various county courthouses from Jasper to Macon County, Georgia, by John S. Williams. Upon realizing that he was to be investigated on charges of peonage, Williams ordered his de facto black trustees to help him murder the men. Many of the prisoners were thrown into the Yellow River, while still alive, with trace chains and one hundred pound rock-filled sacks wrapped around their necks. Another was buried alive after being chopped with an ax. Williams's ultimate conviction actually highlighted the unredressable positionality of the black southern population since, as Pete Daniel (following Mary Frances Berry) points out, Williams was "the first Southern white man since 1877 to be indicted for the first-degree murder of a black [person]—and he would be the last until 1966." Daniel, *The Shadow of Slavery,* 110–31. For a detailing of the various aspects of the "test" aspect of *Reynolds,* see Schmidt, "Principle and Prejudice," 691–701.

56. Brief for United States at 10–11, *United States v. Reynolds,* 235 U.S. 133.

57. Hartman, *Scenes of Subjection,* 164–206.

58. We still have no idea exactly how many black people were at some point literally held in a state of peonage—that is, not only in fictive debt to a "master" but coerced into performing involuntary servitude at the threat of death, rape, and other forms of terror. However, what estimates are available dramatically alter our understanding of the genesis of mass incarceration in the postslavery United States (remembering of course that pre-1865 chattel slavery represented the original prison–industrial complex of the Western hemisphere). In 1907, an investigator surmised that over 33 percent of white planters in Georgia, Mississippi, and Alabama, who had anywhere from five to one hundred black subjects "working" for them, were holding "their negro employees to a condition of peonage." Daniel, *The Shadow of Slavery,* 22, 108. To put this in perspective: in 1900, there were a total of approximately 2.9 million black people in these three states, of which at least 85 percent, or more than 2.4 million, would have been in rural areas where peonage was rampant. If we take 15 percent of that total (less than half of the 33 percent estimate of the investigator) as the most conservative estimate of the number of black people likely to have been held in this socially incarcerating structure, the total number of black peons in these three states alone would reach approximately 360,000. If this total were to include the entire geography of southern racial apartheid, the conservative estimate would easily approach one million "privately" imprisoned bodies. The scale of the public/private neoslavery complex signals how the entire southern landscape *remained* a literal open-air prison after emancipation—a fact that disturbs the current historical consensus in respect to the PIC that cites the late 1970s as the birth-time of racialized mass imprisonment in the United States.

59. Daniel, *The Shadow of Slavery.*

60. Letter from William H. Armbrecht to the U.S. Attorney General (June 10, 1911), in *The Peonage Files of the U.S. Department of Justice, 1901–1945* (microform), ed. Pete Daniel, Reel 13, File 50-106.

61. David Oshinsky offers this description of black neoslavery in the Florida turpentining industry in *"Worse Than Slavery,"* 70–71.

62. As I will discuss in chapters 3 and 4, coerced performance has been a fundamental aspect of black "forced labor" in spaces of neoslavery from the chain gang to the prison plantation, a dynamic that, as Hartman suggests, can be traced back to the call for Africans to "strike it up lively" on the decks of slave ships and while being coffled at public auctions. *Scenes of Subjection,* 17–48. Sexual assault and rape also represent normalized means of sadistic pleasure within zones of "public" neoslavery. In late nineteenth-century Georgia, for instance, this sort of violence was aided by the fact that black women were leased along with men into both state and county facilities, with the number of imprisoned black women

nearly equaling the number of white men. One investigative journalist spoke of coming across a black woman at a jail facility in Atlanta, "an escaped convict [who] had an infant in her arms, probably 5 months old; and said this was her third child that she had given birth to since she was convicted of arson and sentenced to the Penitentiary [lease camp] service of the State for life. She said that her first two children had died and that their remains had been interred by white chain gang bosses, who were the fathers of the children. The [third] child was taken away from her." "Georgia Brutality: How the Convicts in the Penitentiary-Camps Are Treated," *Chicago Tribune,* August 6, 1881, 6. While no such accounts of the lives of black women in Alabama's convict lease camps are available, black women were often held with black men at the state's prison slave camps such as the prison "farm" at Wetumpka, the Pratt Consolidated Mines, and J. Jackson's Rock Quarry and "Farm," wherein they were vulnerable to rape and other forms of gendered carceral repression. Mary Ellen Curtin, *Black Prisoners and Their World, Alabama, 1865–1900* (Charlottesville: University of Virginia Press, 2000), 120. In 1968, the State Penitentiary of Arkansas, otherwise known as Cummins Farm, offered an example of the proliferation of unmarked mass graves in official prisons. While autopsies revealed that each of these men and boys died from acts of physical violence, the officially reported causes of death were utterly absurd: These included "accidental electrocution," "blows from a fallen tree," poisoning with medicine used "to cure colic in horses," injuries from "runaway wagons," and teenaged prisoners dying from "heart failure." Walter Rugaber, "70 Deaths Linked in Arkansas Prison Since 1936 Linked to Violence," *New York Times,* February 7, 1968, 1, 22. The figure of "$11 a head" represents the actual language used in a contract for the lease of black prisoners to a railroad firm, Wallis, Haley & Co., in 1874. The firm became involved in a contract dispute with other companies over the rights to 250 black prisoners, a suit that in the language of the court was made complicated by "the peculiar nature and character of the property" involved. *Georgia Penitentiary Companies Nos. 2 and 3 vs. Nelms, Principal Keeper* 71 GA 301 (1883).

63. Brief for United States at 20, *United States v. Reynolds,* 235 U.S. 133.

64. See, for example, *Garlington v. James* et al., CA 95-0970-CB-C, 1998 U.S. District (Alabama), in which a black man, Lynell Noah Garlington, brought suit against the state of Alabama, charging that his racially based sentence to a modern-day chain gang amounted to involuntary servitude and cruel and unusual punishment as described in the Eighth Amendment. The court dismissed his charges based on a long line of legal precedent going all the way back to *Slaughterhouse,* which has found that prisoners cannot lay claim to Thirteenth Amendment's abolitionist aspect due to its allowance of "slavery and involuntary servitude" as penal sanction. See also *Omatsa v. Wainwright,* 696 F. 2nd (11th Cir. 1983); *Draper v. Rhay,* 315 F. 2nd (9th Cir.); *Ray v. Marbry,* 556 F. 2nd 881 (8th Cir. 1977); and *Lindsey v. Leavy,* 149 F. 2nd 899 (9th Cir. 1945). Indeed, the protective aspect of the

emancipation amendment ended up being wielded more successfully in relation to the white working class in the North than former slaves and their progeny in the South, with most successful cases occurring during the New Deal, when northern labor unions claimed that the right to strike and to refuse coercive labor conditions were enshrined in the Thirteenth Amendment. Goluboff, "The Thirteenth Amendment and the Lost Origins of Civil Rights," 1677.

3. Angola Penitentiary

This chapter is dedicated to my father, Dennis Lee Childs, and to my younger brother, Jerry Seantaurus Barnes's father, Jerry Barnes—both of whom were legally lynched by police for the crime of being born as black males in the United States. The epigraph derives from personal correspondence with Robert Hillary King, September 2011.

1. Passed in 1996, Proposition 209—which also went under the cynical heading of the "California Civil Rights Initiative"—was a ballot measure that amended the California state constitution to prohibit its governmental institutions from utilizing race, gender, or sex in public employment, public education, or public contracting. The supposed "civil rights" law effectively ended affirmative action in public education in the state—a move that led directly to the worsening of an already terrible record vis-à-vis admission of black, Latina/o, and Indigenous students into the state college and university system.

2. The term "two-cent men" refers to the hourly "wage" of plantation field laborers at the prison. The phrase "handcuffed in the back of countless prison buses and shuttled in modern-day coffles" represents a riff with Inspectah Deck, who in "C.R.E.A.M." offers one of the most distinct articulations of the Middle Passage carceral model in modern hip-hop when he performs poetic rememory of the ritualized arrest and upstate carceral disappearance of black males from New York City: "The court played me short, now I face incarceration / Pacin'—goin' upstate's my destination / *Handcuffed in the back of a bus, 40 of us* / life as a shorty shouldn't be so rough." *Enter the Wu-Tang Clan: 36 Chambers*, RCA, 1993. Much can and should be said regarding the connections of early neoslave sound in the forms of the field holler, "work song," and prison blues, and the carceral inner-city blues as performed by modern hip-hop artists in the age of the prison–industrial complex.

3. "Don't come to Angola, this is murder's home," a lyric from Johnny Butler and other anonymous prisoners, "Early in the Morning," *Prison Worksongs*, Arhoolie CD 448, Arhoolie Productions, 1997. Originally recorded circa 1959. "Hell Factory in the Fields" is taken from Mike Davis, "A Prison Industrial Complex: Hell Factories in the Field," *The Nation*, February 20, 1995, 229–34. For a comparison of Angola's geographical area to that of Manhattan, see James Ridgeway, "God's Own Warden," *Mother Jones*, July–August 2011.

4. This phrase refers to Louisiana's version of the overall national juridical and penal trend of committing those convicted of certain felonies to life without the possibility of parole, or "LWOP." Until the 1970s, those who were sentenced to "life" at Angola and other Louisiana prisons were able to gain parole release through what was known as the "10-6" law, which allowed for the parole of prisoners with good-conduct records after they had served at least ten years and six months of their sentence. Louisiana is one of the states that follows the "life means life" creed, which disallows any possibility of parole for anyone sentenced to life in prison. For a discussion of Louisiana's LWOP policy, see Marie Gottschalk, "Days Without End: Life Sentences and Penal Reform," *Prison Legal News,* https://www.prisonlegalnews.org/. This policy has contributed greatly to Louisiana's standing as having the highest incarceration rate in the country: 1,619 adults behind bars (and in the fields) for every 100,000 total adults in the state population (or roughly 1.6 out of 100), a statistic that is dramatically worse in respect to the state's black population. See Cindy Chang et al., "Louisiana Incarcerated: How We Built the World's Prison Capital," *Times-Picayune,* http://www.nola.com/crime/ index.ssf /2012/05/louisiana_is_the_worlds_prison.html.

5. Rodríguez, *Forced Passages.*

6. "Panthers Still Caged in Angola," *Free the Angola 3,* www.prisonactivist.org/angola/support.shtml #mumia.

7. In using the term civilian "freeperson," I am riffing on the epistemically instructive term "freeman" that is used by prisoners at Angola when referring to prison guards and administrators.

8. For an informative treatment of the systematic erasure of the subject of chattel slavery in southern slave plantation museums, see Stephen Small and Jennifer J. Eichstedt, *Representations of Slavery: Race and Ideology in Southern Plantation Museums* (Washington, D.C.: Smithsonian Institution Press, 2002).

9. For an example of this argument, see Mary Rachel Gould, "Discipline and the Performance of Punishment: Welcome to the Wildest Show in the South," *Liminalities: A Journal of Performance Studies* 7, no. 4 (December 2011): 24. Although I appreciate Gould's critique of Foucault's notion that spectacular forms of discipline ultimately became obsolete with the advent of the modern carceral state, her discussion of the prison rodeo ultimately reaffirms Foucault's notion of modernity's transition away from repressive forms of punishment into a *disciplinary* carceral regime. In doing so, it obfuscates the fact that state terror at Angola is punitive/repressive rather than disciplinary/disembodied—that, even in the moments when prisoners are not being gorged by bulls and tossed twenty feet into the air, the entire perverse exhibition rests upon a physically and psychically violent operation of mass civil death, collective disappearance, and legalized neo-slavery of which the rodeo is merely a single "public" expression. Gould's otherwise interesting work ultimately suffers from a lack of engagement with the political

organizing, writings, and songs of Angola prisoners themselves, and an adherence
to Foucault's total elision of race and racial terror within his history of the prison—a fact that partially explains how one can read her entire piece on the "spectacle of discipline" at Angola plantation without once encountering the word
"slavery."

10. It is important to note that the prison minstrel show was a national rather
than peculiarly southern phenomenon—one that I have traced as far back as the
late nineteenth century and that continued well into the twentieth century. See "A
Chain Gang's Sunday: How Georgia Prisoners Are Confined," *New York Tribune*,
October 20, 1895, 30. In this article a northern reporter travels to a chain-gang
camp just outside Atlanta in the context of scandals involving the horrific treatment of black male and women prisoners, high death rates, and profiteering.
While taking her tour, the *Tribune* correspondent notices nothing but good cheer
on the part of the black prisoner, an idea rendered most clearly in her remembrance of the moment in which she and other guests are entertained by a group of
musical captives. She speaks of seeing one particularly gifted "Negro" man dance
the "pigeon wing," the "double shuffle," with "the chain on his leg all the time
making a not unmusical accompaniment to his motion"—and how "no one
enjoyed the exhibition so much as the participant." What went unnoticed by the
tourist was that the song performed by the supposedly jovial neoslaves was in fact
a parable of carceral cannibalism involving a possum (a prisoner) being eaten alive
by his kidnapper while "his sisters and brothers is runnin' around free." As I will
discuss below and in chapter 4, the white tourist's racist disengagement with the
scene of black incarcerated performance represents a "post" slavery redeployment
of the discourses of natural joviality, musicality, and inurement to pain and dishonor that was attached to the African performative body on the decks of slave
ships and on slave plantations prior to emancipation. Hartman, *Scenes of Subjection*, 17–114.

For journalistic coverage of prison minstrel shows in the twentieth century,
see "Joke-Crackers in Prison: Blackface Comedians Entertain Men in Penitentiary," *The Watchman and Southron* (Sumpter, S.C.), December 31, 1913, 8; "Prisoners Give a Play: Many Citizens Attend a Thanksgiving Vaudeville Show in
Auburn," *New York Times*, November 27, 1914, 6; "Sing Sing Prisoners Merry: Convicts Give a Minstrel and Vaudeville Entertainment," *New York Times*, November
29, 1907, 9; "Convicts Entertain Nevada's Governor: Executive Attends Minstrel
Show in Prison—Warden Baker's New Plan," *San Francisco Chronicle*, March 3,
1911, 13; "Convicts Give Minstrel Show: Folsom Inmates Display Talent in Black
Face," *Los Angeles Times*, December 26, 1912, 13. This brief listing of the practice of
prison blackface reveals that most such "entertainments" occurred during holidays.
The warden's granting of captive privilege during holidays issued directly from
the chattel management strategies of masters and overseers on the antebellum

plantation, who often used such "festive" occasions to project the slave's ostensible contentment with bondage. The articles also reveal that many of the northern and western blackface prisoners were actually white—a performative dynamic that represents the state's investment in reproducing white supremacist custom and social stratification even among the civilly dead.

11. Hartman, *Scenes of Subjection*, 17–114.

12. "The bat," which was used at Angola until at least the late 1950s, was a three-foot-long and five-inch-wide strip of sole leather tied to a two-foot-long wooden handle. Along with this torture implement, prisoners in "old" Angola were beaten with "blacksnake" whips, five-foot clubs, and redoubled grass ropes. See B. I. Krebs, "Blood Took Penitentiary Out of the Red: Prisoners Flogged 10,000 Times During Machine Rule," *Times-Picayune*, May 11, 1941, 26–27. Black prisoners at Angola and St. Gabriel prison plantation also suffered the racially restrictive punishment of being chained to punishment posts (a modification of feudal stocks) for as long as thirty-six hours. "St. Gabriel Prisoners Handcuffed to Post for Infraction of Rules" (Baton Rouge) *Morning Advocate*, May 7, 1952. The "sweatbox" was a forerunner to today's "boxcar cells" used in "Supermax" prisons such as Florence, ADX (Colorado). See Raymond Luc Levasseur, "Trouble Coming Everyday: ADX—the First Year," North Coast Xpress (June–July 1996). The sweatbox was a concrete structure containing three separate cells, each with a steel door. The cells were painted entirely black with only two small openings—one at the bottom of the door and another on the ceiling. Though mainly used as solitary cells, at any given time as many as seven prisoners shared one closet-sized cell. Punitive segregation and solitary confinement in architectures such as the sweatbox represented a direct methodological (and supposedly reformatory) replacement for the whip at the level of state policy—a fact that signals both the modern nature of supposedly anachronistic punishments at the plantation and the historical weddedness of the lash and solitary confinement. See "Convicts Prefer the Whip over Solitary Cells," *Times-Picayune*, August 17, 1941. For a brilliant discussion of the terroristic animus underlying the supposedly "humane" operations of the modern carceral state, particularly in respect to the connection of modern solitary confinement and chattel slavery, see Colin Dayan, "Legal Slaves and Civil Bodies."

The "body sheet" is used at Angola today mainly to immobilize mentally ill prisoners. Similar to a straitjacket (aside from the addition of chains underneath), it allows the prison staff to completely immobilize prisoners by riveting them to a four-point or three-point restraining table. Prisoners are strapped into the "sheet" completely nude with the exception of an adult-sized diaper, in which they are forced to defecate and urinate while immobilized for hours. Many prisoners are also shackled either individually or in coffles through implements such as "black box" handcuffs. These "pick-less" restraints include a square-shaped cover made of high-impact ABS plastic and an aluminum alloy; they also include two loops through which a "belly chain" is attached. Prisoner testimony reveals that the "box" regularly leads to deep lacerations and swelling. Wilbert Rideau, "A Matter of Control," *The Angolite,* January–February 1993, 28–34.

13. See "A New Kind of Prison: Designed to Prevent Riots, Save Money, and Help Criminals Go Straight," *Architectural Forum,* December 1954; and "Prison Designs Take on New Look: Architects Are Trying New Methods and Layouts," *New York Times,* January 30, 1966. The construction of the "new" Angola began in 1952. The $8 million project included the building of new cell blocks, an administrative building, and dining hall that featured "an undulating roof" and "spacious, grassy areas." Advertised as a symbol of the state's commitment to penal reform, the structures were designed by Nathaniel Curtis and Arthur Davis of the New Orleans architectural firm Curtis & Davis. The firm gained national and international notoriety for postmodern structural design as a result of the commission. However, one important aspect of the relatively low-cost project belies the notion that the "new" Angola would equal substantively novel treatment for prisoners: every slab of concrete, piece of glass, "dormitory" unit cage, and solitary cell was installed and constructed by prisoners themselves. Furthermore, many of Angola's black prisoners would never be held within the facilities they built with their own hands; a large portion of the prison plantation's "Negroes" would remain in the site's notorious "Jungle Camps" until the late 1960s.

14. The Angola 3 case represents one of many instances of political imprisonment in the United States that occurred as a result of the state's openly declared domestic war against black, Latino, Indigenous, and allied white radical formations via state terror programs such as the FBI's COINTELPRO, or counter-intelligence program. In 1972, Wallace and Woodfox were convicted of killing Brent Miller, a young white prison guard, a charge that Angola's administration managed to link to another Black Panther, Robert Hillary King (aka Robert King Wilkerson), although King was not imprisoned at the penitentiary at the time of the killing. King would spend twenty-nine years in solitary confinement before being released from Angola in 2001, when his conviction for a different murder at the prison was overturned and he pleaded guilty to a lesser charge. Wallace, Woodfox, and King—and the international movement that supports them—maintain that the prison administration framed the three men as a way of derailing the group's organizing efforts on the neoplantation. In fact, Wallace and Woodfox had started the nation's only prison-based chapter of the Black Panther Party in 1971, a year before Miller's murder. The chapter organized campaigns against the prison's segregation policy, the horrific conditions in the plantation fields, and the administratively ignored (and facilitated) system of prison rape. Hillary King has been speaking and organizing both nationally and internationally for the release of Wallace and Woodfox since he was released from Angola, while Wallace and Woodfox continue to organize for their own liberation from within spaces such as Camp J

and the CCR "dungeon." For more information on the case, see http://www.angola3.org/.

Herman Wallace was released from the Louisiana State Penitentiary (the Elaine Hunt Correctional Facility at St. Gabriel) on October 1, 2013, after his original conviction was ruled unconstitutional by a federal judge in Louisiana. He died three days later from terminal liver cancer. Nothing expresses the intimacies of living death, premature death, and neoslave resistance more than Wallace's indefinite political solitary confinement, his (continued) spectral haunting of the state through his national and international activism, and his de facto murder at the hands of the white supremacist carceral state. As of the date of this writing, Albert Woodfox is enduring his forty-second year of solitary confinement.

15. Herman Wallace, "On Solitary Confinement," *Free the Angola* 3, http://prisonactivist.org/angola/.

16. For a discussion of how prison blackface symbolizes what I call "criminal minstrelsy," or the overall structural blackfacing of crime in the United States, see Dennis Childs, "Angola, Convict Leasing, and the Annulment of Freedom," in *Violence and the Body*, ed. Arturo Aldama (Bloomington: Indiana University Press, 2003), 199–203.

17. Hartman, *Scenes of Subjection*, 17–114.

18. "In every line item, I saw a grave. Commodities, cargo, and things don't lend themselves to representation, at least not easily. The archive dictates what can be said about the past and the kinds of stories that can be told about the persons cataloged, embalmed, and sealed away in box files and folios. To read the archive is to enter a mortuary." Hartman, *Lose Your Mother*, 17.

19. Jamaica Kincaid, "In History," *Callaloo* 20, no. 1 (1997): 1–7.

20. Hartman, *Lose Your Mother*, 118, 133.

21. As stated above, "Unhistorical Events" derives from a poem of the same name by the black surrealist poet Bob Kaufman. See note 8 in the Introduction for a description of the poem.

22. Beginning in 1901, when the official practice of convict leasing ended in Louisiana, black women prisoners (along with a small number of white women prisoners) were used as cooks, laundresses, seamstresses, and field workers. Some "worked as servants to the prison employees and 'nannies' to their children." "Louisiana's Prisons," *Angolite* [rodeo addition], 1983 (unspecified month), 41. As I will discuss below, black men and transgender women were also used as "nannies" when submitted to domestic neoslavery.

23. Fred Moten, *In the Break: The Aesthetics of the Black Radical Tradition* (Minneapolis: University of Minnesota Press, 2003), 197.

24. Odea Mathews, "Somethin' Within Me," Arhoolie CD 448, "Angola Prisoner's Blues" (arhoolie.com). Tradition Music Co. (BMI), administered by Bug Music c/o BMG Rights Management. Originally recorded circa 1959.

25. The phrase "loophole ... of retreat" is borrowed from Harriet Jacobs, *Incidents in the Life of a Slave Girl,* ed. Jean Fagan Yellin (1861; Cambridge: Harvard University Press, 1987), 114–17. In Jacobs's narrative, it refers to the nine-foot-by-seven-foot space built into the attic of her grandmother's home wherein she quarantined herself for seven years in order to facilitate her escape from enslavement. Jacobs repeatedly uses the words "hole" and "prison" both in relation to her individual "garret" and to the collective racial/spatial predicament of enslavement—a discursive signaling of the future orientation of chattelism in the form of modern prisons and the solitary "holes" of today's prison–industrial complex.

26. Allen Feldman describes the body-self split of the tortured prisoner as both a function of state power and a locus of resistive possibility: The prisoner's "capacity to survive is dependent on surrendering his body to the objectifying violence that is inflicted upon it. The ... elementary divestiture of the body, as much as it presages death, also becomes the condition of resistance." Feldman, *Formations of Violence: The Narrative of the Body and Political Power in Northern Ireland* (Chicago: University of Chicago Press, 1991), 119. One wonders, however, what sort of resistive possibilities are contained in such moments of state death rehearsal (and execution) when no publicly recognizable radical "movement" is occurring from which the individual tortured prisoner can draw a sense of collective political strength. Indeed, within the context of today's PIC, the radical potentialities of the tortured body are that much more foreshortened because racialized criminalization and stigmatization have so bombarded the social field of the "free" as to render the political, artistic, and social practices of the incarcerated publicly unknowable even when such practices do exist. The word "torture" here refers to the act of human encagement itself along with other acts of bodily rupture associated with it. I would like to thank Dylan Rodríguez for furthering my understanding of the problematic aspects of the liberal discourse of human rights that restricts the definition of "torture" to isolated moments of illegal bodily rupture and "abuse" rather than understanding imprisonment itself as a form of mass, legalized, torture.

27. Spillers, "Mama's Baby, Papa's Maybe: An American Grammar Book," 67.

28. In conceiving of my encounter with the lives and unceremonious deaths of McElroy, Mathews, and others at Angola, I am indebted to the (un)historical practice of Saidiya Hartman in *Lose Your Mother,* particularly as expressed in "The Dead Book," wherein she excavates a "musty trial transcript" and other historical documents in order to recover something of the experience of an anonymous West African girl who was lynched aboard the slave ship *Recovery* in 1792. In so doing, Hartman was forced to attend, in an "imaginative" fashion, to what she describes as a spectral "shadow" left by the slave girl within the historical archive— that is, the unrecoverable feelings and experiences of a stolen and desecrated life for which slave narratives, testimonies, legal cases, and other hypermediated terrains of the master archive are forced to stand in as legible signifiers.

29. "blood to the scraps." Toni Morrison, *Beloved*, 78.

30. John McElroy to Louisiana attorney general Bolivar Kemp Jr., Louisiana State Penitentiary General Correspondence (microform), 1951–52, Louisiana State Archives, Baton Rouge.

31. My use of the term "stenciling" to describe the state's branding of prison slave's derives from Malcolm X's articulation of this process as he experienced it in the Charlestown State Prison in Massachusetts (1946–52): "[Y]our number in prison became a part of you. You never heard your name, only your number. On all your clothing, every item, was your number, stenciled. It grew stenciled on your brain." El-Hajj Malik Shabazz (Malcolm X), *The Autobiography of Malcolm X* (New York: Ballantine Books, 1992), 176.

32. Gordon, *Ghostly Matters*, 64.

33. Hartman, *Scenes of Subjection*, 36.

34. McNair (who was eleven) and Collins, Robertson, and Wesley (each of whom was fourteen) were attending Sunday School class at Birmingham's 16th Street Baptist Church on September 15, 1963, when a KKK-planted bomb exploded, killing them and injuring twenty-two other church members. For an important meditation on the social ramifications of the bombing, particularly in respect to the way in which it was representative of an overall structure of American racial terror, see Angela Y. Davis, *Angela Davis: An Autobiography*, 128–31. For Douglass's discussion of the immense social, emotional, and philosophical meaning of slave songs and how their semantic depth belied contemporary notions of slave contentment, see *Narrative of the Life of Frederick Douglass* (1845), in *Frederick Douglass: Autobiographies* (New York: Library of America), 23–25. "Reaching for it he thought it was a cardinal feather stuck to his boat. He tugged and what came loose in his hand was red a ribbon knotted around a curl of wet wooly hair, clinging still to a bit of scalp." Morrison, *Beloved*, 180.

35. The phrase "publicly slain black boy" refers to Trayvon Martin, a seventeen-year-old black male who was killed by a self-proclaimed neighborhood-watch patrolman on February 26, 2012, after the latter had stalked Martin through a gated community in Sanford, Florida. Martin's killing ultimately sparked a national and international campaign to force the state of Florida to press charges against George Zimmerman, the teenager's killer. Zimmerman was ultimately acquitted on all charges related to Martin's death. However, the phrase also describes another young black male, Ramarley Graham, an eighteen-year-old, who was murdered on February 2 of the same year with relatively little public notoriety. Graham was killed in the bathroom of his family's home in the Bronx, New York, after members of NYPD's narcotics unit trailed him to his apartment in broad daylight, beat down his back door, and shot him as he stood, or sat, or kneeled, unarmed in his family's bathroom. Notwithstanding initial claims that the officers saw a gun on Graham's person, the official police report said that the teen had no gun. Officers

on the scene also stated that the teen represented a threat because he had allegedly flushed a bag of marijuana down the toilet before he was killed. At issue in the relative lack of attention Graham's case is the degree to which acts of state criminality are immediately shuttled within the U.S. media apparatus, and how they are often recorded as "justifiable homicide" at law and custom when committed against congenitally suspect black and brown bodies. Space will not allow me to list every black person murdered by police, security guards, and vigilantes in the first seven months of 2012, a national killing spree of 313 men, women, and minors as of July 16, that is, one black person murdered every twenty-eight hours. Malcolm X Grassroots Movement, "Report on the Extrajudicial Killing of 313 Black People by Police, Security Guards, and Vigilantes," www.operationghettostorm.org.

36. Hartman, *Scenes of Subjection,* 49–78; Feldman, *Formations of Violence,* 85–146.

37. Bolivar Kemp Jr. to John McElroy, Louisiana State Penitentiary General Correspondence (microform), 1951–52, Louisiana State Archives, Baton Rouge.

38. See "Angola Officials Deny Brutalities: Inmates Cut Heel Tendons as Accusations Fly," *Times-Picayune,* February 26, 1951; "More Convicts Slash Heels as Angola Trouble Spreads," *Times-Picayune,* February 28, 1951. See also Anne Butler and C. Murray Henderson, *Angola: Louisiana State Penitentiary, a Half Century of Rage and Reform* (Lafayette: University of Southwestern Louisiana, 1990), 7–33. For the most thoroughgoing exposé of conditions at Angola at the time of the "heel-string" action, see Edward Stagg, "America's Worst Prison," *Colliers Magazine,* November 22, 1952. However, terroristic conditions at Angola were revealed more than ten years earlier by a New Orleanian reporter without a hint of state or national scandal—namely, because the article dealt exclusively with the prison plantation's systematic torture of black bodies. Krebs, "Blood Took Penitentiary Out of the Red," 26–27.

39. Krebs, "Blood Took Penitentiary Out of the Red," and Butler and Henderson, *Angola,* 39.

40. Hartman, *Scenes of Subjection,* 17–114.

41. The coercive extraction of black musical performance on the neoplantation is documented most explicitly within the field of American Folklore. Indeed, two of the most important figures in the field, John and Alan Lomax, often benefited from such methods during their inaugural tours of southern prison plantations such as Angola, Sugarland, Cummins, and Parchman in the early 1930s—trips that not only brought the father and son pair into academic prominence but also signaled a methodological and topical turning point in folklore and ethnomusicology in the United States. Alan Lomax recalls the horrifying circumstances under which one particular black prisoner named Joe Barker was convinced to sing into the white visitors' microphone: "The black [trusty] came out, pushing a Negro man in stripes along at the point of his gun. The poor fellow, evidently

afraid he was going to be punished, was trembling and sweating in an extremity of fear." Alan Lomax, "Sinful Songs of the Southern Negro: Experiences in Collecting Secular Folk-Music," *Southwest Review* 19 (1933–34): 130. As I will discuss in more detail, such scenes unveil the imbrications of the white folkloric enterprise of "discovery" in respect to officially and socially incarcerated black blues and folk musicians and the very conditions of terror and surveillance that made such academic exploration possible. That is, the Lomaxes' transmutation of fields of neo-slavery into sites of "authentic Negro" field recording suggests the degree to which the fungibility, or infinite utility, of the black neoslave extended well beyond the gates of the neoplantation and into academic and popular cultural arenas. No relationship underlines this connection more than that of the Lomaxes and their most prized "find," Huddie Ledbetter (aka Lead Belly)—a folk and blues virtuoso whom the Lomaxes "discovered" on their tour of Angola in 1933, and whom they used as an exoticized musical showpiece, chauffer, cook, driver, laundryman, etc., after his release from Angola in 1934.

42. Hartman, *Scenes of Subjection,* 43–44.

43. Butler and Henderson, *Angola,* 40. The phrase "all-purpose black man" is from Toni Morrison, *Playing in the Dark: Whiteness and the Literary Imagination,* 78.

44. Raymond LeBlanc, "Selected Limitations on the Organization of Treatment in a 'Modern' Prison," Master's thesis, Department of Sociology, Louisiana State University, 34.

45. Goodell, *The American Slave Code,* 77. Emphasis in original.

46. For an example of the treatment of American penal neoslavery as a peculiarly "southern" and "past" phenomenon, see Blackmon, *Slavery by Another Name.* Blackmon concludes his otherwise informative and well-researched study by asserting that the "real" end of slavery in the United States "finally" came in 1951, when Congress issued supposedly definitive statutory proscriptions against involuntary servitude (381). However, as I point out in chapter 2, those "duly convicted" of a crime could not lay claim to the supposed definitive protection that these new statutory edicts offered because they were only applicable to "private" forms of involuntary servitude, or "peonage." That is, whether one was sent to Angola or Attica in the years following this postwar affirmation of the Thirteenth Amendment's proscriptive power, the amendment's exceptional loophole—a "duly convicted" person can be legally submitted to "slavery or involuntary servitude" as "punishment for a crime"—still left one *publicly* enslavable whether the "due" conviction occurred in the South or the North. For another example of the treatment of racialized "convict labor" as a purely southern/past problem, see Mancini, *One Dies, Get Another.* Mancini's otherwise important study also falls under what I refer to as a "liberal" tendency insofar as he restricts his definition of atrocity to a statistical analysis of biological death counts. For Mancini, the fact that the death rate of southern black prisoners between 1866 and 1928 was higher

than that of slaves in the United States before 1865 qualifies the lease as distinct, separate, and "worse" than its predecessor. He argues that, under convict leasing, "black prisoners would suffer and die under conditions far worse than anything they had ever experienced as slaves." While the historical import of the very real ramping up of legalized murders of black people after emancipation cannot be overestimated, a more nuanced approach demands acknowledging that biological death was not the only form of death experienced by slaves. As I noted above, chattelized incarceration, whether experienced in 1771, or 1871, or 1971, represents a necropolitical system in which "life" itself is transmuted into an approximation of death. In fact, the industrialization of biological reproduction during pre-1865 slavery—with the master either "breeding" one slave with another or raping his human commodity himself and producing more human commodities—is the most clear-cut example of how chattelism has always turned both on the production of premature death and *the reproduction of death in life*. Leaving aside Mancini's problematic statistical comparison of a forty-two-year time span of prison slavery to an over four-hundred-year period of chattel slavery (which actually saw periods of extremely high biological death rates, especially in non-U.S. plantation societies such as Brazil and the Caribbean), the restriction of the enormity of slavery to its putatively low biological death count in the United States unconsciously upholds the master mythos that maintained that the plantation was a "protective" and paternalist geography for its (sub)human commodities. More important, this mode of argumentation fits into a larger liberal humanitarian framework that identifies atrocity only where masses of biologically dead or bloodied bodies can be located.

For examples of studies that downplay the relationship between modern carcerality and chattel carcerality on the basis of a "labor"- and/or "production"-centered definition of slavery, see McLennan, *The Crisis of Imprisonment,* 9; Gilmore, *Golden Gulag,* 20–21; Christian Parenti, *Lockdown America* (London: Verso, 199), 211–44. To his credit, Parenti's analysis does leave room for discussion of enslavement as it takes place within the internal relations of prisoners via the administratively sanctioned prisoner sex/rape trade. However, his reduction of prison slavery to a matter of sexual commodification, rupture, and predation discounts the degree to which the prison–industrial complex represents a generalized public/private "trade" in—and rupture of—bodies whom he correctly describes as the sacrificial surplus of the neoliberal labor market. Again, the main object of (in)human commodification and speculation in today's neoslavery is not the prisoner's *labor* but her warehoused *body* and the nexus of public/private profitability and social utility resulting from mass natal alienation, entombment, and civil death. These studies also generally make the error of considering only market-oriented labor—that which produces commodities for sale on the open capitalist market—when discussing the day-to-day work done by the incarcerated. A market-centered approach to the issue of prison slave labor discounts the central role of ostensibly *unproductive travail* to the functioning and reproduction of the carceral state. In other words, the majority of a prisoner's average daily "labor" output in today's prison involves the everyday "smooth" operation of the institution itself—for example, food production (not only growing food but also cooking and serving it), custodial services, prisoner-on-prisoner supervision, clerical work, construction/maintenance of the physical plant(ation), prisoner-run programs such as counseling, legal aid, and religious services, musical/athletic performance, and "consensual" or openly coerced sex "work." Indeed, prisoners often "choose" to perform such unmarketed tasks because "good time"—or a parole-initiating good-conduct report—is often tethered to their perceived consent in performing them. From the purview of prisoners, semantic niceties as to whether the infinite labors associated with "doin' time" should be defined as productive or unproductive does nothing to diminish the fact that any species of work (or apparent prison industrial idleness) clocked within walls, cages, razor wire, or plantation fields amounts to *neoslave labor.* For my knowledge of the centrality of unproductive travail within today's prisons and jails, I am indebted to Saranella R. Childs (Volunteer Coordinator/Case Manager for Friends Outside, Century Regional Detention Facility for Women [CRDF, Linwood, Calif.]).

47. The term "cultural imposition" derives from Frantz Fanon: "In Europe the Negro has one function: That of symbolizing the lower emotions, the baser inclinations, the dark side of the soul. In the collective unconscious of *homo occidentalis,* the Negro—or, if one prefers, the color black—symbolizes evil, sin, wretchedness, death, war, famine.... [The collective unconscious] is the result of what I shall call the unreflected imposition of a culture." Fanon, *Black Skin, White Masks* (New York: Grove Press, 1967), 190–91.

48. Hartman, *Scenes of Subjection,* 17–114.

49. Krebs, "Blood Took Penitentiary Out of the Red," 42.

50. On whether the officially reported figure for whippings at Angola during the 1930s represents an accurate tabulation, Robert Hillary King commented that "if they said it was 10,000 whippings, then it was more like 100,000." Interview with the author, November 29, 2011.

51. Here I should be clear that my raising the specter of the World War II Holocaust should not in any way be read as a contribution to the discourse of exceptionalism that surrounds that moment of atrocity; rather, my articulation of the imbrications of perverse pleasure and abject terror on the neoplantation as related to the concentration camp is in keeping with Aimé Césaire's intervention in this regard in *Discourse on Colonialism,* in which he points out that what was thought to be an example of unprecedented state terror during World War II actually represented a European installment of genocidal "colonialist procedures" that had been enacted in colonial Africa, Asia, Latin America, and the Middle East for centuries leading up to "the" Holocaust. As Césaire makes clear, it was the

culturally manufactured status of the colonized as sub- to nonhuman foils to the Euro-American liberal humanist concept of "man" that disqualified colonialism and slavery from being counted as crimes against humanity. Indeed, as stated above, it is the continued manufacture of blackness as metaphysical affliction that represents the condition of possibility for the social acceptance and social plea-sure that continues to accrue to the modern-day slave plantation/prison. What the practice of these genocidal procedures at Angola represents is that what is most often depicted as an exceptional moment of atrocity during the 1940s was in fact reflective of a nonexceptional project of mass (living) death, imprisonment, and enslavement whose genealogical routes are traceable to the Middle Passage, slavery, and colonial genocide.

52. *Louisiana Municipal Review,* January–February 1943, 2.

53. Douglass, *Narrative of the Life of Frederick Douglass,* 66.

54. It is important to note that Douglass does indeed acknowledge something of the insurrectionary, or at least the subterranean, in moments of apparently seamless plantation hegemony at other junctures of the 1845 narrative—namely, at the moment in which he describes the infinitely complex, poignant, and re-cessed meaning of the slave/sorrow songs he heard as a child on the plantation. Let me also be clear that while I wish to problematize Douglass's generalization regarding the anti-insurrectionary effects of the plantation holiday on the major-ity of his fellow slaves, I also recognize that the deployment of punitive privilege does indeed represent a powerful if incomplete mechanism of dominative control within domains of chattelized incarceration. Herman Wallace discusses the prag-matic utility of prison privilege in the form of a warning to those entombed along with him in protracted or indefinite solitary confinement: "Beware of prison priv-ileges which are designed to manipulate and control your lives. Watching televi-sion or listening to the radio is acceptable only if it doesn't preoccupy your mind or prevent mental growth. As soon as you begin to think you need anything, the prison authorities will use this need against you. Give them nothing to use against you that you are unable to mentally control and you can survive. A high level of self-discipline, self-denial and self-pride are the key to surviving solitary." Wallace, "On Solitary Confinement," 3. Note how Wallace equates personal survival with the total abdication of needs associated with the bodily "self." Again, such testi-mony signals the way in which the chattelized carceral submits the prisoner to an overdetermining simulation of death, or civil death in life, such that even one's attempted assertion of "selfhood" rests on the radical embrace, furtherance, or counter-deployment of the very body-self severance that is performed by the state.

55. I use terms such as "bi," "questioning," and "transgender" fully aware that they were likely not a part of the late 1940s public lexicon in places such as Baton Rouge, New Orleans, and Angola. While granting the discursive and social speci-ficity of past historical moments, I also recognize that any perceived circumscription

as to discursive markers of gender or sexual identity (or other ontological modes) within past social formations in no way translates into a lack of complex lived experience within those formations. Indeed, any such assumption would amount to a presentist myopia.

56. The story of James Dunn, a white male prisoner who was transported to Angola at the age of nineteen, perfectly illustrates this dynamic. He recalls a particular day approximately one month into his sentence in 1960—and how another prisoner "shoved [Dunn] into a dark room where his partner was waiting. They beat me up and they raped me. That was to claim me. . . . When they finished, they told me that they had claimed me. . . . [Once] it happened, that was it—unless you killed one of them, and I was short [i.e., had a short sentence] and wanted to go home. So I decided to try to make the best of it." He goes on to describe another incident that convinced him to assent to be his rapists' "turn-out" or "whore": "During my first week here, I saw fourteen guys rape one youngster 'cause he refused to submit. They snatched him up, took him into the TV room and, man, they did everything to him—I mean, *everything,* and they wouldn't even use no grease. When they finished with him, he had to be taken to the hospital where they had to sew him back up; then they had to take him to the nuthouse at Jackson 'cause he cracked up. . . . I didn't want none of that kind of action, and my only protection was in sticking to my old man, the guy who raped me." Wilbert Rideau, "The Sexual Jungle," in *Life Sentences: Rage and Survival Behind Bars,* ed. Wilbert Rideau and Ron Wikberg (New York: Times Books, 1992), 77. At the point when Dunn finally attempted to free himself from sexual slavery through violent self-defense, he was submitted to solitary confinement and lost his chances at parole. When reading such unspeakable testimony, it is vitally important to understand that ostensibly isolated and individualized acts of rape and sexual violence in prisons and jails are actually de facto elements of one's sentence. See A. Davis, "Public Imprisonment and Private Violence." Not only does penal and juridical law effectively condone such acts, but guards and administrators often participate in them directly, whether through actual physical violence or organizing and profiteering on the trade in sex slaves.

57. For an insightful and critically important treatment of the subject of hyper-criminalization and gendered/sexualized violence as experienced by incarcerated transgender and intersex persons in the context of today's PIC, see Sylvia Rivera Law Project, "'It's War in Here': A Report on the Treatment of Transgender and Intersex People in New York State Men's Prisons," Sylvia Rivera Law Project, New York, 2007.

58. Stagg, "America's Worst Prison," 16.

59. Ibid., 15.

60. See Micki McElya, *Clinging to Mammy: The Faithful Slave in Twentieth-Century America* (Cambridge: Harvard University Press, 2007).

61. Such displays of the incarcerated black body at the twentieth-century prison plantation bear striking resemblance to portraits from early modern England depicting African slaves along with their masters or mistresses. As Kim Hall suggests, when cast in such white supremacist portraiture, the African body functions as a visual emblem of, and foil for, the nobility, wealth, and phenotypical beauty of the white aristocratic subject. Indeed, as in the Angola "trusty" photographs, such imagery often exhibited the black attendant or groom along with an assortment of other possessed living objects, such as monkeys, dogs, horses, and birds—a visual menagerie that was meant to reinforce both the elite status of the owner and the exoticized objecthood of the living stock that he possessed. Kim Hall, *Things of Darkness: Economies of Race and Gender in Early Modern England* (Ithaca: Cornell University Press, 1995), 211–53. My use of the phrase "possessive investment" in respect to the continued socialized desire for such images derives from George Lipsitz's important work on the structured dynamics of white supremacy in U.S. culture, *The Possessive Investment in Whiteness: How White People Profit from Identity Politics* (Philadelphia: Temple University Press, 1998).

62. Butler and Henderson, *Angola*, 41, 44.

63. Toni Morrison uses the absurdist phrase "moving their dirt from one place to the other" to describe a ritualized aspect of the quotidian drudgery that black women faced as domestic servants in apartheid America. "What the Black Woman Thinks about Women's Lib" (1971), in *Toni Morrison: What Moves at the Margin, Selected Nonfiction* (Jackson: University Press of Mississippi, 2008), 27.

64. Butler and Henderson, *Angola*, 39, 41. Henry Lytle Fuqua Jr. has similar memories of his time growing up in a plantation mansion at Angola before his father ascended from the wardenship of Angola to the governorship of Louisiana in 1924. He describes a typical day as an Angola child: "After breakfast we would get on . . . horses, and we would ride all over Angola plantation without any fear of anything. And, of course, the free captains . . . had children. We would . . . visit different camps, and sometimes we would go and have dinner with these folks, and we'd get on horses and ride." And like JoAn Spillman and Patsy Dreher, Fuqua's articulation of childhood happiness is linked to the private possession of black public slaves at both the prison plantation and the governor's mansion: "We had a butler and a cook. And, of course, the state had a colored man, who was a prisoner, that did the lawn, the yard work. And we had, if necessary we could call on a prisoner to drive, but I drove most of the time." Henry L. Fuqua Jr., Oral History Interview, Louisiana State University Special Collections, Henry L. Fuqua Jr., Lytle Papers, Baton Rouge.

In a later segment of the interview, Fuqua reveals how "colored men" from Angola were used to construct roads around the campus of Louisiana State University before its official opening in 1926. The black prisoners were made available for the project after Angola's river levee broke during the Mississippi River flood of 1922. "To keep them busy . . . they had them constructing some of the streets. For instance, Highland Road, they put the curb and gutter down . . . and put in the gravel. And they stayed [on the site of LSU's campus] in these big, surplus World War One aviation tents." The public utilization and exhibition of the black neo-slave at LSU and other "free-world" state institutions continues to this day in Lou-isiana (and other states throughout the United States). In fact, on every single day of my research in Baton Rouge, I walked by black male prisoners, draped in orange jumpsuits, doing landscaping work on the grounds of LSU, the State Library of Louisiana, and the State Capitol building—a repetitive and horrifyingly banal scene that emblazoned the present/future orientation of my "archival" study of neoslavery forever in my mind. Even though I only saw the buses that had trans-ported them to these sites, I am also aware that imprisoned women—the over-whelming majority of whom are black—are used to move "dirt [and shit] from one place to the other" inside the buildings of these same institutions.

65. Butler and Henderson, *Angola*, 41.

66. On the degree to which rape and sexual violence represent "invisible" ele-ments of imprisonment in the United States, particularly in respect to women, see A. Davis, "Public Imprisonment and Private Violence."

67. For an important discussion of the high incidence of homophobic and transphobic sexual violence and physical brutality in U.S. prisons, see Sylvia Rivera Law Project, "'It's War in Here,'" 16, 19, 32–33.

68. The term "freak" was commonly used in black urban communities in the mid-twentieth century to describe nonheteronormative gender and sexual behavior. Marybeth Hamilton, "Sexual Politics and African-American Music; or, Placing Little Richard in History," *History Workshop Journal* 46 (Autumn 1998): 170. In her discussion of Richard Pennimen's transformation from a drag queen named Princess Lavonne into "Little Richard," the self-described "king and queen of the blues," Hamilton discusses the unaccounted-for central role of black drag artists in blues music and the performative venues in which it was crafted. She describes the way in which black urban sociality in cities such as New Orleans represented both a relatively accepting arena for nonheteronormative bodies, rep-resented in its annual "Gay Ball," and a zone of heteronormative sanction against those bodies, symbolized graphically in signs posted outside spaces of public accommodation in black neighborhoods, such as "NO FEMALE IMPERSON-ATORS ALLOWED: COLORED ONLY" (166).

69. The phrase "sexual eccentricity" is from Roderick Ferguson's brilliant work on the heteronormative vectors of the Euro-American sociological imagina-tion, *Aberrations in Black: Toward a Queer of Color Critique* (Minneapolis: Univer-sity of Minnesota Press, 2004), 21. See Sylvia Rivera Law Project, "'It's War in Here,'" for a discussion of the hypervulnerability of today's racialized queer, trans-gender, and intersex persons to economic and social dispossession, and how the

related predicaments of homelessness, joblessness, and natal dislocation often lead to arrest and imprisonment for these subjects.

70. Julie Raimondi, "Space, Place, and Music in New Orleans," PhD diss., Department of Ethnomusicology, University of California, Los Angeles, 2012, 50.

71. See Zagria, "Patsy Valdalia" entry in "A Gender Variance Who's Who: Essays on trans, intersex, cis and other persons and topics from a trans perspective," http://zagria.blogspot.com/2009/08/patsy-valdalia-1921-1982-performer.html; Jeff Hannusch, "The South's Swankiest Nightspot: The Legend of the Dew Drop Inn," ikoiko.com, http://www.satchmo.com/ikoiko/dewdropinn.html; and Hamilton, "Sexual Politics and African-American Music," 167–68.

72. Hamilton, "Sexual Politics and African-American Music," 162.

73. Kenneth Jackson, the grandson of Frank Pania, the club's owner, recalls how the New Orleans city police regularly raided (and patronized) the Dew Drop as a consequence of Pania's open flouting of the city's Jim Crow ordinance, which prohibited interracial association in nightclubs and hotels: "Whites weren't allowed in the building, according to the law. But my grandfather never did discriminate. They used to come in and raid the place. . . . They actually pulled up with paddy wagons outside, and just hauled off everybody out the place, you know. They would arrest *everybody* in the building, everybody in the place at that time, because they were mixing with the opposite race. . . . The majority of the judges and the elected officials were regulars here. The police were regulars. But I guess they had to make an example at some point, saying they couldn't turn a blind eye to the fact that the law was on the book. And according to the way the law was written, they were actually in violation. But it was so crazy, because everybody just came to have a good time." Raimondi, "Space, Place, and Music in New Orleans," 51. On the state's simultaneous creation and disciplining of interracial nightclubs, or "black and tan's," and the racialized urban planning modality of quarantining the public expression of nonheteronormative sexual and gender behaviors to black neighborhoods, see Ferguson, *Aberrations in Black*, 39–43; and Laura Grantmyre, "'They lived their life and they didn't bother anybody': African American Female Impersonators and Pittsburgh's Hill District, 1920–1960," *American Quarterly* 63, no. 4 (December 2011): 983–1011.

74. For an insightful discussion of the elision of narratives of black queer men from histories of black cultural production going back to the Harlem Renaissance, see Essex Hemphill, Introduction to *Brother to Brother: New Writings by Gay Black Men* (Los Angeles: Alyson Books, 1991).

75. Butler and Henderson, *Angola*, 36.

76. Ibid.

77. Ibid., 42.

78. Mary Prince, *The History of Mary Prince: A West Indian Slave, Related by Herself*, ed. Moira Ferguson (1831; Ann Arbor: University of Michigan Press, 1997), 66.

79. Anne Butler mentions the steel plate in Bruce's head in her narrative, a fact she gleaned from an unidentified white "free" resident of the prison plantation. Butler and Henderson, *Angola*, 42.

80. "Search Still Presses for Slayer of Wife of State Prison Officer: Posse Hunts for Trusty Believed Hidden in Woods," *Morning Advocate* (Baton Rouge), October 21, 1948. See also "Posse Continues: Big Manhunt for Prison Houseboy," *Morning Advocate*, October 22, 1948; and "Search for Trusty Moves into EBR," *Morning Advocate*, October 23, 1948.

81. In a move that highlights the differential relation between what was seen as an isolated occasion of personal white tragedy and natural black criminality, and the more "important" business of neoplantation sugarcane production, the state called off the full-scale manhunt for Bruce five days after it had began so that "more than 100 prison guards and employees" could return to overseeing Angola's field-working neoslaves—bodies that had been rendered temporarily "idle" after the Spillman killing. "Posse Disbanded in Trusty Hunt, Search Continues," *Morning Advocate*, October 26, 1948.

82. Mary Fonesca and Steven Brooke, "Afton Villa Gardens: St. Francesville," in *Louisiana's Gardens* (Gretna: Pelican Publishing, 1999), 13–16. See also *Afton Villa, A French Gothic Chateau, 1790–1849: Yesterday's Gift to Today* (St. Francesville, La.: [s.n.], 1900).

83. William Craft, *Running a Thousand Miles for Freedom; or, the Escape of William and Ellen Craft from Slavery* (London: William Tweedie, 1860).

84. I should be clear here that in discussing the lack of an organized liberal or radical society of white antislavery advocates to whom an escaped prisoner could turn in 1948, I am in no way suggesting that there were absolutely no avenues of subterranean aid, concealment, or familial/community understanding available within black (or allied white/brown/Indigenous/Asian) urban or rural communities for a fugitive neoslave. Considering the ubiquity of legalized racial violence against black people, it is not difficult to imagine that most of them would have remained helpfully silent, if not openly defiant, vis-à-vis the law's attempted reclamation of Bruce's fugitive body. I am only attempting to suggest the degree to which—in the context of a nearly wholesale white/public consensus regarding the supposed end of slavery—racialized and sexualized criminal stigmatization would have precluded any such underground political practice from attaining widespread social currency or "aboveground" political viability.

85. "Posse Continues: Big Manhunt for Prison Houseboy," 8.

86. Butler and Henderson, *Angola*, 41.

87. What Louis Althusser calls "preappointment" denotes the preprogramming sector of ideology whereby an "individual is always-already [interpellated as] a subject, even before he is born." Althusser, "Ideology and Ideological State Apparatuses." In a manner akin to antebellum preappointment where nearly every

black person was automatically tagged "slave" before birth—*every black child shall take on the condition of the mother*—black men, women, and children in the postbellum national white supremacist imaginary have been preappointed as metaphysically criminal. Significantly, in clarifying his definition of state interpellation, or what he calls the ritualized "hailing" of the subject, Althusser conjures a scene in which an individual automatically knows when he or she is being addressed on the street by a policeman with the call: "Hey, you there!" (118). Indeed, this articulation of the state's creation of civil subjects represents an all-too-accurate portrayal of racial subjection in the United States and other nation-states. However, what is missing in Althusser's interpellative allegory is the fact that the hailing process represents a collective rather than individualized experience for the precariously civil racialized subject. That is, the story of a single person "recognizing" that he or she is the one being picked out of a crowd by a policeman on the street would have to be adjusted for the experiential reality of those black or brown persons preappointed as always-already suspect subjects—i.e., when the policeman yelled out "Hey, you there!" in a black or brown community, *everyone* would properly assume that they could be the suspect being hailed. Indeed, this collective recognition actually forces another important change to the allegory: instead of turning around 180 degrees in response to the policeman's call, many racially criminalized subjects would run in the opposite direction in hopes of escaping a *hail* of baton blows, tazer shots, bullets, and/or days in a cage.

88. I should note here that the state would have in no way depended on pathologizing Bruce as queer or trans in order to commit this justifiable homicide. Indeed, no captive gender/sexuality has been branded as more disposable than black straight maleness in the postbellum history of U.S. prison slavery. In discussing the degree to which sexual/gender aberrance was ascribed to Bruce, I am pointing out how such difference would have added another layer of social acceptability to Bruce's always already murderable status as black "male" prison slave.

89. "Body of Trusty Found in River Morganza: 'No Signs of Violence,' Jury Reports," *Morning Advocate* (Baton Rouge), October 31, 1948.

90. "Search Still Presses for Slayer of Wife of State Prison Officer," 1. The "dogboy," or "dog sergeant," represented one of the neoplantation roles assigned to "trusty Negroes." Indeed, the particular black man that held this role at St. Gabriel plantation (an auxiliary of Angola) during Bruce's escape is pictured in a photograph that accompanied the *Morning Advocate*'s coverage. He is shown holding one of the penitentiary's scores of bloodhounds, and standing next to the rifle- and pistol-bearing sheriff's deputies and Angola guards, under the caption "MANHUNTERS." "Search for Trusty Moves into EBR," 1. In describing the training method for Angola's variety of English, Cuban, and crossbred dogs, another article, written three years after Bruce's initial arrival at Angola, describes how bloodhound puppies were trained to "tree," hunt, and bite "Negro" prisoners:

"The method of training is simple. The pup is taken to the woods and left, to fol-
low the dog sergeant home by scent. Later the pup is held, while a prisoner lays
down a trail as he makes his way back to camp. By stretching the interval between
the time the trail is laid and the time the dog is set on it, the problem of working
out the trail is made increasingly difficult for the animal. Later still, the pup is
taught to tree his man by having prisoners leave the ground and climb." Albert
Proctor, "Fear of Huge Dogs, Law's Unsung 'Arm,' Helps Keep Order, *Progress*
(Shreveport), 1938 (unspecified date). Angola continues to use dogs as a modality
of terror to this day. The penitentiary even currently practices the crossbreed-
ing of dogs and wolves in order to create an even more terroristic "manhunter."
See Terry Jones, "Wolf Dog to Patrol Angola," *Advocate* (Baton Rouge), May 2,
2012, http://theadvocate.com/ news/2720715-123/wolf-dog-to-patrol-angola. For
a superb treatment of the historical use of dogs as a modality of racial terror from
slavery through the current U.S. invasion and occupation of Afghanistan and Iraq
(and elsewhere), see Johnson, "'You Should Give Them Blacks to Eat.'"

91. "While babysitting at another guard's home, JoAn would unwittingly see
photographs of the convict's body on the sandbar where it was found." Butler and
Henderson, *Angola,* 48.

92. For critically important assessments of neoslavery, and the "(neo)slave
narrative," as expressed within radical black, Latina/o, Asian Pacific Islander
(API), and allied white political formations, see Joy James, ed., *The New Abolitionists* and *Imprisoned Intellectuals.* See also Rodríguez, *Forced Passages.* However, the
experiences of those such as McElroy, Mathews, and Bruce underline the importance of our centering the forms of anti-neoslavery practice that were enacted by
those who have never entered into the pantheon of "black radical politics," and
whose entombment represented the condition of possibility for the modern
white supremacist prison state.

93. The "Salt Pit" was a code name for a CIA-run secret prison, or "black
site," constructed on the remains of an abandoned brick factory north of Kabul,
Afghanistan, after the United States invaded, bombed, and occupied the country
in October 2001. With Afghan guards acting as proxies, the CIA used the site to
torture Afghan detainees. One prisoner, Gul Rahman, froze to death after being
stripped naked from the waist down, chained to the floor of his cell, and left to
freeze overnight. Dana Priest, "CIA Avoids Scrutiny of Detainee Treatment:
Afghan's Death Took Two Years to Come to Light," *Washington Post,* March 3,
2005. The United States has operated such sites throughout the Middle East, Central Asia, and Eastern Europe since its invasion of Afghanistan and its invasion
of Iraq in 2003. One cannot gain a full understanding of U.S. state terrorism
and criminality in "black sites," or in openly declared international prisons such
as Guantánamo Bay and Abu Ghraib, without recognizing that such practices
have issued directly from conditions of neoslavery "at home." Four years after

becoming the first member of the Angola 3 to be released, Robert Hillary King underlined this point by expressing his mystification at the international shock and bewilderment that attended the release of photographs depicting torture of prisoners at Abu Ghraib. "What amazes me is, when the photos were exposed by the media [in May 2004], it seemed as if people were appalled. . . . I wondered: Am I an alien or something? This is something that has been going on in the United States since the inception of prisons. Prisons are torture chambers." Speech given at the "From Attica to Abu Ghraib" conference, University of California, Berkeley, April 23, 2005.

4. The Warfare of Northern Neoslavery in Chester Himes's *Yesterday Will Make You Cry*

1. Chester Himes, *Yesterday Will Make You Cry* (New York: W. W. Norton, 1998), 96, 99.

2. Ibid., 163.

3. Ibid., 165–66.

4. Ibid., 320–21.

5. Two earlier examples of northern narratives of neoslavery are Harriet Wilson, *Our Nig; or Sketches of the Life of a Free Black* (1859; New York: Vintage Books, 1983), and William Walker and Thomas Gaines, *Buried Alive (Behind Prison Walls) for a Quarter of a Century: Life of William Walker* (Saginaw, Mich.: Friedman & Hynan, 1892). In expressing how chattelism infused the lived experience of the life of "free" black people in the North, Wilson's text offers an originary testament to the socially incarcerating structure of U.S. apartheid. Walker's virtually unknown text is critically important given the fact that he experiences both chattel slavery in the South (Virginia) and penal neoslavery in the North (Jackson Prison in Michigan). Tellingly, Walker describes the regime of solitary confinement and cellular cargoing that he experienced in the North as decidedly more abject than its southern counterpart. To read Walker's text, see the Documenting the American South Collection, University of North Carolina Library, Chapel Hill, http://docsouth.unc.edu/neh/gaines/summary.html.

6. For a detailed account of the Easter Monday Fire, see Elise Meyers Walker, David Meyers, and James Dailey II, *Inside the Ohio Penitentiary (Landmarks)* (Charleston, S.C.: History Press, 2013), 90–102. I have incorporated the term "tight-packing" here to highlight the degree to which the warehousing of nearly five thousand prisoners into a prison designed for fifteen hundred bears haunting resemblance to the cargoing methodology of chattel slavery (see chapter 1), which called for the "tight-packing" of slave holds with as many bodies as possible notwithstanding the extremely high death rates this practice inflicted (with the idea that the profitability of this method would outstrip the costs associated with

masses of dead cargo it produced). The most infamous example of this Middle Passage carceral model imprisonment technique is offered in the sketch of the British slaver *Brookes*, which was designed to hold 454 African captives, but which transported as many as 740. Here we should take note of the degree to which the "modern" northern land-based slave ship far outstripped its eighteenth-century forerunner in the close "stowage" of chattelized bodies. However, in so doing we should also be careful not to adopt a liberal human rights ideological framework that would read a "correctional" recalibration of human cargoing facilities to their "proper" proportion of captive bodies per cubic feet as just, humane, and progressive. In short, even one body in a prison, jail, or immigrant detention facility equals carceral overcrowding and state terrorism.

While the Ohio Penitentiary fire remains the most deadly prison fire in U.S. history, the people of Honduras were recently made to witness a grim echo of the Depression-era holocaust when 358 prisoners (and some of their family members) burned alive inside their cells at the National Penitentiary in Comayagua on February 14, 2012. It supplanted the Easter Monday Fire of 1930 in Ohio as the worst prison fire in recorded history. As in the case of the Ohio fire, the discourses of administrative neglect and tragedy that arose after the Honduran prison catastrophe serve to elide state culpability for submitting poor people to a system of carceral living death without which such "tragedies" could never have occurred.

7. "Mutinous Convicts in Ohio Shot Down by Prison Guards," Associated Press, *Times-Picayune* (New Orleans), April 30, 1930, 1; "Tunnel to Home of Ohio Warden Found by Guards," Associated Press, *Times-Picayune*, May 1, 1930, 1; "Machine Gun Kills Two Convicts," *New York Times*, May 9, 1930, 15.

8. On September 13, 1971, New York governor Nelson Rockefeller ordered the New York State Police and New York National Guard to storm Attica Prison in western New York state in response to a multiracial prisoner uprising that had resulted from the atrocious conditions at the prison and from the assassination of George Jackson at San Quentin Prison in California on August 21, 1971. After failing to negotiate in good faith with the 2,200 rebellious neoslaves, the state culminated its siege on Attica by dropping tear-gas bombs from helicopters into the yard and murdering 29 prisoners and 10 guard hostages. Those deemed to be the leaders of the uprising (the majority of whom were black) endured days of torture after the massacre. Prisoner testimony reveals that these men were kicked in the testicles, burned with cigarette butts, and forced to run on top of broken glass through what the state police called "nigger stick" (i.e., baton) gauntlets of twenty to thirty troopers. The Attica rebellion and massacre represents both a spectacular example of U.S. fascism and a significant representation of the unintended consequences of punitive homogenization—that is, the multiracial aspect of the uprising expresses how the prison performs a relative deconstruction of whiteness through civil death. As such, such moments of prisoner uprising represent

flashpoints of rebellious opportunity in which cross-racial solidarity functions as an unaccounted-for excess of collectivized civil death. For more on this process of repressively born solidarity potential in U.S. prisons, see Staughton Lynd, *Lucasville: The Untold Story of a Prison Uprising* (Oakland: PM Press, 2011), 85, 133–34. See also Gilmore, *Golden Gulag,* 244–45.

I do, however, take serious issue with Lynd's utilization of the example of white prisoners seeing themselves as part of a "convict race" in the case of the Lucasville, Ohio, uprising of 1993, as overturning what he considers to be an "essentialist" construction of whiteness proffered by those such as W. E. B. Du Bois, David Roediger, and Cheryl Harris, who have argued for the propertied, psychic, and material interests associated with white working-class racial becoming in the United States. See Du Bois, "Back Toward Slavery," in *Black Reconstruction, 670–709;* David Roediger, *The Wages of Whiteness* (London: Verso, 1991); and Cheryl Harris, "Whiteness as Property," 106 *Harv. L. Rev.* (1993): 1709–95. Lynd states that interracial solidarity in the cases of prison uprisings demonstrates how there is nothing "essential" about racial difference and how race is the product of "specific historical circumstances." However, he fails to recognize that the scholars mentioned above each argue in systematic ways for the exact opposite of essentialism: they each point out how, for white people, race is nothing if not a historically constructed, if ideologically sedimented, mode of social being; and a legal, political, and cultural "property," whose lived materiality is felt at the level of economics, politics, culture, and, I would add, a *relative* racialized protection from state repression.

What the examples of Lucasville and Attica underscore is the fact that, unfortunately, it often takes a great deal more than economic exploitation for the white working-class subject to relinquish some of the material, cultural, and psychic property of whiteness in the name of collective human liberation. Lynd's citation of a repressively borne situation of interracial solidarity in the prison actually ends up underlining the embeddedness, tenaciousness, and materiality of race as a structurally ossified social construct in the "free" world. That is, the examples of Lucasville, Attica, and the Ohio Penitentiary fire exemplify the tenaciousness of race insofar as they reveal how the free white civil subject often has to endure civil death, and a perilous experiential approximation of biological death, in order to—in the words of James Baldwin—really *believe he is not white.* As I will discuss below in reference to the fire scene in *Yesterday Will Make You Cry,* interracial solidarity in the case of prison uprisings is less of an example of an achievement of color-blindness, or a suspension of racial difference qua blackness, than a representation of the ways in which white prisoners undergo a process of virtual *niggerization* through criminal stigmatization. However, to this we must add that the continued retrenchment of racial antipathy and white supremacy in US prisons through formations such as the Aryan Brotherhood and racist prison administrations suggest how the process of prisoner solidarity is most often outflanked by the state's strategic refabrication of racial apartheid and punitive difference within the walls.

9. Mutulu Shakur, Anthony X. Bradshaw, Malik Dinguswa, Terry Long, Mark Cook, Adolfo Matos, and James Haskins, "Genocide against the Black Nation in the U.S. Penal System (Abridged)," in James, *Imprisoned Intellectuals,* 190–97; Robinson, *Black Marxism,* 81; Gilmore, *Golden Gulag,* 86, 238–39.

10. On the racialized aspects of northern imprisonment relative to black migrants and other poor black people, and how this component of U.S. carceral history has largely been ignored in extant discussions of the North's supposedly "modern" answer to southern systems of racist policing and imprisonment, see Khalil Gibran Muhammad's excellent study, *The Condemnation of Blackness: Race, Crime, and the Making of Modern Urban America* (Cambridge: Harvard University Press, 2010).

My use of the term "articulation" to describe the dialectical interfacing of racial, class, gendered, and sexualized terror in the U.S. prison derives from Stuart Hall's discussion of the interconnections and divergences of racial dominance and class exploitation—particularly as found in apartheid South Africa—in, "Articulation and Societies Structured in Dominance." This term is directly related to Kimberlé Crenshaw's concept of "intersectionality," although Krenshaw uses a critical race-theory epistemology to center the determinant role of gender violence in social and legal relations. Krenshaw, "Mapping the Margins: Intersectionality, Identity Politics, and Violence against Women of Color," *Stanford Law Review* 43, no. 6 (July 1991). For a black feminist approach to the discussion of intersectionality, see Patricia Hill Collins, *Black Feminist Thought: Knowledge, Consciousness, and the Politics of Empowerment* (New York: Routledge, 2000). And for a hugely important treatment of articulating structures of racial, class, gendered, and sexualized terror under the U.S. carceral state, especially in relation to transgender women of color and intersex people in the New York prison and policing system, see Sylvia Rivera Law Project, "'It's War in Here': A Report on the Treatment of Transgender and Intersex People in New York State Men's Prisons," Sylvia Rivera Law Project, New York, 2007.

11. Michel Fabre, "Chester Himes Direct," in *Conversations with Chester Himes,* ed. Michel Fabre and Robert Skinner (Jackson: University of Mississippi Press, 1995), 131.

12. Chester Himes, *The Quality of Hurt* (New York: Paragon House, 1971), 117.

13. Chester Himes to Carl Van Vechten, February 18, 1947, *Van Vechten Papers,* James Weldon Johnson Memorial Collection, Beinecke Rare Book and Manuscript Library, Yale University.

14. Robert Bone, *The Negro Novel in America* (New Haven: Yale University Press, 1965), 169. Marlon Ross offers a brilliant refutation of this line of argument in his essay "White Fantasies of Desire: Baldwin and the Racial Identities of Sexuality,"

in *James Baldwin Now,* ed. Dwight McBride (New York: New York University Press, 1999), 20–24.

15. H. Bruce Franklin, "'Portrait of the Artist as a Young Convict': *Yesterday Will Make You Cry,*" in *Andromeda,* Rutgers University, http://andromeda.rutgers .edu/~hbf/ himes.html.

16. Fabre, "Chester Himes Direct," 125.

17. Himes, "Prison Mass" (1933), in *The Collected Stories of Chester Himes* (New York: Thunder's Mouth Press, 2000), 147.

18. Dayan, "Legal Slaves and Civil Bodies," 59 (italics in Blackstone; underlining is my emphasis).

19. Agamben, *Homo Sacer,* 159.

20. Angela Y. Davis's earlier referenced point regarding the de facto social crime of blackness, and black maleness in particular, bears repeating here. In speaking of the fact that more than one-third of young black males were either in prison or under some form of direct carceral state control (i.e., parole or probation) as of 1995, she states: "One has a greater chance of going to jail or prison if one is a black man than if one is actually a law-breaker. While most imprisoned young black men may have broken a law, it is the fact that they are young black men rather than the fact that they are law-breakers which brings them into contact with the criminal justice system." Davis, "Racialized Punishment and Prison Abolition," 104.

21. See, for example, Assata Shakur, *Assata: An Autobiography* (Chicago: Lawrence Hill Books, 1987); Jackson, *Soledad Brother*; A. Davis, *Angela Davis: An Autobiography*; Leonard Peltier, *Prison Writings: My Life Is a Sundance* (New York: St. Martin's Press, 1999); Abu-Jamal, *Live from Death Row*; Viet Mike Ngo, "Grave Digger," *Amerasia Journal* 29, no. 1 (2003): 180.

22. Jackson, *Soledad Brother,* 23.

23. A fairly recent study found that there were three times more seriously ill people in prisons and jails than in hospitals as of 2005. "More Mentally Ill Persons in Jails and Prisons Than in Hospitals: A Survey of the States," Treatment Advocacy Center, Arlington, Va., May 2010.

24. Himes, *Yesterday Will Make You Cry,* 77–79.

25. Wynter, "On Disenchanting Discourse," 446–47.

26. The racist brand "nigger" represents one of the more devastating examples of what Hortense Spillers describes as the practice of nominative violence, or white supremacist and misogynist (dis)naming of African persons. She suggests how this violent discursive system is dialectically connected to the serialized rupture of "black flesh" under formations of chattelism, and how white supremacist misogynist "naming [serving] as one of the key sources of a bitter Americanizing for African persons." Spillers, "Mama's Baby, Papa's Maybe," 73.

27. Kimberly Phillips, *AlabamaNorth: African-American Migrants, Community, and Working-Class Activism in Cleveland, 1915–1945* (Champaign: University of Illinois Press, 1999), 12.

28. For a brilliant discussion of the criminalization of black migrant subjects in the North, and the sociological consensus regarding the "shiftless," "diseased," and "immoral," black migrant, see Khalil Gibran Muhammad, *The Condemnation of Blackness*. For a site-specific treatment of the pattern of ghettoization, criminalization, and the public defamation that was visited on black migrants to Ohio, see Kenneth Kusmer, *A Ghetto Takes Shape: Black Cleveland, 1870–1930* (Urbana: University of Illinois Press, 1976); Beverly Bunch-Lyons, *Contested Terrain: African American Women Migrate from the South to Cincinnati, 1900–1950* (New York: Routledge, 2002); and Phillips, *AlabamaNorth*. For an account of the practice of northern Jim Crow in Ohio against free and fugitive black people in the nineteenth century, see Frank Quillin, *The Color Line in Ohio: A History of Race Prejudice in a Typical Northern State* (Ann Arbor: F. G. Wahr, 1913). See also Litwack, *North of Slavery*, 71–75. Phillips's account is particularly important insofar as it traces the degree to which black migrants imported to northern cities the sort of cultural/survival practices that they had cultivated in the South, practices such as religion, music, and political activism. It is important to point out, however, that such practices were that much more essential to the northern black migrant experience given the high incidence of police brutality and imprisonment these migrant bodies faced—experiences that served as haunting rememories of southern Jim Crow, the chain gang, and the prison plantation.

29. Kusmer, *A Ghetto Takes Shape,* 165.

30. Edward Margolies and Michel Fabre, *The Several Lives of Chester Himes* (Jackson: University Press of Mississippi, 1997), 19–20.

31. Himes, *The Quality of Hurt,* 18, 64.

32. Himes is not alone is his problematic and exceptionalist self-portrait in relation to common black folk. Indeed, his prison autobiography falls directly in line with what Valerie Smith has described as a dynamic of simultaneous representivity and exceptionality within black male writing going back to Frederick Douglass's 1845 autobiographical slave narrative. For Smith, many literate/literary black male writers, from Olaudah Equiano, to Douglass, to James Weldon Johnson, to Richard Wright, tend to position themselves as liminal figures, who are at once representative of a subjugated black population but who are intellectually superior to that very population. Valerie Smith, *Self-Discovery and Authority in Afro-American Narrative* (Cambridge: Harvard University Press, 1991). As Smith's important study makes clear, this pattern should not be conceived as an individualized pathology; that is, the exceptionalist mode of self-narrative had a great deal to do with the black writer's attempts at belying white supremacist notions of black subhumanity, "unmanliness," and intellectual inferiority through the performance

of literary and intellectual acumen—a fact that suggests how in portraying themselves in an exceptional manner these black writers actually performed a racially representative act in serving as proof of black "manhood." As in the case of Frederick Douglass, however, Himes did recognize that black folk culture contained forms of artistic genius that are unaccounted for according to the very elitist standards of literacy and education that he attempted to meet in his own work. "I have talked to black sharecroppers and convicts and various black people who could tell, without stopping, better stories than Faulkner could write. Some of them couldn't even read or write, but they had the same genius for telling stories that Faulkner had, and they could tell continuous stories, too. The narrative would go on and on, and they would never lose it. But then these people couldn't write, you see. So I believe that the black man certainly has a creativity that is comparable to the highest type of creativity in America . . . [and] probably even greater." John A. Williams, "My Man Himes: An Interview with Chester Himes" (1970), in Fabre and Skinner, *Conversations with Chester Himes*, 64.

33. Moten, *In the Break*, 197.

34. "There is no document of civilization which is not at the same time a document of barbarism." Walter Benjamin, "Thesis on the Philosophy of History," in *Illuminations*, 256.

35. Moten, *In the Break*, 208.

36. Unpublished Notes, c. late 1930s, *Chester Himes Papers*, James Weldon Johnson Memorial Collection, Beinecke Rare Book and Manuscript Library, Yale University.

37. Quillin, *The Color Line in Ohio*, 55–56.

38. Ibid., 57.

39. Litwack, *North of Slavery*, 72. Again, Litwack's work represents a pathbreaking treatment of the North's version of the Black Codes—the Black Laws of states such as Ohio, Illinois, and Indiana—along with how northern states inaugurated many of the Jim Crow laws that are associated with the "Jim Crow South" during the nineteenth century (see also chapter 2 above).

40. Ibid., 72–73. Lynchings and other forms of extralegal violence against black migrants were an all-too-common occurrence in Ohio throughout the nineteenth century. For instance, in Waverly, a town approximately fifty miles south of Columbus, black migrants were driven away by a regular occurrence of lynching. However, the black subjects did not leave the town without offering resistance. In his book *The Color Line in Ohio*, Frank Quillin quotes at length from the early twentieth-century Ohio historian Henry Howe: "A lot of Virginia negroes [*sic*] settled up on Pee Pee creek, in the neighborhood of the Burkes and the Downings. Some of them prospered nicely, and this enraged their white neighbors. Downing's crowd got to burning the hay and wheat of the colored farmers, harassing their stock, interfering in their private business. . . . One night they organized a big

raid into the colored settlement, with the avowed purpose of 'clearing out the whole nest of the d—d niggers.' They went fully armed, and didn't propose to stop short of doing a little killing and burning. One of the first cabins they surrounded was that of an especially hated colored man. They opened fire upon it, hoping to drive the negro out. But the darkey, —an honest, peaceable fellow, —wasn't too frightened. He, too, had a gun, and taking a safe position near one of the windows of his cabin, he blazed away into the darkness.... A wild cry of pain followed his shot. The buck shot from his gun plunged into the right leg of Tim Downing's brother, cutting an artery." After the white man bled to death, the lynch mob returned to the black man's house and shot his son in the head, killing him. The black man fled from the town soon after. Other "darkeys" were lynched through-out Ohio until (at least) the end of the nineteenth century for alleged sexual "out-ragings" of white women. Quillin, *The Color Line in Ohio,* 112–15.

41. Scott Christianson, *With Liberty for Some: 500 Years of Imprisonment in America* (Boston: Northeastern University Press, 1998), 228.

42. Incarceration rates are drawn from *Prisoners, 1923: Crime Conditions in the United States as Reflected in Census Statistics of Imprisoned Offenders* (Washington, D.C.: U.S. Bureau of the Census, 1926), 245. Total population statistics are taken from Campbell Gibson and Kay Jung, *Historical Census Statistics on Population Totals by Race, 1790 to 1990* (Washington, D.C.: U.S. Bureau of the Census, 2002). It is important to point out, however, that though the per capita rate of imprison-ment was decidedly higher in Ohio than Alabama, the southern state far outstripped its northern counterpart in terms of the sheer size of its racialized neoslavery regime, with black prisoners totaling 2,062 out of the 2,976 prisoners in the Ala-bama system, or 70 percent—which was double the size of the black penitentiary and reformatory population in Ohio for 1923.

43. Alan Lomax supplies us with an example of the liberal romantic folkloric treatment of the prison plantation and chain gang as "preserves" of authentic "Negro" culture in an article from 1934, in which he describes his initial trips with his father, John Lomax, in the early 1930s. For him, the prison preserved the "Negro" in his authentic, "premodern," vernacular form: "We had found the edu-cated Negro resentful of our attempt to collect his secular folk-music. We found other Negroes afraid for religious reasons to sing for us, while the members of the younger generation were on the whole ignorant of the songs we wanted and inter-ested only in the Blues . . . and in jazz. So it was that we decided to visit the Negro prison farms of the South. There, we thought, we should find that the Negro, away from the pressure of the churchly community, ignorant of the uplifting educa-tional movement, having none but official contact with white men, dependent on the resources of his own group for amusement, and hearing no canned music, would have preserved and increased his heritage of secular folk-music. And we were right. In two months we recorded approximately a hundred new tunes from

the singing Negro convicts: work songs from the levee camp, the section gang, the workers in the woods and the fields, and the chain gang—ballads, reels, field calls." What Lomax leaves out of this pastoralized and romantic view of the scene of neoslavery is that the main reason the Lomaxes were more successful in gaining access to "authentic Negro" culture in the prison plantation than on the streets was that the imprisoned black person could not say "no" when ordered to perform for white folkloric tourists by his prison master—a fact that Lomax himself revealed later in the same piece when he describes how a certain black man was compelled to sing a particular ballad that the father-and-son pair were "hunting": "The Superintendent wouldn't sing it, but at last he sent a trusty with a shotgun into the dormitory to find somebody who knew the song. Presently the black guard came out, pushing a Negro man in stripes at the point of a gun. The poor fellow, evidently afraid he was to be punished, was trembling and sweating in an extremity of fear." Alan Lomax, " 'Sinful' Songs of the Southern Negro," in *Alan Lomax: Selected Writings, 1934–1997*, ed. Ronald Cohen (New York: Routledge, 2003), 22, 30. Again, whether articulated through the liberal romantic racism of Alan, or the more open white supremacy of his father, John, the primitivist mode of folklore that the most renowned folklorists of black incarcerated music produced was both dependent on and part and parcel of the neo-enslavement of black people as field, mine, domestic, and "musical" prison slaves.

44. Muhammad, *The Condemnation of Blackness*, 4–5.

45. As I will discuss below, "Prince Rico" is actually based on a real person, Aubert LaCarlton Collins. Rico's biography represents something of a mystery, for while he is described as hailing from Georgia in press reports, his fictive persona in *Yesterday Will Make You Cry* claims to be from Los Angeles—a claim that has possible validity since he and Himes did indeed meet in Los Angeles after Himes's release from the Ohio Penitentiary. Margolies and Fabre, *The Several Lives of Chester Himes*, 48. Interestingly, as the only other well-developed (and obviously intelligent) black character in the text (besides the "white-faced" Himes), Rico is also described in very ambiguous racial terms in *Yesterday Will Make You Cry*. He is described as having "olive skin" with an "exotic," Spanish look, and having a "Mongolian cast to his features." Himes, *Yesterday Will Make You Cry*, 265–66.

46. In my discussion of the creative power that emanates from the erotic bond between Rico and Jimmy, I am drawing upon the definition of the erotic proffered by the black feminist theorist Audre Lorde: "The erotic has often been misnamed by men and used against women. It has been made into the confused, the trivial, the psychotic, the plasticized sensation. For this reason, we have often turned away from the exploration and consideration of the erotic as a source of power and information, confusing it with its opposite, the pornographic. But pornography is a direct denial of the power of the erotic, for it represents the suppression of

feeling. . . . The erotic is a measure between the beginnings of our sense of self and the chaos of our strongest feelings. It is an internal sense of satisfaction to which, once we have experienced it, we know we can aspire. For having experienced the fullness of this depth of feeling and recognizing its power, in honor and self-respect we can require no less of ourselves." She adds that it "is never easy to demand the most of ourselves, for our lives, from our work." Audre Lorde, "Uses of the Erotic: The Erotic as Power," in *Sister Outsider: Essays and Speeches* (New York: Random House, 2007), 54. However, the embodied and epistemic force of the erotic is rendered circumscribed at best in the space of civil death, wherein intimate "touch" is often indistinguishable from sexual violence, rupture, and enslavement.

47. Chester Himes to Carl Van Vechten, March 11, 1953, *Chester Himes Papers*, James Weldon Johnson Memorial Collection, Beinecke Rare Book and Manuscript Library, Yale University.

48. See Regina Kunzel, "Situating Sex: Prison Sexual Culture in the Mid-Twentieth Century United States," *GLQ: A Journal of Lesbian and Gay Studies* 8, no. 3 (2002): 253–70. Kunzel's study offers an amazing historical analysis of the homophobic ideological currents that created the reduction of all sexual encounters in prisons into a heteronormative framework that pathologized those bodies branded as sexual pathological before imprisonment, and that treated those bodies that were read as "heterosexual" as simply performing a repressed biological necessity when having sex with a "punk," "kid," or "girl-boy" in the sexually restricted space of the prison. For her, the pathologization of same-sex encounters in the prison, and the attempt by sociologists and psychologists to treat prison sexual culture as totally distinct from sexual dynamics of the "free-world," expressed unconscious anxieties on the part mid-twentieth-century researchers, and the public at large, regarding nonheteronormative behavior in general at a moment when "the homo/heterosexual binarism was growing more rigid" (259). As Kunzel notes, many of the sexual patterns that were exhibited in U.S. prisons from the beginning of the twentieth century actually mirrored the sexual culture of the streets, especially within so-called vice districts, which were most often located in working-class and black neighborhoods. See also George Chauncey's informative study, *Gay New York: Gender, Urban Culture, and the Making of the Gay Male World* (New York: Basic Books, 1994). Himes himself testifies to this fact in his official autobiography: "Nothing happened in the prison that I had not already encountered in outside life. . . . [Aside] from masturbation, all sex gratification [in the prison] derived from sodomy, and I had encountered homosexuals galore around the Majestic Hotel and the environs of Fifty-fifth Street and Central Avenue in Cleveland. The pansies called it 'pussy without bone' when soliciting. . . . But I always preferred my pussy with all of its pelvic bone intact, whether it was sharp or cushioned. In prison the female of the species, known as 'boy-girls,' were not

much different in behavior patterns and emotions from their counterparts out-side, the black prostitutes, only their anatomy was different." While Himes's queer desire is totally disavowed in this homo/transphobic description of Scovill's sex-ual culture (indeed he fails to mention his sexual relationship with Rico in these remembrances), his prison autobiography and letters to Van Vechten unveil that he was much less certain about his sexual preferences than his reactionary com-ments allow.

While I completely concur with the intervention Kunzel makes regarding the problematics of the "situational sex" model, I do feel that her method tends to evacuate the centrality of sexual violence, sexual slavery, and human trafficking within the "desire" matrix of the prison. That is, while all same-sex encounters in the prison cannot be reduced to "situational" or "forced" intimacy, we also need to be wary of a too-easy grafting of the theoretical modalities we bring to "free-world" sexual desire, identification, and practices onto the zone of civil death, ritualized rape, and neoslavery—aspects of prisoner "sexual culture" that are completely absent from Kunzel's study. For further thoughts of caution along these lines, see the work of Stephen "Donny" Donaldson, a former prisoner (and prison rape vic-tim), who directed the national organization "Stop Prison Rape" until his death in 1996. For instance, in one piece, Donaldson derides any attempt by unimprisoned academics to dismiss the primary role of sexual deprivation in respect to prison sex/rape: "Many of the reasons for [same-sex] involvement go beyond the neces-sity of relieving the sex/intimacy drive, though I should add before leaving the subject that those armchair theorists who claim that sexual deprivation is not one of the many factors in prisoner rape, as distinguished from rape in the community, are mistaken." Stephen Donaldson, "A Million Jockers, Punks, and Queens," in *Prison Masculinities*, ed. Don Sabo, Terry Kupers, and Willie London (Philadel-phia: Temple University Press, 2001), 122.

49. Himes, *Black on Black: Baby Sister and Selected Writings* (Garden City, N.Y.: Doubleday, 1973), 7.

50. Himes to Carl Van Vechten, March 11, 1953.

51. Himes, *Yesterday Will Make You Cry*, 259.

52. Ibid., 317, 304.

53. As Regina Kunzel points out, those subjects who were identified as sexu-ally "abnormal" upon imprisonment were often described as the cause of all non-heteronormative sexual practice in prisons—as a kind of miasmal, degenerating, threat to otherwise "normal," i.e., heterosexual, men. Kunzel, "Situating Sex," 258–59. Indeed, the notion that the "girl-boy," or "fairy," amounted to an ontology of contagion within the prison was upheld by none other than Cesare Lombroso, one of the most influential criminologists in history, at the turn of the twentieth century: "Homo-sexual offenders whose crime has been occasioned by residence in barracks, or colleges, or by a forced celibacy, plainly will not relapse when the

cause is removed. It will be sufficient in their case to inflict a conditional punishment, for they are not to be confused with the homo-sexual offenders who are born as such, and who manifest their evil propensities from childhood without being determined by special causes. *These should be confined from their youth, for they are the source of contagion* and cause a great number of occasional criminals." Cesare Lombroso, *Crime, Its Cause and Remedies* (London: W. Heinemann, 1911), 418. Note the connection here between the homophobic discourse of criminal contagion and the white supremacist discourses of racial contagion/criminality that attached to black bodies. In fact, Lombroso made similar claims regarding the innate incorrigibility, atavism, and indolence of "Negroes" and other "savage" peoples (207). Indeed, the connections between white supremacist and homophobic discussions of the prison were stated outright in some cases, such as one early nineteenth-century study in which the sexual "degeneration" of white women at a northern prison was found to be a result of the "mesmerizing" lasciviousness of the black women with whom they formed intimate attachments. Margaret Otis, "A Perversion not Commonly Noted," *Journal of Abnormal Psychology* 8, no. 2 (June–July 1913): 113–16.

54. Himes, *Yesterday Will Make You Cry,* 259, 315.

55. Like much of his relationship with Rico, Himes's (Jimmy's) moments of sexual and gender questioning that occurred *before* his imprisonment were completely excised from *Cast the First Stone.* In one such pre-prison remembrance in *Yesterday,* "He began to wonder why he was so strange and different from other boys. It wasn't just being girlish-looking with silly yellow hair and big blues eyes with long gold lashes; it wasn't having dimples either, although that was something that gave him plenty of fights. It was something else and he didn't know what it was. But whatever it was, it worried him a lot because he didn't want to be different" (120). It is in a conversation with Rico about his past that Himes/Jimmy finally allows himself at least partially to confront the "it" that dared not speak its name earlier in the text: "I was different from everybody and didn't exactly know why. I didn't want to be. That was what caused my trouble; I didn't want to be different. I've never wanted to be different. It was then that I began feeling that I had to prove something; I don't know, prove I wasn't different, I guess; prove I wasn't scared; prove I wasn't a sissy, I guess that was it" (311).

56. Ross dispatches with this myopic notion in his discussion of the critical work associated with the social category of normalcy in the writings of James Baldwin: "Baldwin's contribution to African American culture lies in his ability to imbalance the cultural conception of normalcy and in his linking of normalcy to racist ideology. The concept of normalcy, according the Baldwin, is the legacy of a European American system of racism. White supremacist culture needs a norm in order to trust its own illusion of black inferiority and white supremacy. More

precisely, it needs a sexual norm in order to perpetuate the myth of whiteness as a racial norm." Ross, "White Fantasies of Desire," 44.

57. On the "ruptural" and "critical possibilities" of explorations into nonheteronormative racial difference via queer of color critique, see Roderick A. Ferguson, *Aberrations in Black: Toward a Queer of Color Critique* (Minneapolis: University of Minnesota Press, 2004), 17, 21–22.

58. For critical analysis of the vital import of incorporating radical queer, queer of color, and transgender analyses into theorizations of the racial capitalist hetero-misogynist incarceration and into the politics of prison abolition, see Sylvia Rivera Law Project, "'It's War in Here'"; Eric A. Stanley and Nat Smith, eds., *Captive Genders: Trans Embodiment and the Prison Industrial Complex* (Oakland, Calif.: AK Press, 2011). For black, brown, and Third World feminist analyses of the prison–industrial complex, see Julia Oparah (aka Julia Sudbury), ed., *Global Lockdown: Race, Gender, and the Prison-Industrial Complex* (New York: Routledge, 2005).

59. In his study of queer life in early to mid-twentieth-century New York, George Chauncey discusses how criminalization, arrest, and imprisonment were regularly faced by queer subjects in the city's "vice districts," particularly in Harlem, a space in which class exploitation and (public) racial/sexual difference were isolated into one urban location. In elaborating this point, he speaks about how black drag queens who were stars of Harlem's renowned cabaret performances and drag balls were a particular target of racialized-gendered-sexualized legal violence: "Over the course of two weeks in February 1928 the police arrested thirty men for wearing drag at a single club, Lulu Belle at 341 Lenox Avenue near 127th Street." Chauncey, *Gay New York*, 249. See also Ferguson, *Aberrations in Black*, 41–42; and Laura Grantmyre, "'They lived their life and they didn't bother anybody': African American Female Impersonators and Pittsburgh's Hill District, 1920–1960," *American Quarterly* 63, no. 4 (December 2011): 983–1011.

The legal brutalization, arrest, and imprisonment of nonheteronormative racialized bodies—many of whom are homeless at the time of arrest—is a fundamental, if largely overlooked, aspect of today's PIC. See Sylvia Rivera Law Project, "'It's War in Here.'"

60. Ferguson, *Aberrations in Black*, 41.

61. Sylvia Rivera Law Project, "'It's War in Here.'" See also Lori Saffin, "Identities under Siege: Violence against Transpersons of Color," in Stanley and Smith, eds., *Captive Genders*, 141–64.

62. My language here is indebted to Ruth Wilson Gilmore's brilliant phrase in respect to the political geography of the PIC: "The expansion of prison constitutes a geographical solution to socio-economic problems, politically organized by the state which itself is in the process of radical restructuring." Gilmore, "Globalisation and US Prison Growth: From Military Keynesianism to Post-Keynesian Militarism," *Race & Class* 40, nos. 2/3 (1998–99): 174. The phrase "dangerous

heterogeneity" is a riff on/with Roderick Ferguson's articulation of the simultaneous critical possibility and social danger that attends to the nonheteronormative racialized body—or what he calls "material heterogeneity." Ferguson, *Aberrations in Black*, 21.

63. The practices of sexual panopticism and sexualized homo/transphobic segregation have been endemic to the U.S. modern penitentiary from its outset—punitive modalities based upon the quarantining of bodies presumed to be abnormally "feminine," or overtly "homosexual," into ontologically mobilized punishment units in light of their presumed degenerative effect on "normal" men. This is elaborated clearly by a former inspector of federal prisons at the very time that Himes and Rico were in the Ohio Penitentiary: "These are the types of known homosexuals which one will find in varying numbers in every large penitentiary. They comprise both those convicted of homosexuality or some offense growing out of it, as well as those committed for other offenses so patently homosexual that the prison officers 'spot' them at a glance. . . . In almost every big penitentiary an attempt is made to segregate this colony of known homosexuals from the main body of prisoners. . . . The mere presence of one ['known homosexual'] in the main body of prisoners . . . is a serious menace to discipline." Joseph Fishman, *Sex in Prison: Revealing Sex Conditions in American Prisons* (New York: National Library Press, 1934). Here the words of Cesare Lombroso on the matter of the degenerating effect of presumably queer imprisoned bodies bears repeating: "*These should be confined from their youth, for they are the source of contagion* and cause a great number of occasional criminals." Lombroso, *Crime, Its Cause and Remedies*, 418.

64. Shakur, *Assata*, 130.

65. The punitive segregation of prisoners branded as "girl-boy," or "punk," has continued through today's PIC. Wilbert Rideau offers a window into this practice at Angola prison plantation—a practice that is performed under the euphemizing label of "protective" segregation: "Protection cases are always segregated from the rest of the prisoners, denied the kind of freedom and wide range of activities afforded ordinary inmates. They are denied access to the prison's education and vocational programs and, so long as they are confined in protective custody, they carry the social stigma of being a 'catch-out,' a 'rat,' a 'coward.' The regulations and restrictions governing their existence are the same as those governing the prisoners locked in Cellblock A, across the hall from them, for 'punishment.'" Rideau, "The Sexual Jungle," in *Life Sentences*, ed. Rideau and Wikberg, 97.

66. Himes, *Yesterday Will Make You Cry*, 360.

67. See "'It's War in Here,'" Sylvia Rivera Law Project.

68. For discussion of how rape represents a de facto element of punishment in women's prisons see A. Davis, "Public Imprisonment and Private Violence." For a study of the regularity of rape in men's prisons see Human Rights Watch, *No Escape: Male Rape in U. S. Prisons* (New York: Human Rights Watch, 2001).

69. Donaldson, "A Million Jockers, Punks, and Queens," and Rideau, "The Sexual Jungle."

70. From the late 1960s to 2002, the U.S. prison and jail population rose from approximately two hundred thousand to more than two million. A. Davis, *Are Prisons Obsolete?* (New York: Seven Stories Press, 2003). Ruth Wilson Gilmore places this prison binge into the specific context of one of its epicenters: the "golden" state of California, in which the "state prisoner population grew nearly 500 percent between 1982 and 2000." Wilson Gilmore, *Golden Gulag*, 7. On the white supremacist ideological currents of the Nixon/Goldwater "law-and-order" brand of "statecraft," see Rodríguez, *Forced Passages*, 19–24.

71. Anonymous, "The Story of a Black Punk" (excerpts from letters to Stephen Donaldson), in *Prison Masculinites*, ed. Kupers et al., 129.

72. Donaldson, "A Million Jockers, Punks, and Queens," 122–24.

73. Himes, *Yesterday Will Make You Cry,* 358.

74. "Prisoners' Songs Go Into His Opera: Negro Convict in Ohio Pen Memorizes Words, Music of Working Chanteys," *Cleveland Plain Dealer,* January 20, 1935. Amazingly, the black Communist political prisoner Angelo Herndon learned a different version of this black neoslave song while entombed in Atlanta's Fulton Tower prison, at nearly the same time that Rico sang it in the Ohio Penitentiary. His version of the tune appears in the epilogue of his hugely important but largely invisible neoslave autobiography, *Let Me Live: Look a-yonder, yonder / Hard boiling sun / Is turning over, / It won't come down, O Lawd, / It won't come down . . . Every mail day—mail day / I get a letter, / Son, come home / O son, son, come home."* However, in Herndon's version of the self-directed chain-gang dirge, the speaker addresses the fact that certain biological death would be the cost of attempted natal dis-alienation through escape: "How can I go? / Shotguns and pistols / All around me / To blow me down / O lawd, to blow me down." Herndon, *Let Me Live,* 327–28. That this collectively authored song was performed by two different black neoslaves at the same time, with Rico in a northern prison and Herndon in a southern prison facing a chain-gang sentence, analogizes the degree to which neoslavery was indeed a national phenomenon. As importantly, the haunting south to north (and back again) reverb of this song expresses how the redressive force of black neoslave sound migrated along with the black bodies who would be entombed on both sides of the mythical divides of North and South, and slavery and freedom.

75. For one of the first sustained articulations of the practice of racially gendered medical terrorism against pregnant women in U.S. prisons (post-1865), and pregnant women of color in particular, see Shakur, *Assata*. During her pregnancy, Shakur was not only held in solitary confinement, but she was also beaten, shackled, and separated from her baby immediately following her birth. In one of the more stunning moments of medicalized terror, Shakur was advised by a prison

doctor to have an abortion in response to her complaints of stomach pains. After Shakur demanded to see a gynecologist, the "doctor" offered these instructions: "My advice to you is that you should go to your cell and lie down. Just lie down and rest your mind. Just lie down and stay off your feet. And if you go to the bathroom and see a lump in the toilet, don't flush it. It's your baby" (126). The repressive medical regime that Shakur endured as a black radical political prisoner in the late 1970s represented a haunting prefiguration of the sort of violence that women of color and poor women face under today's PIC—a regime of violence that, in its rupturous bearing toward black, brown, and poor women's bodies, represents one the most devastatingly clear indicators of what I have described as the Middle Passage carceral model. For discussion of the current state terrorist practice of shackling pregnant women during childbirth in U.S. prisons, see Anna Clark, "Giving Birth in Chains: The Shackling of Incarcerated Women during Labor and Delivery," RH—Reality Check: Reproductive & Sexual Health and Justice, News, Analysis & Commentary, http://rhrealitycheck.org/, July 6, 2009. For a piece dealing with the genocidal practice of forced sterilization in California women's prisons, see Corey Johnson, "Female Inmates Sterilized in California Prisons without Approval," Center for Investigative Reporting, http://cironline.org/reports, July 7, 2013. In a forward-haunting rememory of practices of forced sterilization against Indigenous women in California and other states, the California Department of Corrections and Rehabilitation (CDCR) has ordered the sterilization of at least 148 women at the California Institution for Women in Corona between 2006 and 2010. These numbers do not include the large number of black and brown women who have been sterilized in California prisons and jails after being counseled into participating in "elective" sterilization programs. See Robin Levi and Vanessa Huang, "Prison Proposal Is Disturbingly Akin to Eugenics," *Los Angeles Daily Journal,* January 8, 2007.

76. Zaharibu Dorrough, J. Heshima Denham, and Kambui Robinson, "Feeling Death at Our Heels: An Update from the Frontlines of the Struggle (from the NCTT Corcoran SHU)," *Prisoner Hunger Strike Solidarity: Amplifying the Voices of CA Prisoners on Hunger Strike,* Prisoner Hunger Strike Solidarity Coalition and California Families to Abolish Solitary Confinement, http://prisonerhunger strikesolidarity.

Index

DENNIS CHILDS is associate professor of literature and an affiliated faculty member of ethnic studies at the University of California, San Diego.